THE SHOTGUNNER'S BOOK

A MODERN ENCYCLOPEDIA

The Author

THE
SHOTGUNNER'S
BOOK

A MODERN ENCYCLOPEDIA

By
Colonel Charles Askins

BONANZA BOOKS · NEW YORK

This book is appreciatively dedicated to that
great Spanish sportsman
DON AGUSTIN ARANZABAL

AUTHOR'S NOTE

It is generally believed that the writer who would essay a tome on the shotgun finds there is precious little to be said that is new. The scattergun—like morals in Macao—has remained unchanged lo these many years and altho we demand an auto new from glistening bumper to high-flaring fishtails every twelvemonth we tamely submit to the acceptance of a fowling piece that as for design was around when Sheriff Pat Garrett provided Billy the Kid with that well-known one-way ticket. Modern shotgun design first saw the light of day when Prince Albert was getting his likeness on all those tobacco tins.

It is further believed that writers who attempt book or article on the smoothbore needs must trade with the tyros to the sport. The oldtimers are satiated with the trite stuff that is hashed and rehashed by every guns-writing man in the business. There are those who argue that the shotgun has been brought to such a state of perfection as to need, virtually, no further refinements. This is indicated, they contend, by the happy uncomplaining attitude of its users.

This ain't so. The squaw gun is an inefficient machine so primitive in its development as to be incapable of similar performance twice in a row. You may drive two successive bullets into the same hole with the rifle but do you think you can shoot two patterns from a shotgun exactly alike? You cannot. A shotgun can profess to be a full choke but will it always shoot 70% patterns? It will not. It may shoot anything from 50% to 85% and do it with successive shots. If the bench-rest rifleman had a rifle that performed thus eratically he'd bend it over the gunmaker's bows.

Despite this, all is not lost. There are some faint glimmerings of hope. This past pair of years there have been some indications that the wingshooter's tool is being bettered, if but slightly.

Of more encouragement is the shotshell picture. Cartridges have been improved very measurably and in fact are now capable of higher performance than the guns. To turn the thing around a bit, the shell now does such an efficient job it makes the gun look good and in fact covers up some of the obvious shortcomings of the latter.

I am encouraged.

As a matter óf fact a sizable portion of this book is concerned with the improvements discernible here of late in gun and load.

As well, this opus toward the tag end gets pretty deeply into the art of shotgunology—the business of straight gun pointing. The Fish and Wildlife Service tells us we have 15,000,000 shooters, obviously most of 'em are *aficionados* of the smoothbored tube. It is toward these fellows that I have taken dead aim, intent on helping them to point and swing, guess off the forward allowance and whip in the second barrel.

Some of the copy, with revision, first saw the light of day in my Guns and Ammunition column in the *Skeet Shooting Review,* official publication of the National Skeet Shooting Association. The indulgence of the Editor, George W. White, is appreciatively acknowledged. Likewise the cooperation of the *Gun Digest* and *Guns Magazine* is acknowledged in the matter of certain copy which first appeared in those journals.

CONTENTS

CONTENTS

THE SHOTGUNNER'S BOOK

A MODERN ENCYCLOPEDIA

Chapter 1
TODAY'S SHOTGUN PICTURE

OUR TASTE IN SHOTGUNS, like our taste for powerful autos, Bourbon whisky and loud shirts, is peculiarly American. While the remainder of the shotgunning world is content to shoot just twice, we like to bang 'em out rat-tat-tat. To do this we have developed scatterguns that load themselves. Some are automatics, others need a little shuffle amidships; but the end result is the same. There are those who contend that these corn-shellers have decimated our game and this may be so. Be that as it may, we are a country of pump-gun and auto-loader shooters and we are apt to remain such for a long time to come.

The spark that generated the repeating shotgun is a weak flame today. I speak of that lush half-century—1875 to 1925—when beefsteak cost two-bits the two pounds, when whisky sold for a buck the gallon, when hunters were numbered in the thousands and game in the tens of millions, when game laws were made but not enforced, when market hunters peddled plump mallards by the barrel—and everyone cried for a shooting iron that would hold more than two shells.

The repeater was the answer. An efficient killer that held five or six and sometimes seven cartridges, it was not as pretty and as well balanced as the double but was infinitely more lethal.

Today this magazine arm is so remarkably popular the majority of our scatter guns are repeaters of one kind or another. Of some thirty-six basic models currently in production some twenty-two are magazine weapons. The breakdown runs as follows: Seven auto-loaders, nine pump repeaters, and six bolt-action repeaters. The remaining fourteen models are divided: Seven single-barrel single shot, five double-barrel, and two over-and-under shotguns.

The repeater is singled out by our legislators for special treatment. They discriminate against the weapon. The Federal Government restricts magazine capacities to two cartridges. Most of the States have enacted similar laws; it is only a matter of time until all the forty-eight will fall into line. Drastically reduced bag limits have called another strike on this scatterbore. It was developed primarily as a wildfowler's tool. That was when 50 canvasbacks were considered an average day's bag. Now with limits set at four

1

or five ducks and half that number of geese, what advantage lies in shooting a gun capable of raking a full limit out of the first flock that wings in?

There will be those sanguine hombres who will hold that the game is coming back. We'll see again duck limits of 25 birds per day, and 15 geese; there will be live decoys once more and baited blinds; the season will stretch from October until March and the plugs will all be jerked out of the magazines. Then the repeater will be in its heydey once again!

The edge the repeating shotgun has held over the double lies, in the main, in its increased shell capacity. Now that margin has been reduced to a single additional cartrdige. In many ways it is inferior to the double. It lacks the good handling qualties inherent in the side-by-side shotgun; it weighs more, does not point as naturally, and is infinitely more ugly. In fairness to the gun, however, it should be pointed out that slim though the margin be between two shots and three, that third round in the hands of a skilled wing gunner can be made to pay real dividends!

There isn't anything new about the repeating scatter gun. A

The Winchester Model 12 pump repeater and the Browning Superposed shotguns. The late Major Charles Askins, father of the author.

The Stevens Model 311 double shotgun. This shotgun is identical with the Fox except that it has double triggers.

The Stevens Model 59 bolt-action shotgun.

repeating model was first patented by the Spencer Arms Co. in 1882; the following year Burgess patented a second repeater; and in 1887, based on developments of the immortal John Browning, the Winchester Co. announced their first magazine shotgun.

This was the Model 1887, a lever-action, tubular magazine, 12-gauge, outside hammer, 5-cartridge shotgun. The following year the weapon was chambered for the 10-gauge shell. The gun was modified slightly in 1901 and the name changed to the Model of 1901, the 12-gauge was dropped and the shotgun continued of manufacture in 10-gauge until 1920.

In 1897 Winchester brought out a pump-action repeater, a visible-hammer, tubular magazine gun known as the Model 1897. This was an improved version of the Model 1893, a weapon developed by John Browning and sold to Winchester. The Model 97 was made for 60 years, has only just recently been discontinued.

In 1907, possibly before, the Stevens Co. brought out the first of the successful hammerless repeating shotguns. This was the Model 520, a 12-gauge, tubular-magazine takedown; the gun was another Browning design, sold to Stevens. The weapon was shortly followed by Remington who bought the Pedersen design for their Model 10 pumpgun. This Remington contribution appeared in 1907.

During 1912, considerably later, Winchester had ready their hammerless repeater. This was the Model 1912. It was first announced in 20 gauge, but a year later was ready in 16 and 12 gauges. This is the most famous, best liked, and very probably the most sturdy repeating shotgun.

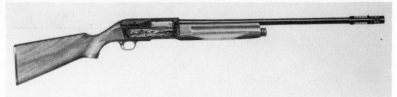

The Savage Model 775sc auto-loader shotgun.

The Remington Model 31 pump repeater, now obsolete.

In 1934 the gun was adapted to the 28 gauge; in 1942, it was slightly modified to accept the 410 cartridge. In 1947 a cheapened version of the M12 was made and this gun was designated the Model 25. It has since been discontinued.

About the turn of the century the Marlin Firearms Co. introduced a trombone-action repeater that was quite reliable and equally popular. The Model 10 Remington, as I have said, was of the same vintage, generally. This shotgun was a departure from convention in that the only opening in the receiver was at the bottom. The gun was loaded through the bottom and ejection was through the same opening. The Model 17, which followed the original gun, employed this same design; it was a stronger and more satisfactory weapon.

The Model 17 gave way to the Model 31 pump repeater. Here, for the first time, Remington swung to the side-ejection principle.

While pumpguns were passing through this developmental period, Remington purchased from that remarkable Mormon, John Browning, the license rights for the American manufacture of an auto-loading shotgun.

This weapon operated on the long-recoil principle. It was a tubular magazine, 5-shot, self-loading shotgun that became known as the Model 1911. It was continuously manufactured by the Remington Co. from 1911 until 1948. During '48, Remington announced a new automatic shotgun, the Model 48. With the advent of this new shotgun they discontinued the old Browning.

While no longer under production by the Remington Co., the gun is still very much alive. It is under production by the Browning Arms Co. of Ogden, Utah, and by the Savage Arms Corp.

The now obsolete Winchester Model 40 Auto-loader.

During the long years when the M1911 was the American property of the Remington Arms Co., it was manufactured and sold abroad by Fabrique Nacional d'Armes de Guerre of Belgium. It is one of the most widely distributed shotguns in the world.

During the developmental years of the Winchester and Remington pumps and auto-loaders other firms were busy. Savage made a pump gun for a number of years; this was during the 1920s. Stevens also had a trombone action, and today as a subsidiary of Savage, still produces a sturdy repeater.

The Ithaca Gun Co., formerly exclusively dedicated to an outstanding line of side-by-side double guns (also single-barrel trap models), turned to the manufacture of a pump repeater. This was before World War II, and with the end of hostilities the company has continued with the slide-action repeater known as the Model 37. The receiver on the M37, like the Remington 10 and 17, is a solid piece. Ejection is through the bottom of the action. So intensive has been the demand it appears the firm will never return to the manufacture of double shotguns.

The Noble Manufacturing Co. is in production of a slide-action, tubular-magazine repeater. Sears, Roebuck and Co., through their subsidiary, the High Standard Mfg. Co., produce a very sturdy pump gun, the Model 20. This pretty well completes the picture except for the bolt-action numbers which are offered currently by Mossberg, Marlin, Stevens, Sears, and Harrington and Richardson.

Since the end of World War II, the Remington Co. has produced a family of original and remarkably interesting magazine shotguns. The first of these was a pump repeater, the Model 870. This slide-action has a number of innovations about it never before seen on an American firearm. Stampings are freely used in the action.

The Germans, during the fisticuffs of 1939-45, turned to the use of stampings in the manufacture of many of their military small arms. Remington's design teams took a leaf from the Kraut book and the M870 was the first result. The use of pressed steel parts, die-castings, and stampings means the firearm can be made more quickly and cheaply.

Quite as interesting in the case of the 870 is the new action. The breechblock locks up directly behind the shell-head, much after the fashion of our high-intensity rifles. This feature is an excellent one and largely obviates headspacing difficulties.

A second shotgun soon followed the new pump, this was an auto-loader dubbed the Model 48 (it appeared in 1948) and later on called the 11-48. It was evident the same crew that did such a bang-up job on the Model 870 had had their hands on the new automatic. It has essentially the same receiver. This receiver is as smoothly streamlined as a racing Jaguar. The horrific shoulder which characterized the receiver on the old Remington auto was entirely missing. The result was a weapon appealing to the eye and light to the hand. The weight has been trimmed to pump-gun proportions.

Prices of the two new Remingtons reflect the speed and cheapness with which they can be built; both are substantially less costly than competitive models.

It goes without saying that a pressed steel part, stamped out like a pop bottle cap, simply cannot give the performance nor possess the life expectancy of a similar part that is machined from good steel. Granted this is true, we must then ask ourselves just how much shooting does the average wing gunner do these days?

The startling truth is that the ammunition manufacturers tell us but two boxes—50 cartridges—represent his per-season expenditure.

This being the average it is easy to see how a shotgun utilizing

Fox Model BST, one of the two side-by-side shotguns under manufacture in the U.S. today.

The L. C. Smith, a fine double gun no longer made.

Stevens Model 77sc pump repeater.

stampings in certain parts of the mechanism will prove entirely satisfactory for a great many years.

For some obscure reason we think nothing of investing a small fortune in a new automobile which within a handful of months will need a new set of plugs, new distributor points, oil filter, tires, etc.; but on the score of a shooting iron, a relatively inexpensive machine, we expect a performance little short of perfection. If a gun gives the slightest indication of malperformance during the first decade of usage we cry to the heavens.

It would be better, most certainly, to pay only half as much for our shooting hardware and thereafter expect a normal replacement of worn parts just as we do on our auto.

Before the war there were a number of manufacturers of side-by-side double shotguns. The twin-tube model was with us long before the corn-shellers and despite the demand for the latter the double remained popular. However, as skilled labor- grew more costly, and since the double shotgun requires a great deal of hand-fitting and finishing, manufacturers were compelled to turn to the repeating types.

The side-by-side has gradually faded, as may be appreciated, for these reasons: (1) the demand of a certain class of shooter, essentially the wildfowler, for a magazine arm; (2) the inability of the manufacturer to produce a double at a going price, due to the high cost of skilled labor.

Once double shotguns were made by Parker, L. C. Smith, Baker, Ithaca, Fox, Lefever, Savage, Remington, Colt, Winchester, and others. Today, side-by-sides are made by but two firms, Winchester and Savage. The Savage Corporation owns Fox and Stevens; each subsidiary produces a double-barreled shotgun. As for Winchester they produce one parallel barrel model. This is the Model 21, probably the best shotgun in the world in the barrel-beside-barrel type.

Remington Co. before 1942 made a splendid over/under shotgun, the Model 32. Browning also marketed a superposed model. Marlin and Savage each had an O/U; the Marlin version was made in 12, 20 and 410 gauges. Since the war the only superposed models to continue of manufacture have been the Browning and the Marlin.

The Browning over-and-under is one of the finest shotguns made. The action, the very heart of any firearm, is characterized by a simple yet sturdy lockup that never shoots loose. The external lines of the receiver are a delight to the eye and the lack of depth of this action, considering it vertically, contributes very markedly to the good performance of the gun. Browning builds the Superposed in six grades. The Grade VI, the most costly of the models, is the kind of a shotgun Indian potentates used to indulge in BN (Before Nehru); seldom is such magnificent walnut, such exquisite engraving, and careful attention to detail found in any shotgun regardless of the price tag.

The war, and the years since, have seen some major changes in the shotgun picture. While the fracas was in full swing enterprising GIs accumulated countless thousands of Continental scatter-barrels and shipped them home as booty. Many of these guns had twist and Damascus barrels, others were pin-fires; numbers were chambered for the short 12-gauge case. Sharp combs, splinter fore-ends and other peculiarities rendered the prizes not only largely worthless but in many cases actually dangerous.

But not all the liberated hardware fell into this category. Countless Continental twelves and sixteens were first-rate shooting irons.

Directly after the war enterprising American importers trekked to Europe and there commenced to buy, taking advantage of the less costly labor, fine workmanship, and excellent designs of the Continental gunmakers.

Very soon we commenced to see double shotguns, both side-by-side and over/under, as well as auto-loaders in America again. Abercrombie and Fitch, the great New York sporting-goods house, again stocked the fine Francotte, Belgian double with a long and enviable reputation. Continental Arms also offered Belgian and Italian smoothbores in both doubles and auto-loaders; Ferlach-made side-by-sides and over-and-unders from Austria arrived in numbers. Firearms International imported the sterling AYA shotguns made by the leading Spanish manufacturer, Aguirre y Aranzabal. Sears Roebuck, who now dominate retail sales of all firearms in this country, sell the AYA double shotgun in the model known as the J. C. Higgins, Model 100.

Stoeger Arms Corporation, publishers of that unique catalog, *The Shooter's Bible,* import the Sarasqueta, Bernardelli, Franchi and Sauer shotguns.

That the conventional and time-honored double shotgun has lost none of its appeal is attested by the fact that these many importers are doing a booming business. Most of the foreign houses providing

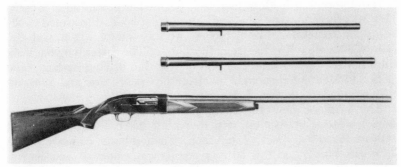

The Winchester Model 50 auto-loading shotgun. Gun is short-recoil operating and features a radically new "floating" chamber.

arms to guns-hungry America are comparatively small, at least measured by our standards, and for that reason are hard put to fill the orders received.

None of these "Europeans" slip into this country and finally into the hands of the sportsman without the payment of some exceedingly steep import duties. This duty is so considerable as to see the Continental arm fetch 50% more on this side of the Atlantic than at home. This means, many times, that the asking price is as high or higher than a US-made similar model. Despite these price tags the influx continues and gives evidence of growing stronger.

Very recently interest has grown for the 10 gauge. Presently no 10-gauge shotgun is made in this country; however, ammunition is still loaded, and what's more interesting is that a walloping load of two full ounces of shot is available. This trifling charge is poured into a case as long as a politician's promise, and is pushed along by a half-hatfull of powder. The resulting combination has almost as much recoil as the new .458 elephant gun but it is a duzy for high-flying ganders!

The gun for this 3½-inch 10-gauge shell is called a 10 Magnum and it is properly named. The Firearms International Corporation import a magnificent AYA double 10, single trigger and selective ejectors, to fire this Roman Candle; Continental Arms also import Magnum 10s, both in side-by-side and superposed models; still a third is the Silver Co. of San Francisco, who feature the sturdy Neumann (Belgian) Big 10; Frank Clark, the Wyoming importer, rounds out the picture.

During early 1955, the Browning Arms Co. of Ogden, Utah (and St. Louis, Mo.) announced a new shotgun that shook the whole shotgun world. This was an automatic. Unlike all its predecessors— long-recoil operated to the last model—this revolutionary new gun operated on the short-recoil principle.

Heretofore self-loaders had locked the barrel and the breech-bolt together, and on the explosion the two had traveled rearward for something like 3 inches. At the end of this travel the bolt was cammed apart from the barrel. The latter moved back into battery under the compulsion of the driving spring. The bolt hesitated long enough to eject the spent case and pick up a live round.

The brilliant new Browning did not follow this cycle. The barrel, instead of recoiling together with the breechblock, moved only a fractional part of an inch. Then it was cammed apart from the block; and this latter piece moved rearward and accomplished the necessary chores of flipping out the empty and picking up the live round. Val Browning, the designer, achieved a whale of a sweet balance between his operating springs to cushion the backward slam of the breechblock so that the recoil neither disturbed the firer nor battered the mechanism.

Although the shotgun represented the first of the short-recoiling self-loaders, maybe what was more revolutionary was the fact that it held only two cartridges. The weapon had no magazine. The first round was carried in the chamber, the second on the shell carrier. A handy slot in the left side of the receiver permitted the rapid loading of the gun, it also provided a window where the gunner could see at a glance whether the second round was in place.

It takes a lot of guts to build an automatic shotgun that only shoots twice.

To my notion this Val Browning-designed scattergun presages the future. My prediction is that eventually all smoothbores will be reduced to two shots. As our game diminishes there will be more and more pressure exerted on our legislators to reduce magazine capacities. The Browning Co. has simply built tomorrow's shotgun today.

After springing the new weapon on a delighted sporting world, the firm went ahead and produced a lightweight model. This No. 2 sported an alloyed receiver and was pleasingly lighter than the standard all-steel model. Not content with this, Brownings then shook the wing-gunning clan to its very roots by bringing out the new gun—called the Double Automatic due to its two-shot capacity—in colors!

There was a choice of colors ranging from silver through black, green and autumn brown. The receiver is Dural, a kind of high-tensile-strength aluminum alloy. It takes an anodized color very well. Naturally no attempt was made to alter the blued color of the barrel, and the walnut stock and forend remain in their conventional patterns. The new automatic, from the be-

Marlin bolt action, 12 gauge, Model 55.

$2,500.00 Grade Ithaca Repeater.

ginning, sported a very fetching dollop of English scroll engraving. With a background in color this engraving looked handsome indeed!

No sooner had the new Browning been announced than Sears Roebuck, the great mail-order house, piqued the interest of wing gunners with a fowling piece quite as extraordinary in many ways as the new Browning.

This was a 12-gauge self-loader that functioned by the use of the propellant gases. Rifles and machineguns have utilized gas pressure to operate the mechanism for many years. It remained for the High Standard Mfg. Co., a subsidiary of Sears, to develop the first successful gas-powered shotgun.

The Model 60, as the "J. C. Higgins" is called, taps the gas a little less than midway of the barrel and permits this jet of hot propellant to impinge on a collar-shaped piston. This piston, unlike the conventional type, surrounds the tubular magazine, and once set into motion actuates a driving rod which in turn drives the breechbolt backward.

The first models of the new gas gun did not always function satisfactorily. However, High Standard continued to improve the shotgun and soon had it so that performance was very reliable. The weapon is the heaviest of the present crop of automatics, it weighs 8 pounds 6 ounces.

Directly after the J. C. Higgins contribution, the Winchester Co. pulled the wraps very proudly off their entry in the auto-gun race. This was a powder-burner quite on a par with the Browning and the Sears insofar as original design was concerned.

The Model 50, as Winchester elected to call their new auto,

is a second short-recoil arm. Browning, if you will recollect, produced the first in the Double Automatic. Winchester's engineers (among others the famous "Carbine" Williams) arrived at the short-recoil system by a most ingenious method. The barrel on the 50 gun was anchored solidly in the receiver. Within the breech end of the barrel-tube an auxiliary chamber was fitted. This assembly is quite separate of the barrel and is held in place by a short extension which serves the double purpose of acting as a portion of the breech lock. When the weapon fires, this auxiliary chamber recoils. The barrel remains in place. After some hundredths-of-an-inch movement the breechblock cams out of lock with the chamber extension and moves to the rear, ejecting the empty shell, and on its return chambers a live cartridge.

An inertia weight in the buttstock and a double-coiled spring about this weight serve to cushion the bolt. Recoil in the M50 is especially mild. Not only the system of weights and springs but the overall poundage of the weapon all serve to produce a kick that is noticeably non-jarring. The M50 is butt-heavy. This is due to the inertia weight, the springs, and the aluminum housing, all of which are stowed in the stock. Once the gunner grows accustomed to this rather odd distribution of the weight he will shoot the latest Winchester very satisfactorily.

Not to be outdone by the local competition, the Remington Co., in the Spring of 1956, announced the second gas-operated auto shotgun. This newest offering in the self-clattering field is called the Model 58. Stack the 58 beside the Model 11-48 and it is hard to tell 'em apart. This is considerable of a tribute to the ingenuity of the boys who whumped up this gas gun. Dig a bit under the surface and there are differences, however.

Gas is tapped from the barrel where the magazine ring joins the tube. This gas is jetted into a cylinder that fits into the end of the magazine tube. It hits a hollowed-out piston and the force works on a forked operating rod. This rod is linked to the breech block. Remingtons had trouble with this gas-operated fusee when they switched from light skeet loads to the heavy standard Magnum 1½-ounce busters. To get around this problem they simply put some gas vents in the end of the magazine cap. By screwing the cap a portion of a turn, orifices are lined up which divert the unwanted gases. It is simple and ingenious.

The new Remington has all the good balance and handling qualities of the Model 870 pump gun, and I predict it will eventually supplant the M11-48, which after all, is long-recoil operating and pretty obsolescent thereby.

Chapter 2
HOW THE SHOTGUN IS MADE

THE AVERAGE SHOOTER knows about as much about the manufacture of a modern firearm as he does about the inner machinations of the Sicilian Mafia. He is told the gun is machine-made. That is, mass-produced. To him this means that maybe they are stamped out like pop-bottle caps. He accepts this industry-inspired propaganda that the firearm is machine-made.

Actually the cost of manufacturing the garden-run pump shotgun, a standard dog to the last nut and bolt, will see 70% of the cost eaten up by hand-fitting and finishing. One of our finest double shotguns fetches a staggering sum simply because 95% of the king's ransom goes into its cost for hand-finishing.

Machine-made indeed!

The shotgun has been slow of development. Right after the first integration effort, now variously referred to as the War Between the States (Southern version) or Civil War (Northern preference), the scattergun was notable for a pair of tubes that had to be charged at the muzzle, a stock as crooked as old Bugle's hindleg, outside hammers, and Magnum bores like 4, 6 and 8.

During the shank end of the 19th Century some changes took place.

The Anson and Deeley action, a true hammerless, replaced the antiquated, dog-eared and muzzle-charged fusee, and other changes possibly even more revolutionary became commonplace. Best of these changes may be attributed to the inventive genius of John Browning, who produced both pump-action and auto-loading scatterguns. It was during this epoch period that shotgun barrels lost their straight cylinder dimension and gained a constriction at the muzzle. This vastly improved lethality.

Just who it was who hit on the happy business of pinching down the muzzle, adding a "choke" as it is called, is the matter of considerable debate. The English say they first discovered this handy constriction; but there are other claimants, none probably with a more legitimate case than Fred Kimble.

This Illinois market gunner used a 6-bore single-barreled shotgun and frequently sacked up a hundred mallards during a morn-

13

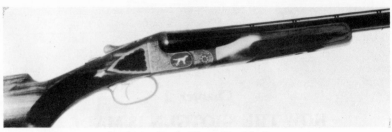

$1,700.00 Grade Ithaca Double Gun.

$2,500.00 Grade Ithaca Repeater.

ing in the brakes along the Mississippi. His old 6-gauge had a straight cylinder barrel—as did all scatter guns of the day—and was short-ranged. Kimble pondered the limitations of his weapon and determined to improve its lethality. He made and bored another barrel and in this new tube he purposely left a considerable amount of muzzle constriction.

When he patterned the new barrel he found it scattered the pellets all over a barn door. Disgusted and convinced he was on the wrong track, he returned to the lathe and determined to remove all the choke. This he did and again patterned the shotgun.

Much to his delight he found he now had a remarkably close shooting gun. It would, according to Kimble (this has never been accomplished since!) place the entire shot load in a 30-inch circle at 40 yards. He again measured the bore and checked the muzzle and found that instead of removing all the choke he had inadvertently left something like .065-inch of constriction. Thus was choke-boring discovered.

Word got around fast. The 'smiths on either side of the Atlantic were not slow to employ the pinched-in effect on their scatter guns. This was back during the days when Custer got his hair lifted. Surprisingly, or maybe I should say, disappointingly, precious little has been done to improve the shotgun tube since the Kimble discovery.

Those were the days when shotgun tubes were made of Damascus steel. A Damascus barrel was made by twisting alternating bands of iron and steel about a mandrel. As the ribbons were slowly wound about the core the work was hammered to weld and flow the metal into a homogeneous mass. Various patterns were created in the outer barrel surfaces depending on how the strips of iron and steel were interwoven. The quality of the tubes could be told almost at a glance by the pattern. The finer and more graceful the design the more costly the barrels.

A fine Damascus shotgun was indeed a handsome piece of ordnance!

Twist steel barrels and laminated steel barrels were the poor cousins. Both were made after the fashion, essentially, of the Damascus; neither were as good. Of the two, however, the laminated was the stronger.

Damascus barrels were made in a variety of grades and patterns. These were:

Horseshoe, Rose, Bernard, Crolle, Moire and Laminette.

So popular was the Damascus that a decalcomania was created so that an imitation pattern could be affixed to the cheap twist steel barrel. It is questionable who this must have fooled, but at any rate the discerning sportsman would sooner have been caught abroad without his pants than been found sans his fine Damascus double.

Fueled with black powder, the Damascus, laminated, or twist barrel was as sound as the Monroe (not Marilyn) Doctrine. With the advent of progressive-burning smokeless powder the old tubes could not cut the mustard. All had the inherent fault of sidewall thin spots. The very business of hammering ribbons of iron and steel about a shaft made for variances in barrel-wall thickness. As a result, when sportsmen attempted to swing from black powder cartridges to the potent new smokeless loads, soft spots showed up in the barrels and often these let go with disastrous results.

52 Grade Ithaca single-barrel trap gun.

7E Grade Ithaca single-barrel trap gun.

The gunmakers had kept pace with the development of progressive-burning smokeless powders and when the new propellant commenced to gain acceptance, the Damascus tube was dropped in favor of the fluid steel barrel. This latter is the gun tube we use today. It will withstand our heaviest modern loadings. However, the fly in the soup remains in the shape of the thousands upon thousands of old twist, laminated, and Damascus guns that are still kicking around.

With the obsolescence and final retirement of these old guns, the ammunition manufacturers immediately launched a campaign

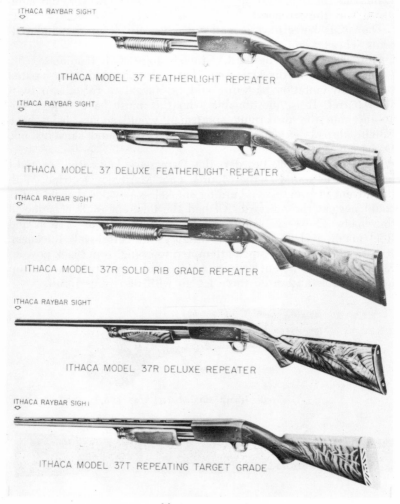

Ithaca repeaters.

to educate the gun's owners. Now, some sixty years later, the educational program is still going on. Look on the shotshell box and you'll find there a warning not to use the cartridges in the old Damascus boobytrap.

High carbon-content steel, alloyed with nickel, molybdenum, chromium and other high tensile-strength metals are poured into today's gun tubes. The gunmakers are a tightmouthed crew and would sooner let you examine their last year's income tax than reveal the alloy used in their shooting hardware. As a propaganda device each has some special name for his barrel steel. It may be "Ordnance Steel" or "Nickel Steel" or "Nitro Steel" or some other equally innocuous sobriquet. This is just gentle fun; doesn't mean a thing, but maybe fools the tyro into the belief that he is getting something special.

It used to be that nickel steel was accepted as the last word in barrel steel. It was boomed by one of our largest rifle-shotgun manufacturers. Actually it wasn't nickel steel at all but an alloy which contained about 3¼% of nickel. The Yankees who made sportsmen nickel steel-conscious, with typical reticence, never revealed the contents of their alloy; but it was generally carbon .35% to .45%, manganese .50% to .80%, phosphorus maximum not over .04%, sulphur about the same, *i.e.* .04%, and finally nickel from about 3.1% to 3.75%.

Nickel-steel barrels were excellent, and still are. When used in breechbolts this alloy, especially in the bolt-action rifle, tends to be "sticky." Whether this characteristic has caused the manufacturer to shy away from such high-content nickel alloys isn't known, suffice it to note the turn is now to alloys containing more chrome and molybdenum.

Present alloys shape up like this:

Carbon	.45%	to	.50%
Manganese	.60%	to	.90%
Chromium	.80%	to	1.10%
Molybdenum	.15%	to	.25%
Silicon	.15%	to	.35%
Phosphorous maximum	.04%		
Resulphurize to	.04%	to	.09%

Not all scatter-gun manufacturers go for the chrome-moly barrel. At least two, to my knowledge, stick to nothing more tough than ordinary high carbon-content steel. This is perfectly okay. The shotgun develops about 12,000 p.s.i., and despite the fact that the tube is considerably thinner than the high-intensity rifle, with its 50-60,000 pounds of breech pressure, there is an ample safety margin.

The claims of many arms makers on the Continent that they are using alloyed steels is largely poppycock. They are using high-carbon steels alloyed with nothing heavier than a lot of sales propaganda. Both here and abroad high-carbon steel will run about as follows:

Carbon	.45% to .55%
Manganese	1.10% to 1.35%
Silicon	.25% to .35%
Resulphurized to	.06%
Phosphorous maximum	.06%

In connection with barrel strength it is interesting to note that the Nazis made several million Mauser rifles, Model '98, cal. 7.92 m.m., during the Late Unpleasantness and when we got around to an analysis of the steel in barrel and receiver we found it to be plain high-content carbon. A steel somewhat equivalent to our SAE No. 1035, carbon content .30% to .40%.

Of equal interest were similar checks run on the Japanese military rifle. It was found to be high carbon-content steel, running .80% to .90%.

General Julian S. Hatcher, one of our arms authorities, before his retirement from the Ordnance Corps, turned down a Springfield '06 barrel until it had a sidewall thickness just over the chamber of but 1/16-inch. He fired three service loads (about 50,000 p.s.i.) through this paper-thin barrel and it digested 'em perfectly. The normal barrel thickness, let it be noted, is 5/16-inch. A fourth round, a blue pill turning up 75,000 pounds per square inch, wrecked the tube. All of which gives rise to the suspicion that maybe our manufacturers overdo this business of using costly chrome, molybdenum and nickel in the fabrication of the snorkel-end of the shooting iron.

A shotgun barrel is scarcely recognizable as it comes from the steel mill. It is in the shape of a billet, a billet that must be heated and given a number of rolls to bring it roughly to size. After that it is subjected to a series of machining operations to bring it to exact dimension. Before the final machining it is drop-forged, tempered, and carefully inspected to assure that an entirely homogenous mass has been achieved.

While most rifle barrels are broached, or button-rifled these days, to the best of my knowledge this has not been found desirable with the spaghetti-like shotgun tube. It is a straight-boring job and interestingly it comes out of this operation with no more choke in the muzzle than you'll find in the Holland Tunnel. The choke is added by swaging the last several inches of the muzzle.

We used to conclude that a swaged choke was pretty shoddy business. It was believed it would shoot out, gradually the barrel would return to its original dimension. Maybe it will too if not stress-relieved. There is a lot of economy practiced these days to

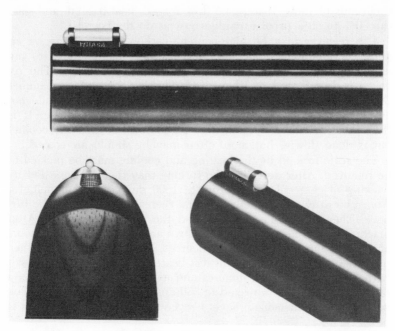

Ithaca Raybar sight.

keep the price of the firearm within reason. Swaging the choke instead of cutting it is one among many.

The barrel is given two blue pills as proofing rounds. The first, while the tube is in the semi-finished state, the last, the definitive proof, when finished. If it is going to develop any flaws they want to be found as quickly as possible to preclude further costly machining. Proof loads usually run an overload of 30%, may go as high as 50%.

As an indication of the goodness of our scatter guns, Winchester once fired 2,000 blue pills souped up to 50% overcharge in the Model 21 double. The gun took 'em without sign of pain or strain.

Our manufacturers accomplish their own proof firing. They have always attended to this chore. In Europe, proof firing is done by the various Governments. Each has a Proof House and the manufacturer must submit his weapon, getting back the gun and a certificate attesting that it withstood the tests. Not so here. Our gunmakers test-fire their own, and the goodness of our firearms attests to the honesty of our makers.

A shotgun receiver, the very heart of the firearm, must be made from an alloyed steel that has great tensile goodness so as to soak up the shock of the heaviest cartridge and be able to do this for thousands of shots. It must be drop-forged, heat-treated, and pass the 30% to 50% proof cartridges just as do the barrels.

The receiver may be high-content carbon steel or may be an alloy containing molybdenum. At least one manufacturer to my knowledge uses both moly and chrome in his receivers. The receiver is drop-forged, as I have said. This is done under a hammer that delivers a ¾-ton blow. After forging, it is trimmed while hot and then goes back under the hammer to correct warping. It is then permitted to cool, sometimes in charcoal so that the cooling out is done slowly; but more often may be simply air cooled.

The scale formed by the heating and cooling must be pickled to be removed. After descaling the forging may then be annealed by packing in charcoal and heating to 1600 degrees, Fahrenheit, for from two to two and one-half hours, thereafter cooling in the furnace. Then it is again descaled and the machining begins. After machining, it is heated in bone for two and one-half to three hours at temperatures of 1500-1600 degrees, Fahrenheit, and is then quenched in oil. Following this it is heated to 1250 degrees in a salt bath for a period of six minutes and again quenched in oil. As a final tempering it is subjected to 350 degrees, Fahrenheit, in an oil bath and then air cooled. Such a receiver will show a Rockwell C of 32 to 45.

Not all manufacturers follow this method exactly. However, generally speaking, it is the method adhered to. The resulting receiver possesses great tensile strength, has an extremely tough skin that will accept a good polish, possesses a resilient core, and indicates a resistance to fatigue that contributes to long, trouble-free performance.

One of the reasons double-barreled shotguns are so scarce on the manufacturer's list is because of the skill that is needed in joining the two tubes. The barrels are machined separately and afterward joined by a mechanic who must have had years of experience in doing that very thing.

Ordinarily the tubes are joined together by brazing. Winchester, however, on the Model 21, do an exceedingly clever job of mechanically interlocking the barrels.

The criticality of the operation is not in evidence until the weapon is targeted. One tube may shoot to center and the other strike over by the apple orchard. This means the joiner has bungled his job. The cure is to break the braze and commence over again the job of joining each barrel to a common center.

I one time shot a fine, imported over/under 12-gauge that had the lower barrel dead on at 40 yards but the upper tube would not pattern within 18 inches of its twin. This is a fault far more common than many shooters realize.

The new Remington "Sportsman-58F" Custom-Grade skeet gun; 3 shot; 12 gauge.

Once the barrels are regulated the ribs are attached. These are usually sweated into place. Soldering is sometimes resorted to but it is none too satisfactory and when a rib loosens, as sometimes happens, an examination of the break invariably reveals a soldered joint.

Statistics indicate the average wing gunner only fires 50 cartridges yearly. At this rate it would take a long time to place any material strain on the shotgun. But there are exceptions. Like the trapshooter who may very well consume 20,000 cartridges in a season. Once a Winchester Model 12 pump gun was fired 500,000 times. The shotgun when it passes over the counter may fall into the hands of Mr. Average Sportsman who poops off a couple of boxes of hulls per annum, or it may become the property of the hombre who will never let it cool. In any case it has got to be able to take it.

Savage, before World War II, was the first of our large manufàcturers to swing to aluminum alloys for the manufacture of shotgun receivers. Now a number of our gunmakers are utilizing the light, tough metal, none probably more widely than the sixgun manufacturers. After the war, Savage lost little time in swinging back to the use of alloy. What the contents of this particular aluminum alloy may be is a well-kept secret, but it is reasonable to presume that the mixture runs about: copper 3% to 5%, magnesium .3% to .6%, manganese .4% to 1.00%, with the remainder of the alloy aluminum.

Chromium may also be present in minute quantities. When it is present the alloy responds more readily to surface burnishing with a consequent improved appearance. Even so it is difficult to get a satisfactorily blued surface, a fact which has induced the Browning Co. to anodize the skin of their receivers in colors. This electrolytic slight-of-hand has shaken the Old Guard to their roots. Nonetheless the resulting finish is so deeply joined in the very metal itself it will outlast any bluing yet discovered.

The aluminum alloy does not flow as well as steel but responds to drop-forging quite satisfactorily. Forging temperatures range from 880 to 920 degrees. The alloy is rather critical at high tem-

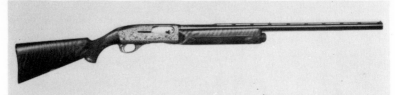

The new Remington "Sportsman-48F" (Premier Grade) auto-loading skeet gun.

The new Remington "Wingmaster" Model 870. Custom built with gold inlay.

peratures, and if the high range is not carefully controlled the alloy is inclined to crumble. Whether worked hot or cold, or in a combination of both, it can be given additional strength by heat treatment. It may also be annealed when that is desirable. Because of repeated drawings, annealing may become necessary; after annealing, heat treatment will restore all the maximum physical properties.

I think we have just seen a beginning of the use of aluminum alloys in firearms manufacture. Heavy ordnance is unpopular. Today's shooter wants a zephyrweight, a shooting iron no more ponderous than a piccolo, something with about the heft of a Daisy air rifle. The stuff we have always associated with the manufacture of kitchen pots and pans seems to be the answer.

Another interesting phenomenon that has horrified the Old School has been the introduction of die-castings and outright stampings in our shooting irons. Remington with its remarkable new family of guns has led the pack.

A die-casting is made by forcing a suitable alloy—those with an aluminum base being among the best—in a molten state into a mould. It goes without saying that this must be done under tremendous pressure, the force applied from a mechanical or pneumatic source, and when the mould is once filled, the casting is permitted to cool. When removed, it is ready for buffing with little or no machining remaining to be done. Not only is the process quite rapid but it is also economical and surprisingly precise. Tolerances remain within useable limits, the necessity for the employment of highly skilled labor is largely obviated, and speed is attained for quantity production.

The alloy used in Remington firearms is a trade secret but it is safe to assume that it runs pretty close to the following: SAE Alloy No. 312, a composition of copper 7 to 9, iron maximum 2.5, silicon 2%, remainder aluminum. Tensile strength will range in the neighborhood of 33,000 ps.

While stampings and die-castings can materially reduce the manufacturing cost, most of our gun builders prefer forged and machined parts. Although some parts of a shotgun may be turned out of low carbon content steel, many others must be of alloyed stock, drop-forged, tempered several times during manufacture and finally hand-fitted. Breechbolts, firing pins, hammers, ejectors, and extractors are forged, turned, finish-machined, inspected and finally assembled to the gun. An understanding and appreciation of the time and effort involved makes it easier to realize that fully 70% of the cost of the weapon must be accounted to skilled hand labor.

During the innumerable operations that are part and parcel of the manufacture, an endless amount of control and inspection is maintained. There are inspectors in every division, in every department, almost literally in every bay. And while the machine operator isn't carried as an inspector, actually he is one of the most important. He knows best what he is doing, is most familiar with the part he is making, and if something goes sour he is first —or should be—to pick it up.

Additional inspections are constantly done by the bay foreman, still others by the department foreman, and finally by the inspection branch of the plant. These latter perform the most rigid inspections of all.

Col. Shelly Smith, chief guru of the Ithaca Co., third generation of the gun-building Smiths (not to be confused with the cough-drop Smiths), says a very conservative estimate of the number of inspections on a single Model 37 pump repeater would show that not less than 10,000 are made!

Besides these inspections accomplished by the bench operator, who, just for the sake of illustration we will say is finishing firing pins, there comes around the department inspector. He will pick over a basket of pins and apply his "go" and "no go" gauges. This particular operation is permitted a certain percentage of firing pins as rejects. An allowable rejection rate will run about .05%.

If the inspector finds on making his check that the allowable rate is being exceeded, he immediately commences an energetic investigation to pin down the trouble. The production of the pins may be halted until the trouble is localized. This is a costly proceeding, for very soon the lack of pins will be felt on the benches where breechblocks are being assembled. It is a chain-reaction sort of thing. Let it be noted that this is an example and would be a rare happening indeed. Inspection and manufacturing control is so rigid and so continuous that major troubles are largely avoided.

One of the final operations is bluing. Each manufacturer has his own process and the secrets of the bath are guarded like the stuff we keep underground at Fort Knox. Once blued, the piece is completely assembled and goes along for final inspection. Before the bluing and after having been completely finished it has the second and definitive proof-load. After that the weapon gets the proof mark stamped on it. Usually a number of functioning rounds are fired through it. After that it is ready for a light oiling, packaging, and a trip to the jobber.

Chapter 3

THE SHOTGUN IS AN ENGINE

WALLACE COXE, for 40 years the chief ballistician for Dupont, says the shotgun is an engine. It is an apt description. The barrel, says Coxe, represents the cylinder, the shotload is the piston and the wadding the piston ring.

Provided the cylinder walls are straight and true, just as with the auto engine, and further provided the wadding forms a seal both strong and secure, again like the conventional piston ring, the performance of the "engine" will be satisfactory.

The truth is the shotgun "piston ring"—the wadding—performs in mediocre fashion. It has lagged behind in the development of our shotgun-engine.

Now we are interested in the "cylinder" of the shotgun, that is, the barrel. The shotgun develops low breech pressures, from 8-12,000 pounds per square inch, and for this reason may be constructed quite safely of a thin, light tubing. Some extra metal must be retained about the chamber, but an abrupt taper toward the muzzle permits the use of a tube with side walls that are quite light. During manufacture the barrel must be straightened a number of times because of its lightness. Unlike the rifle the scattergun tube is easily straightened.

Some barrels are made of high carbon steel, others of chrome nickel; at least one manufacturer uses chrome molybdenum, and there are other alloys employed. High tensile strength alloys such as chrome, nickel, and chrome-moly permit the manufacture of a barrel that is lighter in weight than one made of straight carbon steel. This in turn means that weight may be safely reduced and an improved balance attained.

Regardless of the kind of alloy used, all shotgun tubes are made very much after the same process. The tube after pouring is submitted to the drop-forging hammer while in a heated state. It is then pickled to remove scale, is machined, stress-relieved, heat treated, and finally bored, chambered, finish-reamed, and polished, the step-by-step manufacture following pretty generally the same pattern whether accomplished by Winchester, Remington or Browning.

There is a great deal of broach and button-boring of rifle and pistol barrels these days, but to the best of my knowledge these latest practices have not been found practicable with the smoothbore.

The inside dimensions of the shotgun barrel are as fixed 'mongst American makers as a Southern Baptist's conception of Hell. A good many years ago the gunmakers got together and formed a tight little circle known as the Arms and Ammunition Manufacturers Institute. At monthly intervals representatives of all the larger arms and ammunition companies meet in New York and among other things establish the minimum and maximum dimensions for the shotgun barrel. This was done long ago. They permit

Checking equipment preparatory to checking velocities of duck gun.

Elaborate equipment for recording muzzzle velocities of military weapons.

Checking velocities of the 10-gauge 3½-inch magnum cartridge.

some deviations from the standard since neither man nor machines work to zero tolerances, but the variances permitted are small.

In Europe, including England, no such hard and fast agreements exist between manufacturers. As a result the buyer never knows just what he is getting. The gun may be stamped "12 gauge" but this does not mean the tubes will measure .729-inch by any means.

Attempting to improve performance, Continental shotguns are sometimes under-bored. We experimented with this business a long time ago and learned to our full satisfaction that there is little to commend it. Here barrel measurements as followed generally by our makers are:

410 gauge	.410 inch
28 gauge	.550 inch
20 gauge	.615 inch
16 gauge	.662 inch
12 gauge	.729 inch
10 gauge	.775 inch

The manufacturers do not reveal what tolerances they permit themselves from the agreed-upon standards. It is to be presumed that a variation of about .006-inch is probably permitted. In this connection some interesting stories are being bandied about by at least one of our leading firearms writers to the effect that 12-gauge guns are being under-bored as much as .722-inch and over-bored to .748-inch. If there is any truth in these tales, I am inclined to believe the guns that were measured by this gun-writing hack represented lone specimens and are not indicative of a trend to either over-bore or under-bore.

The barrel, properly speaking, is divided into several well defined sections. These are: (1) the barrel proper, (2) firing chamber, (3) forcing cone, and the (4) choke.

Chamber measurements as followed by the members of the Arms and Ammunition Manufacturers Institute are:

Gauge	Chamber Length	Chamber Width At Breech	Chamber Width At Cone
410	3 inch	.478 inch	.463 inch
28	2.875 inch	.6284 inch	.614 inch
20	2.750 inch	.6988 inch	.685 inch
16	2.750 inch	.7458 inch	.732 inch
12	2.750 inch	.8118 inch	.798 inch
10	2.875 inch	.8554 inch	.841 inch

These measurements are minimum figures in every case. What the allowable maximum may be is not revealed.

An interesting comparison with figures provided by the Government Proof House, Eibar, Spain, is as follows:

Gauge	Chamber Length	Chamber Width At Breech	Chamber Width At Cone
410–10.4 mm°	50.8 mm.	12.05 mm.	11.8 mm.
28–14. mm.	63.5 mm.	15.9 mm.	15.6 mm.
24–14.7 mm.	63.5 mm.	16.8 mm.	16.5 mm.
20–15.6 mm.	69.8 mm.	17.73 mm.	17.4 mm.
16–16.8 mm.	69.8 mm.	18.92 mm.	18.6 mm.
12–18.5 mm.	76.2 mm.	20.7 mm.	20.30 mm.

° 25.4 millimeters equals 1 inch.

A chronograph of field type used to record shotshell velocities.

Making ready to take velocity reading.

It is interesting to note that both ourselves and the Spanish do not cut chambers with a negative chamber but maintain a uniform narrowing of the chamber from the breech to the forcing cone. This is to expedite extraction.

Fifty years ago we had a variety of chamber lengths in all the gauges. Since then we have largely eliminated the freakish lengths. The 12 gauge is standardized at 2.75 inches with some Magnum guns made for the 3-inch casing; the 16 and 20 gauges are standard at 2.75 inches. The 28 gauge, as well as the standard 10 gauge, both at 2⅞ inches; the 410 at 3 inches; and on special order the Magnum 10 at 3½ inches.

Directly ahead of the firing chamber is a short, tapered section in the barrel. This is called the forcing cone, or sometimes more simply the cone. It is a funnel cut into the gun-tube which serves to shunt the shotload from the cartridge into the barrel proper.

When the shell opens the crimp unfolds under the impetus of the powder gases and as the edges of the case-mouth straighten they make contact with the forcing cone. As the shot commences to pour out of the cartridge the sloping shoulders of the cone funnel the pellets into the bore.

It would appear from this that the cone performs a simple chore. Actually it is an extremely important function in the step-by-step delivery of the shot to the target. The cartridge is larger than the bore; it follows that the shotload is likewise of greater diameter. When the sledge-like blow of the gases sets the several hundred pellets into motion they do not move smoothly and evenly into the barrel but are jam-packed, hurly-burly.

This action is accomplished in an infinitesimal part of a second and to say that the funneling is done gently would be like describing nuclear reaction in the same terms.

The soft leaden pellets are in a lump, a core which is larger in diameter than the gun bore and during a passage of approximately .250 inch must be constricted and elongated to fit into the smaller diameter of the barrel. All this the cone must accomplish. It is a tough chore and not only does this all-too-short "neck" take a beating but so, too, do the shot.

In a 1¼-ounce load of No. 6 shot there are some 279 pellets, of these approximately 130 are mutilated in the cone; in a 1⅛-ounce load of No. 7½ shot there are 388 pellets, of these 156, approximately, contact the cone and are rubbed out of round. The soft, tiny spheres of lead in the outer edges of the shotload are rubbed against the unyielding steel surfaces of the cone on the one side and are compressed against the stubbornly resisting mass of the shot on the other. Mutilated, out-of-round pellets are largely worthless in the pattern. These lop-sided members trail behind the bulk of the load, penetrate poorly if at all, and account for the scattered pellets to be observed on every pattern sheet.

Any number of amateur ballisticians have decided that the solution is a longer cone since it follows that if the passage of the shot from the larger diameter firing chamber to the bore could be accomplished slowly and gradually, the mutilation of the pellets would be markedly reduced. This idea is wholly sound except for one thing.

The wadding between shotload and powder is not sufficiently flexible as to instantly expand to the diameter of the cone, thus effectively blocking the gases. Nor does the wadding have the virtue of again contracting once the true bore is reached.

Wadding is so designed as to expand considerably under the anvil of the gases, but this expansion does not effect a seal between propellant and lead until it has entered the bore. The idea then of a long cone tapering gradually for several inches is not valid.

It is mandatory that the cone be short and that the angle of its approach (5 degrees, 30 minutes) be acute. Despite the fact that such sharply angled cones do harm to the shot, it is something we must, perforce, bear with. The shotgun is not a perfect machine and in no part of its design is there more room for improvement than here.

Attempts have been made to eliminate the cone altogether. This is done by building what is called a chamberless gun. Brass cases must be used, which permits a cartridge casing with a very thin side-wall. While the chamber is actually larger than the bore, the difference is negligible. Reports have it that such guns perform very well. The cone of course is non-existent. The distortion of the shotload in the cone is thus obviated.

So far as I am aware chamberless guns have never been made except in England, and then only in the larger gauges, 10 and 12. Obviously our cartridge manufacturers aren't going to consider anything as costly as a brass case. Especially in view of the rela-

A chronoscope for recording velocities of shotshell loadings.

tively small gains in pattern goodness. Many improvements could be made to both gun and cartridge if we disregarded entirely the commercial aspects of the problem. These, unfortunately, cannot be forgotten by the cartridge people.

As the shotload travels down the bore it tends to elongate somewhat; not greatly, but some lengthening of the column occurs. During this passage the powder gases are working powerfully against the obturators, *i.e.* the wadding. The gas leaks about the badly fitting wads and when it enters the shot column it wreaks no small harm. These gases are burning at temperatures of several thousands degrees and it is theorized by some ballisticians that some fusion of shot occurs when the gases sweep around the wadding.

I do not accept this, for the interval is too short; but what really does happen is that there is considerable disruption of the orderly arrangement of the pellets.

If there has been any measurable leakage about the wadding on the instant the shotload passes the muzzle the gas tends to flair and scatter the pellets. It is violent stuff and since it exerts force in all direction, laterally as well as forward, it disrupts the shot-column once it is free of the gun.

It may be seen from the foregoing that the wadding is a most important item in the scheme of things. If it isn't composed of such material as to be instantly as expandable as rubber, closing the bore very effectively against the gas, trouble is sure to develop. Many materials can be found that will perform quite satisfactorily as obturation agents. The rub is that far too many of them cannot be considered because of the cost involved, or for other reasons equally cogent. The manufacturer must use some material that is reasonably satisfactory but not too expensive.

There isn't any part of the shotgun cartridge more urgently in need of improvement than the wadding.

Chapter 4

THE ABC OF CHOKES AND BARREL LENGTHS

A CHOKE-BORED SHOTGUN develops more velocity than a cylinder bore. To explain this the water hose is a good example. When the nozzle is opened the stream has little force; screw the nozzle down so that the pressure builds up behind the narrowed stream and you immediately get greater distance and speed from the flow. It is similarly true with the choke-bored shotgun.

Burnside Laboratories of the Dupont Co. found, after a series of tests, that there is a difference of approximately 30 feet per second in the velocities of full-choke and modified-choke shotguns of the same gauge. However as between modified and full cylinder there is little difference at all. A matter of only 5 or 6 feet per second.

There are only three standard shotgun chokes today: (1) improved cylinder; (2) modified; and (3) full choke.

There are other chokes, but these may be had on special order only and are limited to custom-turned arms. The manufacturers no longer build full-cylinder barrels. A shotload from a true cylinder delivers a pattern that is patchy and unreliable. It will indicate concentrations of shot here and there and holes with no pellets at all in other parts of the pattern.

The improved cylinder has a slight choke at the muzzle. In the 12 gauge this constriction is usually about .004 to .007 inch. This slight reduction in muzzle diameter improves the pattern very markedly. It eliminates the sketchiness of the true cylinder and yet permits a dispersion of the shot to maximum diameters even at close range. A shotgun bored improved cylinder will open up about 1 inch per yard of range at 22-25 yards; and at 30 yards will cover a 40-inch circle. It is a most excellent executioner at skeet. And on such close-rising game as bob-white quail, snipe, woodcock, sora, and like game it is sweet indeed!

The improved cylinder performs best in 12 gauge, delivers a fairly effective pattern in 16, is patchy in 20 gauge and should not, as a matter of fact, be selected for the 20 at all. In 28 and 410 gauges it is largely worthless.

An improved cylinder barrel will place 45% of its shotload, regardless of the size of pellet, charge of powder, or length of cartridge, in a 30-inch circle at 40 yards. In testing for an improved boring, little attention should be given the choke dimension by measurement. The shotgun is a queer animal and while the degree of constriction in the tube-mouth in part effects the distribution of the shot charge at the target, it is not, by any means, to be accepted as the final word. The cartridge has the last say.

Some shotguns bored much more closely than improved cylinder will not throw patterns any better than this percentage. The reason lies in the shell. With a careful selection of cartridges it is possible to get better than improved cylinder patterns from a gun choked only .004 to .007-inch. Patterns may run as high as modified choke.

The modified choke is the best in the book. Modified, sometimes referred to as half-choke, means the gun will place 60% of the load in the 30-inch circle at 40 yards. This boring will kill more game, has a wider range of use, will account for more birds brought to bag and fewer cripples, and will be found more satisfactory than any other.

Ordinarily in a 12 gauge the constriction of the muzzle amounts to .022 to .025 inch. With a proper selection of cartridges the modified boring can be made to deliver full choke patterns.

With a poor choice of cartridge, ordinarily with a 2⅝-inch shell in a 2¾-inch chamber, plus the use of drop shot, percentages will fall until the modified barrel will deliver no better than improved cylinder patterns.

If shotgun makers decided to bore all guns to only one choke they would do the shotgunners of the country an immense service by settling on the modified choke. It is unbeatable.

The modified boring performs very satisfactorily in 16, 20 and 28 gauges. In 410 an improved-modified boring is to be preferred.

Last of the chokes is the full. A shotgun so bored and regardless of gauge will place 70%, or more, of the shot charge in a 30-inch circle at 40 yards. Not less than 10 cartridges and more preferably 25 should be fired to determine the average percentage. In testing a shotgun for choke a single round will not suffice. Neither do I consider 5 targets as sufficient, not less than 10 patterns should be fired. The shotgun is an inefficient machine and while it may be bored full-choke this does not mean that every cartridge fired will deliver 70% or more of the pellets inside the 30-inch ring. You will find if you essay the test that some patterns will indicate only 60% and others will range as high as 80%. The average of all rounds fired indicates the true choke.

A 12-gauge full-choke shotgun has little utility these days. It is a wildfowling gun and with bag limits reduced to next to nothing,

The 12-gauge magnum develops a hefty recoil.

as well as other factors which we shall discuss, it is a boring of limited value. In 20, 28 and 410 gauges this, of course, is not true. I am speaking principally of the 12 and in lesser part of the 16.

The full-choke 12 does an overly perfect job of concentrating the shot load. Such a marvelously efficient job, in fact, that the average marksman cannot hit with it!

The full-choke is for 35-50-yard killing. Distances so long the run-of-mill wing gunner misses because of faulty estimation of lead. The full-choke is an expert's tool, it has no place in the hands of the average shotgunner. Due to a dwindling game supply, shortened seasons, the press of modern business, and many other things, the ordinary hunter gets precious little shooting practice. He kills only a modest bag if you can get the truth out of him. As a result of his lack of opportunity to burn powder he is a poor marksman. Certainly far too mediocre to consider the use of a full-choke shotgun.

Despite these obvious truths there are more full-choke shotguns sold today than all the others put together.

The firearms companies would have it differently, for they have known for a long time what a sad shooter Mr. John Wing Gunner is. Surprisingly they have little voice in the matter. The shooting public demands the full-choke gun so the makers serve it up for them.

There are ways and means of circumventing Mr. Average Marksman and all for his own good, however; one of the largest of our arms-ammunition companies indicate these choke borings in their annual shooting manual:

Boring	Percentage
Full Choke	65 to 75
Improved-Modified (¾ choke)	55 to 65
Modified (½ choke)	45 to 55
No. 2 Skeet	50 to 55
Improved Cylinder (¼ choke)	35 to 45
No. 1 Skeet	35 to 40
Cylinder	25 to 35

It has been accepted for many years by all gun makers, ammunition people, writers, and ballisticians that American choke borings are:

Boring	Percentage
Full Choke	70% or higher
Improved-Modified	65%
Modified	60%
¼ Choke	55%
Improved Cylinder	45%
Cylinder	35%

A comparison of the sets of figures shows that this particular arms company is indicating more open patterns. It needs only a moment's reflection to see the strategy. If the shooter can be persuaded to accept a shotgun that is stamped "Full Choke" and the gun will only deliver 65% patterns—actually only a strong modified choke—he is far better off than the individual who insists on the 75% gun.

Again, I have never seen a modified boring as low as the 45% that is indicated by the ammunition booklet. On a variety of game the marksman equipped with a gun so bored, *i.e.* improved cylinder, will kill more game.

The company in question intend to help the shooter, and all through the simple expedient of retaining the old designations while at the same time opening up the various chokes.

The perfect choke is not the one that plasters all the shot load into a 16-inch circle at 40 yards. That isn't what we are seeking at all. What we are striving for is the boring which will deliver the ballistically inferior leaden pellets to the target so that every square inch of the target contains a leaden shot. It's distribution not concentration that counts.

A full-choke pattern, and for that matter any pattern, is full of holes and bare patches. In some spots there are concentrations of pellets and in others there is nothing. And about the fringes of the target there are always stray and scattered hits. These are bad, unwanted characteristics of the shotgun.

The perfect boring, if we ever achieve it, will see the target struck evenly and uniformly over every last square centimeter.

Choke is cut into a barrel in various ways. At least one of our arms makers employs what is referred to as a taper choke. Actually this choke is not a true taper but is cut with a slight radius. Any desired degree of choke (in a single gauge) is cut with one reamer, running it in deeper for a modified barrel than for a full choke, and still deeper for an improved cylinder boring.

Two others of our largest shotgun makers employ what is some-

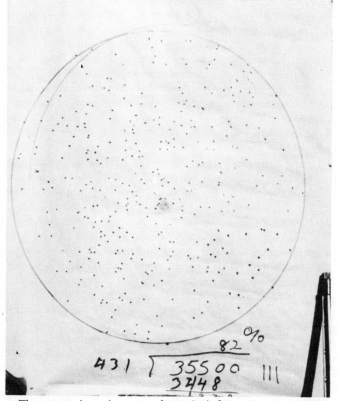

The pattern is an important factor in judging the worth of the choke.

times called the "standard" choke. The barrel commences to narrow some 3.5 inches from the muzzle and this taper continues for about 1.5 inches whereupon the constriction is held, without increasing or diminishing, for the remaining distance to the muzzle. In other words the last 2 inches of the barrel immediately behind the muzzle indicates a constant dimension.

A swaged choke is a cheap and hurried way to incorporate the needed degree of constriction. The barrel while still in the white and in a heated state is placed in a hydraulic press and the muzzle is forced into a die, thus narrowing the mouth. Due to the elasticity of the steel it tends to resume its old dimension unless stress-relieved. There remains the suspicion, whether stress-relieved or no, that the piece may lose a good deal of the supposed choke as time and shooting add years to the gun.

Many shotguns are swage-choked today.

Recess choking is a common practice of our better gunsmiths. This is ordinarily resorted to when the tubes have been cut off and the original constriction has been lost. The 'smith sets the barrel up in a fixture, then rigs a rod to which is attached a slotted and expandable head. The rod is entered into the barrel from the muzzle to a very carefully regulated distance. The slotted head carries the finest emery cloth, or a cutting compound, and is revolved by a slow turning lathe. After the emery, the gunsmith may use jeweler's rouge for the eradication of any scratches left by the emery. Lead lapping sometimes follows the application of the rouge.

The recess is generally cut 1.5 inches behind the muzzle and is, of course, very shallow. The amount of choke gained by this process is sufficient to produce an excellent improved cylinder pattern.

Since the word "choke" indicates that there is a narrowing of the muzzle, and since this is not done in a recess-choked gun, the reader may wonder how the shot is controlled. Actually what occurs is that the enlarged (or recessed) portion of the barrel permits the shot load to flair and broaden laterally. Once this wider lateral dimension is assumed the load is again narrowed as it enters the last 1.5 inches of the gun mouth. Thus by a somewhat different approach the same end is attained.

According to Jack O'Connor, one of our firearms writers, the 12-gauge barrel on the American shotgun is no longer bored to standard dimension of .729 inch. He says that many gunmakers vary from this dimension and that some tubes run as small as .722 inch, while others are over-bored and may be as large as .747 inch.

We have accepted for many years the figure that a full-choke 12 ran around .690 inch, in other words had 40/1000 inch of constriction. This is usually referred to as "forty points" of choke; the improved-modified (¾ choke) had 30/1000 inch or thirty points"; modified 20/1000 inch or "twenty points," etc.

According to O'Connor this is no longer true. "With today's ammuntion," he writes, "any gun with much more than .030 inch (thirty points) of constriction is probably over-choked. Guns marked "full-choke" leave the factory with as little as .035 inch of constriction and actually shoot full-choke patterns."

He attributes these changes in choke dimensions to the folded

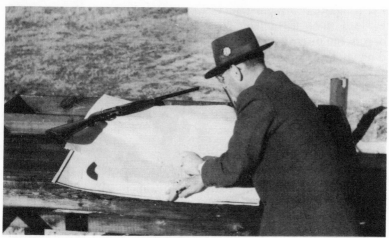

Counting patterns.

crimp, gas-seal wadding, frangible over-shot wad, etc. O'Connor suggests that the manufacturers have quietly altered bore diameters and said nothing about it.

As substantiating argument he tested a friend's 12 that was marked improved cylinder (45% in 30-inch circle, 40 yards). Results ran as follows:

1st shot (Peters 3 drs equiv X 1⅛ oz X 7½)	66%
2nd shot (Winchester 3 drs equiv X 1⅛ oz X 7½)	71%
3rd shot (Remington 3 drs equiv X 1⅛ oz X 7½)	67%
4th shot (Federal 3 drs equiv X 1⅛ oz X 7½)	74%
5th shot (Western 3 drs equiv X 1⅛ oz X 7½)	65%

These percentages indicate the shotgun was delivering patterns that ran from improved modified (¾-choke) to full choke.

I discussed the contentions of O'Connor with one of our leading cartridge manufacturers and he says he has absolutely no evidence to indicate that barrel specifications are or have been subtly altered by the gunmakers.

It used to be strongly supported that the longer the barrels on the shotgun the more lethal the fusee. Joe Falcon, one of the big wheels in the Savage-Stevens Arms Corporation, tells me there is a growing demand for his Model 220 single-barrel 12-gauge with 36-inch tube. Shades of the old Long Tom! At the turn of the century when black powder was still in vogue, wildfowlers thought any shotgun barrel less than 32 inches in length was wholly out of the question. Most preferred the barrel to stretch a full yard. It appears notions die hard.

Wallace Coxe, whom I have mentioned before, says that peak pressures are reached in the shotgun tube by the time the load has progressed a scant four inches up the bore. Further than that he says these extra long barrels actually reduce velocities! This occurs because of the friction and drag of the shot load and wadding as they are pushed up the barrel.

On the other hand you can go too far in the opposite direction. Whack a 12-gauge tube off from 30 inches to, say, 25 inches and what do you do? Why you reduce the instrumental velocity (speed of the shot over a 40-yard range) by an average of 6.5 feet to 7.5 feet for every inch reduced. This is considerable. Where then is the happy medium?

More than 75 years ago, Greener wrote in his *The Gun and Its Development;* "The proportionate length will soon be ascertained from the ratio of length (barrel) to caliber—40 to 1 holds good for shotguns and rifles—the gauge and length of barrel will determine the weight of the weapon; if its weight is not proportionate to the load it will recoil unpleasantly. A safe rule is to have the gun weigh 96 times heavier than the shot load."

The old boy then goes on to list his barrel lengths on the basis of his 40 to 1 ratio. This sees the 12 gauge come out to 29.16 inches; not so far off, really, and especially when you consider that Greener was writing in the 19th Century.

For the 16 he indicates a proper length of 26.48 inches, which is close to the standard 26-28 inches we accept today. In considering the 20, 28, and 410 gauges, however, his formula is all wet. He'd settle for a 20 gauge with a barrel of 24.6 inches, the 28 at 22 inches and the 410 at a mere 16.40 inches.

We build our shotguns with tubes from 24 inches to 36 inches, this variation covers the field from 410 to 12-gauge magnum. In the first days of skeet, now a good 30 years agone, you would occasionally see some student of the smoothbore tube who would visit the field with an abbreviated version of the gun that was going to bust 'em all. Tubes ranged from sawed-offs of 18 inches to 22, 24, and 25 inches. The Model 97 Winchester with the riot barrel of 20 inches was extensively tested; I remember one fine Parker that was utterly ruined by slashing the barrels to a foot and a half. The bucko who did that looked like he should have been riding shotgun on the Wells-Fargo stage with that one!

These abbreviated models besides reducing the velocity very markedly also play hob with the lead, for the shooter finds he can literally swing 'em too fast. Not only that, but the muzzle blast from the foreshortened barrel is an unpleasant factor which seemingly adds to the recoil. This last isn't so important with the attachment of a muzzle brake, but the lack of sighting radius is something so critical that nothing can compensate for those inches that are gone.

Increase the shotload and with it a boost in the quantity of powder to drive that lead and the gunner really notices the carbine-like barrel. A shotgun is effected not only by jump but flip as well. The jump is the turning movement, or upward climb, during those microseconds when the shotload is traversing the barrel. The bend of the stock causes a turning movement about the center of gravity which forces the muzzle upward.

The second phenomenon, which, for the lack of a more apt term, is usually referred to as "flip," is seriously concerned with the shortened barrel. The pressures generated by the burning propellant as it forces the shotload up the barrel set up a series of vibrations throughout the entire weapon. The very manner in which the gun is gripped, the shape and drop of the stock, and most assuredly the length of the barrel have a great deal to do with the duratiaon and violence of these vibratory movements.

The center of gravity of all shotguns is below the axes of the barrels so that the so-called flip is in a vertical plane; with the double-barreled shotgun, in addition, there is a second movement horizontally due to the fact that the axes of the barrels are located to one side of the center of gravity.

Should velocities be increased the amplitude of the vibrations are at once stepped up, and this may cause the gun to shoot either higher or lower. At the factory the front sight is painstakingly calculated to force a certain inclination of the muzzle which is compensated by the presumption that the barrel will remain at its original length and normal loadings will be fired. Any tinkering with the length of the barrel has its immediate consequence in the flip of the piece. And what a lot of people do not know, many times to their sorrow, is that the attachment of a muzzle choke drastically effects the amplitude of the vibratory movements of the barrel. As soon as the front end dingus is in place a careful check should be made on the pattern board and on a good many thrown targets to see what the flip is going to do.

The English for their grouse shooting have long been devotees of the ultra-short 12-gauge barrel. These usually run to a length of 25 or 25½ inches. It is one thing to have a 25-inch tube on a Winchester or Remington pump or automatic and quite something else again to have this same short muzzle adorning a double gun. That double with its runty little receiver makes a veritable pocketpiece of the weapon.

But the English use 'em, and if you have ever observed milord in a bit of hot grouse cover you'll agree that he seems to have the gun for the game!

Bob Nichols, who before his death was guns editor for *Field and Stream Magazine,* and who wrote the shotgunning book *Skeet,* was an advocate of the extra short barrel. Personally I always thought Bob was so blind he wanted a foreshortened tube so he could find the end of it; but be all that as it may, he had his effect on the shooting conscience of a very considerable audience.

According to Nichols, when thrashing out a bit of grouse cover or when gunning for timberdoodle, the 22 inches which he customarily advocated for his uplands guns was just the huckleberry. Tests at Burnside Laboratories indicate a 12-gauge barrel cut to 18 inches cannot be made to pattern effectively at 40 yards. But then no one takes ruffed grouse and woodcock at anything like that yardage.

The shooter who likes his shotgun barrel short can get away with some two inches less length if he sticks with the pump or auto-loader. The greater length of the receiver in effect gives him that much added sighting radius and it serves to place the muzzle sufficient distance ahead of his ears so he does not suffer from muzzle blast. The shotgunner who is addicted to the double or over/under cannot do this. His gun is notable for an action that is most compact; he must provide for the necessary sighting radius by retaining tubes that are never less than 26 inches.

The most popular barrel length today is 28 inches. Despite the fact that this length on a pump gun makes it some inches longer, overall, than its brother, the double barrel, this tube length is common to both weapons. It used to be that shooters demanded 30 inches for the 12 gauge, but this barrel no longer holds its old charm. Although in passing it might be well to harken back a few paragraphs to the words of Joe Falcon, the President of Savage, who points out that he is selling increasing numbers of the 36-inch single barrel.

Many pump repeaters and self-loading models are made in 26-inch lengths; Savage offers both their automatic and pump gun with 27-inch barrels. The new Browning Double Auto has a tube that is 27 9/16 inches in length, and the Breda auto shotgun, made in Italy and imported by Continental Arms Corp., has a barrel of 27 3/32 inches.

Among the 16s barrels range from 26 to 32 inches, with the shorter dimension more popular among the repeaters and the double addicts clinging to the longer models. Barrels in the 20 gauge run 26-28 inches. Personally, I believe the 20 is muzzle heavy, and a lot of whip and speed is lost with the little gun with any barrel over 26 inches. Certainly this is true with the 28 gauge.

The Remington Co. offers the 11-48 auto-loader in 410 gauge with a 25-inch barrel. Winchester adds an inch in their Model 42 pump repeater. The Fox double made by Savage in 410 is 26 inches, and there is a Stevens bolt action with only a 24-inch barrel. Mossberg not to be outdone have a bolt-operated 410 with a 25-inch barrel.

The 10-gauge Magnum, an import, is rising rapidly in popularity among goose hunters, sticks pretty closely to the 32-34-inch tube lengths. This is as it should be. Not only do the longer tubes provide the sighting radius so essential to accurate work at 50 yards, but muzzle blast is minimized by the extra inches. The big Magnums range from 10½ to 12 pounds, they have to be hefty to absorb the 50-odd pounds of recoil. Most of this weight, as in any shotgun, is located in the butt end of the weapon, unless there is plenty of barrel length to compensate, the balance is ruined.

Chapter 5

THE STOCK: THE LINK BETWEEN THE MAN AND THE GUN

IT IS DIFFICULT for the uninitiated to perceive the importance of the gun stock. To the non-shooter it probably appears a rather odd-shaped not to say downright ugly piece of furniture. Wholly apart from its appearance the stock provides a most vital link between man and gun. Depending on how it fits, the link may be strong or weak, literally welding human and machine into a single sweetly-functioning unit—or be quite the contrary.

A gun stock appears to be a simple thing. This is an illusion. While stocks may look as alike so many babes in the late Follies, in truth they are not. There is much about the walnut that does not meet the casual eye. A difference of no more than .5 inch in length can do real harm; a quarter-inch fraction in height can wreck havoc. The width of the comb, the pitch down or up, a toe too long, can render the piece worthless.

Nope. Stocks may seem as alike as TV jokes, but scratch the surface and you will find they are not.

Our gunmakers know a great deal about stocks and how they should be fashioned. As a result of their great experience the dimensions, size, and outline of the standard factory stock approaches perfection. In nine out of ten cases the gunner finds he can pick up an over-the-counter shooting iron and finds the stock fits him very well indeed.

The gun stock has a certain terminology which is best explained so that in subsequent paragraphs we are sure of a mutual understanding.

The place where the stock joins the gun frame is known as the grip, or small of the stock, this portion may be straight or may have a handle which looks very much like the stock on a handgun. If shaped in this latter manner it is called, happily, the "pistol grip." Behind the grip the main stock begins. At its top is the comb. The forward point of the comb is called the shoulder, the rear is known as the heel. The lower side of the stock has a toe. Properly speaking the heel and toe belong to the gun butt. The butt is long and narrow, broadening at its middle and slimming

44

gradually toward the heel and toe. The outline is an elongated oval, an oval three times as long as it is broad.

This then is a brief description of the salient parts of the gun stock. The terminology holds whether considering scatter-gun or rifle stocks.

The length of the stock is a critical measurement; a stock may be worthless if it is a bare half inch too long or too short. The length of the stock is not figured from end to end of the wood. Measurement is calculated from the trigger (the forward trigger if a two-trigger double gun) to the center line of the butt. This is called "length of pull" and not length of stock, although many times we are guilty of carelessely using the latter phrase.

Depending on the make and kind of gun, the trigger is going to be located a bit differently. The repeater has a trigger hung on the aft end of a long receiver· the double, on the other hand, has its trigger positioned below an action notable for its dumpiness. For these among other reasons, length of pull is a measurement which must be figured from trigger to butt and not of the wood alone.

The length of pull for the average shotgun stock is 14 inches. This measurement fits almost everyone. It may vary but the differences up or down are small, ranging from 13⅞ inches to 14¼ inches, and depending upon the type of gun. Some pump repeaters run a mite shy as to length while one of our over-and-under smoothbores has a stock of 14¼ inches.

If a shooter is of average height with arms and a neck of normal proportions he can shoot the 14-inch stock. If, however, he is tall and gangly with a long neck and arms to match, the standard stock will give him trouble. There follows a rough sort of table which indicates pretty closely the length of pull based on the height of the gunner.

Height	Length of Pull
5′ 4″	13½ inches
5′ 6″	13⅞ inches
5′ 8″	14 inches
5′ 10″	14 inches
6′	14¼ inches
6′ 2″	14½ inches
6′ 4″	14¾ inches

A gun to be fired accurately has got to have two sights. One of these sights must be located at the muzzle end and the other near the marksman's eye. The farther apart these sights are, other things being equal, the more accurately the gun can be aimed; a gun with only one sight cannot be aimed precisely. The shotgun has only

one apparent sight. This is the tiny bead at the very business end.
While the weapon seems to possess only this one sight, actually
there are two.

The second sight is sort of an illusive affair. It consists in part
of the gun stock and in part of the standing breech. The shooter

Typical arms at the skeet club. Most of these guns carry the standard factory stock, which will fit ninety percent of all shooters.

brings the weapon to his shoulder, snuggles his cheek down on
the comb and looks over the breech end, the stock arbitrarily positions the aiming eye to a fixed line above the breech, and thus
provides an effective rear sight.

Effective that is if the comb is the proper height and the marksman trains himself to place the cheek in the same position on the
comb each shot!

This may appear at first blush as a crude sort of a rear sight since there is no visible apparatus. In truth it is quite precise. Successful use of the stock as a positioner for the sighting eye depends on the height, shape and conformation of the comb. If it varies as much as one-fourth inch from what we know to be correct, shooting troubles will arise.

A comb with too much drop, that is, one that is too far below the rib line of the gun, will place the eye in such a position as to make it possible to see only the tiny bead at the muzzle. Such a weapon will shoot low. A comb which permits the front sight plus some eight or ten inches of the sighting rib directly behind the bead to be seen will shoot dead on; a comb that allows the gunner to view not only the front bead but all the sighting rib will shoot about 10-12 inches high at 40 yards. Most practiced wing shots prefer a gun that shoots high. Such a weapon permits the marksman to aim not at the target but under it. In this fashion the bird is kept in view at all times, his turnings and twistings followed the better.

Nothing is more fatal than the low-shooting shotgun. The self-anointed wing gunner who has trained himself on the rifle and subsequently switches to the smoothbore ofttimes demands a stock with such an excessive amount of drop as to permit him to aim down the rib. He sees nothing except the front bead, exactly like his .30-06. This rifleman-turned-shotgunner dubs off until he learns that the comb-drop of the rifle won't work on the scatter gun.

I look for a smoothbore that will throw its center of pattern a good 10-12 inches high at 40 yards.

The normal measurement at the comb on all standard shotguns is 1⅝ inches below the aiming rib. For the average this drop at comb is okay. The height of the comb is measured by placing a straight edge along the sighting rib of the gun and then checking the distance from the straight edge to the very point of the comb. Sometimes the drop is a bare 1½ inches, this variation from the standard does no harm. A gun with 1½ inches drop will shoot a bit higher than the weapon with 1⅝ inches. Should the comb indicate as much drop as 1¾ inches it can be shot successfully only by the gunner with a neck as long as a Tom turkey.

By the same token if the comb height is only 1⅜ inches, then look out! Such a stock is said to be "straight" and is made for the trap-shooter, or more popularly for the live-bird marksman, both of whom have need for guns that throw the charge quite high. Sometimes, however, there are exceptions. The shooter with a neck that is no neck, the individual who appears to sprout ears on the top of his shoulders, can handle an extremely straight stock.

The drop of the stock can be easily changed. If the gun has too much drop the comb can be raised by the liberal application of plastic wood, or by lacing on a Jostam cheek pad, or by sawing off the comb altogether and then dowling on a false and higher accessory comb.

By the same token the comb can be lowered. It is altered by cutting it away with a rasp, the rasp followed by successive applications of sandpaper, each finer than the last, until finally the desired height is achieved. The altered section can then be treated with wood filler, stain, and linseed oil to return the stock to its original color.

Occasionally stocks, especially on double guns, are steamed and bent to alter the drop. On some repeaters this can be done by bending the tang, or by altering the position of the retaining bolt which passes through the center of the stock.

Stocks from custom makers can be had, if desired, with what is referred to as cast-off. This means simply that the stock is built with a slight curve or deviation to the right. This curvature is seldom more than one-eighth inch and suffices to place the marksman with beefy jowls more directly behind the sighting rib. There is also such a thing as cast-on in which case the stock is twisted to the left, inwardly that is, toward the gunner's cheek. This is for the shooter with an extraordinarily long and narrow face.

These variations are frequently built into Continental shotguns but are seldom seen in this country anymore, and never on standard models. It would take considerable persuasive powwow, I suspect, to convince one of our custom gun-stockers to carve a piece of walnut with either cast-off or cast-on. In my opinion any "cast" either in or out is pretty much humbug.

A very important detail is the thickness of the comb. This part of the stock must be fat and well-rounded on top. If it has any sharpness about it injury and consequently flinching will result. The Germans, before the war, have been some of our worst offenders in the matter of shaping combs that came up to an almost knife-like edge. Nor were they alone. I bought an over/under 12 several years ago that had been made by Fabrique Nacionale, Herstal, before World War II. Although this gun did not bear the Browning name it was a copy of the Browning Superposed to the last nut and bolt—all except that atrocious splinter of wood! It had a stock fashioned after the best approved kraut pattern. Small and flimsy with a comb that would have punished a granite jaw. Such combs were formerly common in Europe. Today, at least on the arms that are reaching these shores, these abbreviated numbers are seldom seen.

The comb should be broad at the top with plenty of wood to bear against the fleshy part of the cheek and to cushion the up-chuck of the piece. The shoulder, or point of the comb, must carry

The stock must fit if the shooter is to hit.

far enough forward so there is no danger of digging into the face. If a comb is so bobbed-off as to permit the point to dig into the cheek it indicates the stock is too short or else badly designed.

A happy sort of comb is the Monte Carlo. This comb has no drop to it; it is the same height from end to end, there is no sloping toward the heel of the stock. The advantage is that regardless of where the face drops on the comb the eye assumes the same elevation. The Monte Carlo has much to commend it.

The only fault I have to find with this comb is on the score of beauty of line. The Monte Carlo near the heel suddenly makes a horrendous swoop downward and then curves into the butt. It ruins, completely ruins, the graceful lines of any firearm.

Another device that has much to recommend it in so far as positioning the face properly and also protecting the cheek is the cheekpiece. This modification is a raised and extended side on the left surface of the stock. In effect it very positively positions the shooting eye, broadens the comb most comfortably, and while insuring a more precise aim also dampens the blow to the face. The cheekpiece is not nearly so ugly, nor yet so obvious as the Monte Carlo comb, yet in all honesty it must be admitted that it is an unsightly sort of growth which stands out from the side of the stock and gives it an ungainly and lop sided appearance.

Despite this I like the cheekpiece. And even like unto the Zulu and his wooden lip-plugs, I have come to accept it as a rather good-looking accessory.

A comb that is too narrow besides permitting the gun to whack you a disagreeable blow may very well be so sharp as to cause cross-firing. If the comb permits the face to reach beyond the center line of the stock the aiming eye will not look down the

The new Winchester Model 50 automatic has a stock which runs 14"x1½"x2½". It will be found okay for the majority of field gunners.

sighting rib but will be positioned to the right of this line. Then there is the devil to pay for sure! Happily, I do not know of any American shotgun thus sadly engineered.

The gun butt is an important part of the stock. It should measure not less than 5¼ inches in length and not less than 1¾ inches in width. A butt any shorter or narrower will punish the gunner if the caliber be as large as the 12.

The toe of the butt should not be too long. If it is it will dig into the shoulder; as well, it will give the weapon an undesirable amount of up-pitch.

The pitch of the stock is tied very closely to the size and shape of the butt. Suppose we take a look: Place the shotgun on the floor, use care to insure that the butt rests squarely. Move the weapon back to the wall until the breech touches the perpendicular surface, check to see that both the heel and toe of the stock are firmly and squarely planted. Now glance at the muzzle. It should extend outward from the wall some 1½ to 2 inches. This variation from the perpendicular indicates the pitch; a gun with a down pitch of 1½ to 2¼ inches is about normal. Should the weapon, during our test, have touched the wall at the muzzle it would be said to have a negative pitch. Some shotguns, especially for trapshooters and pigeon gunners, are actually pitched upward, these specialists are seeking high-shooting hardware.

Harold C. Russell, one of our finest trap and skeet shots, as well as a smoking hot field gunner, invariably specifies a shotgun with no pitch at all. Billy Perdue, one of the great live-bird marksmen, winner of the 1952 pigeon championship of Europe, shoots a Purdey with a full inch of up-pitch!

The pitch, whether up or down, is regulated by the angle of the butt. If the butt is short at the toe of the stock the gun will have a down pitch; if it is long at this point it may have no pitch a all, or conceivably be up-pitched a little. Happily the standard smooth-bore has about 1½ inches of *down-pitch* which is correct for most of our marksmen.

Guns of 16 bore and larger need recoil pads. The pad is an ugly accessory made for utility and not for beauty, yet so undeniably necessary as to persuade us to bear with the thing even though. it does harm to the good looks of the gun. The pad is ordinarily made of rubber with a hard backing of bakelite and is slotted so that the recoil may be absorbed more rapidly and in greater degree. I have never seen any estimates as to the amount of perceptible recoil eliminated, or taken up, by the pad. It is considerable, how-ever, and is peculiar for the fact that the softening of the blow is not so noticeable the first shot nor during the first dozen shots; but should the gunner fire as many as a hundred rounds, the real value of this rubber attachment is really appreciated.

Some manufacturers offer their guns with the recoil pad at-tached, others do not. If it is decided to attach a recoil pad the job should be given to a competent gunsmith. Excellent recoil pads are made today by Pachmayr, Mershon and Jostam. The pad meas-ures approximately 1¼ inches in thickness, this necessitates a reduc-tion in the length of the stock. This shortening is a tricky chore. Should the owner attempt the job he is very apt to alter the pitch of the gun. Just permit the saw to wander off toward the toe and he will find he has an excess of down pitch, or should he remove too much at the heel and even more disastrous results will ensue!

The over-the-counter shotgun, ordinarily, is provided with a bakelite or hard rubber buttplate. This accessary is cheaply made, is durable, and protects the wood from splintering. However from the standpoint of the shooter it leaves something to be desired. The plate is corrugated, serrated, or in other manner roughened so that the gun is supposedly anchored against the shoulder. Ac-tually the roughening wears slick after a time and permits the gun to crawl ever so little when a hasty mouting is done. On the other hand the rubber recoil pad will cling to the clothing and once the

stock hits the shoulder it stays put. Recoil pads from the best manufacturers are either serrated, grooved, or in other manner provided
with a surface which clings very satisfactorily.

The man with an average hand should have a small-of-stock, or
grip, which measures about 4½ to 4¾ inches in circumference. If the
grip is too large it does not feel secure simply because the gunner
does not get his fingers around it sufficiently. On the other hand a
lady-like grip is a good deal like grasping a broomstick. It is too
waspy and is forever uncomfortable. Beyond that a small-of-stock
that is too slim is always in danger of breakage. My shotgun with
largest grip, a Winchester Model 12, with custom stock, has a grip
which runs 5 inches. Smallest is a grip of 4¾ inches on a Westley
Richards over/under.

The grip needs be deeply checkered. This checkering to provide
the proper surfaces must be sharp and well defined. The checkering on standard model shotguns, if it exists at all, is almost invariably pretty poor. Not only does it fail to provide the necessary
sharpness but as for beauty it fails utterly. Checkering at its best
is seen on custom-turned and deluxe arms. Then it is not only of
good utility but adds measurably to the beauty of the shotgun.
Really first-class checkering must run 22, 24, or 26 lines to the inch;
each small diamond is clear and distinct and comes up to a needle-
like point; borders are cleanly and artistically executed, and the
work when finished adds impressively to the inherent good looks of
the weapon.

The pistol grip is a standard item on the American shotgun. This
ornament comes in three styles: full-pistol, half-pistol, and quarter-
pistol. It is believed that the pistol grip provides something looking
to the better control of the gun. There are those who contend that
the pistol grip provides a more secure support for the trigger hand;
there are others who say quite the opposite, that it positions the
hand to better support the gun. I'll leave it to the reader to take
his choice.

I believe the pistol grip on the pump gun is probably something
of an aid when the slide is shuffled.

On the automatic and the double gun I do not believe it adds
one iota to the handling qualities.

All standard models are currently so equipped. In considering
this penchant for the curving hand-hold it appeals to me that
shooters do not insist on the thing, they simply accept it. Everyone
has a shotgun with a pistol grip, therefore it is the thing. Or maybe
the buyer feels he gets more for his money when the new fowling
piece sports this extra two-bits worth of walnut.

The pistol grip cramps the hand when firing a two-trigger gun.

All our cheap doubles, both side-by-side and over/unders, have two triggers. On the single trigger models the pistol grip does not tie up the hand; neither can I see that it provides anything really worthwhile.

In all the gun world there isn't anything as pleasingly stream-lined as a side-by-side shotgun with a straight-grip stock. What a pretty package! Sleek and clean-limbed, it is a joy to behold.

Take the same weapon and attach a pistol grip and that hernia-like protuberance changes the thoroughbred into a hack. I wouldn't own a double-barreled shotgun with a pistol grip.

An important piece of wood is the forestock, or as it is many times referred to, the fore-end. The hand that guides, directs, swings, points, stops, starts and otherwise controls the powder-burner is the all-important forward one. This hand grips the fore-stock.

It is crucial that the two hands be positioned in the same plane. Too often the forward hand is located below the trigger hand. This makes for poor control and leads to a high shooting gun. The two supporting members have simply got to be in line, horizontally speaking. If they are, better and more consistent hitting results. If they are not, the performance of the gun-and-gunner team leaves much to be desired.

We regularly build several kinds of forestocks. On side-by-side doubles of yesterday the fore-end was a thin and skinny sliver of wood barely large enough to contain the ejector mechanism. Many similar forestocks are standard in Europe today. We deride these wee bits of wood and shout that they are inadequate. Actually they are not quite that bad. The more closely you wrap your hands about the barrels the better you point the gun. The forward hand should be located just as close to the tubes as possible. The tiny fore-end makes this more nearly possible. This whisper of wood has its faults as well as its strong points, its virtues I have just extolled; its faults are that with many fast shots, the gunner gets his fingers burned.

We are addicted to the beavertail fore-end. It is a greatly fat-tened kind of forward stock; some are well designed, others stink. The beavertail that is broad horizontally and quite shallow ver-tically is okay, the one that is fat and rounded, with great depth from top to bottom is objectionable. At least two custom stock makers are turning out beavertail fore-ends for pump guns and automatics that are criminal to behold. These are both of exag-gerated depth, position the forward hand far too low, and by so doing achieve a high-shooting gun.

A properly designed beavertail is found on the Winchester Model 21 double. It is broad yet quite flat. It offers a comfortable handful but due to its flattened underside the hand remains in close proximity to the barrels.

The fore-end on the pump repeaters in the standard grades is a good one. It is not too bulky, does not bulge downward thus increasing the depth, and it permits a nicely controlled gun because it is not too large in circumference. A skeet-type fore-end is made for most of our pump guns. This is built with an extension, reaching rearward, which is made to accommodate the shooter with the short arm, or for those who take a very shortened grip. This fore-end is invariably made as a beavertail.

The forestock on almost all our automatics is too large for most hands. This is well nigh unavoidable as the wood must cover the magazine and the recoil spring. Furthermore it must be heavy enough to withstand a considerable amount of rough handling. Some manufacturers of custom forestocks built this piece even larger than standard, so large, as a matter of fact, as to place the forward hand well below the trigger line, thus creating a high shooting gun.

Chapter 6

STOCK SELECTION, CARE AND REPAIR

STOCKS, both the main and the forestock, are made of American walnut. American black walnut is a plain-grained wood that is notable for strength but has precious little of beauty about it. Throughout the world there are 17 recognized species of walnut. Some trees range to a height of 150 feet and are 6 feet in thickness. Others are no more than shrubs.

The American black walnut is a native of North America and is found, generally, east of the Mississippi. Even during colonial days we exported the wood to Europe, mostly to England and Germany. Our walnut is not notable for a beauty of grain and for that reason was not used by the Europeans for gunstocks but was made into furniture.

During World War I, our walnut was used by the English for airplane propellers. During World War II, we placed such a demand on our dwindling supply that the wood became in short quantity. The American Walnut Manufacturers Association of Chicago commenced a campaign to encourage the planting and growth of more walnut for this very reason.

Other woods are used for gun stocks. Among these are myrtle, maple, cherry, apple, birch, mesquite and rosewood, to name but a few. None of these, to my notion, are as handsome as walnut.

Stocks made for standard shotguns are all cut, essentially, to the same pattern. They are as stereotyped as trigger guards and front sights. All are machine produced; as many as 20 stocks are turned out simultaneously, the blanks resting in individual fixtures but all revolved and cut as one.

The turning is regulated by a master stock, usually of brass, which carries the desired measurements. Around this master stock indexing wheels revolve, thus governing the movement and direction of the cutting edges. So accurate is the stock-turning lathe that all stocks are finished to precisely the same dimensions. Inletting of the action into the stock is commenced by machine and finished by hand. This latter effort is held to a minimum.

Stocks have various designations: Circassian, French, Italian, English and American. Circassian walnut comes from the Caucasus highlands of Southwestern Asia, an area behind the Iron Curtain. It goes without saying that the amount of genuine Circassian walnut currently under importation would not make a set of stocks for an old Peacemaker sixshooter!

French, Italian, and other walnuts, as the name indicates, come from those countries. However, it often happens that stock makers grade walnut as "French" or "Italian," et cetera, because of its appearance and not always based on the origin of the wood. Currently the best available walnut is French.

As might be surmised the majority of our stocks are of plain American black walnut. Most of it is about as appealing as the loose boards in the hen-house door. Some, however, is quite handsome; American crotch walnut very often runs to a beautiful, wavy pattern, and it is appealing indeed.

Wood for gun-stock use should be seasoned slowly, generally not less than five years. Purdeys tell me they are now making up stocks from wood that they have had in their Audley Street shop for 30 years. In our standard grades wood is frequently kiln-dried and it sometimes happens this artificially dried walnut checks and splits. A moisture content of 6% to 8% must be maintained.

Custom gun-stockers come to know wood very intimately. They can tell almost at a glance whether the blank will make a good finished stock. A proper blank will have the grain bending down through the grip and it will continue to flow downward to the very toe of the stock. When looked at from the top side, that is viewed edgewise, the grain should be perfectly straight. If it is not, that is if it weaves and is somewhat staggered, you may be sure it will make up into a stock that will be weak in the grip.

When the blank is in process of being roughed out it sometimes happens that the watermarks are mistaken for the grain. Should it happen during this operation that the watermarks are permitted to run at an angle to the grain, then look out! Grain and watermarks must follow each other.

Long experience has shown that only curly and fiddleback are desirable; by the same token stump or crotch burl must not extend into the small (grip) of the stock.

A rule closely adhered to in selecting a blank is to pick a piece in which the grain is straight and flowing. Sometimes expert stockers do not stick to this rule, but when they vary they do so knowing full well that the finished piece will probably be more handsome but may be somewhat less sturdy.

Those woods which send the discriminating into an ecstasy of delight are: stumpwood figures, curly or fiddleback, birds-eye, striped and ribbon figures.

W. S. Boyle, writing in the *American Rifleman Magazine*, tells us that the hardness of wood depends largely on the fiber content. Walnut to be worthwhile must be very hard, must be finely textured, and quite dense. The hard woods, that is, walnut, myrtle, cherry, apple and maple, are composed largely of fiber cells; also, and of lesser importance, of vessel cells and parenchyma cells. The soft woods possess few vessels and even less fibers. The fiber cells are elongated and have thick, tough walls. The parenchyma cells carry food and water, while the fiber cell, which is actually a dead cell, imparts strength and density to the wood.

Boyle, a ranking authority on gun-stock woods, goes on to say, in effect:

Patterns come from a variety of natural phenomenon, namely the location and direction of the annual ring, the natural coloring, and irregularities created by stump-figure, crotch, and other burls.

When the wood tissues arrange themselves in a long ribbon the resulting combination is called by the trade a wood ray. These rays usually radiate from the cambium to the center of the tree and are of importance in securing a handsome blank. In sawing, the blank can be greatly influenced since the orientation of the annual rings and the rays have much to do with the beauty of the finished blank. If a log be quarter-sawed the annual rings will be seen running parallel, these vertical stripes cut at acute angles by the wood rays. If traced, the wood rays are usually relatively straight. However, they may appear in irregular patterns depending on the distance the plane of section happens to follow them.

Curly or fiddleback figure results from repeated left and right deviations from the vertical alignment of the vessels and fibers. When the undulations are close and abrupt the pattern is called fiddleback. Birds-eye figure is due to local distortion in fiber and vessel alignment caused by conical indentation in the annual rings. These indentations may extend from the bark inward toward the pith and once started are continued in successive annual rings for many years. Sometimes the figures are confined to one side of the tree or to irregular patches. Striped or ribbon figure is caused by interlocking grain. In some species the fiber and vessels are slanted in one direction for several years; then the direction of pitch is reversed for a similar period, after which the alignment again returns to the original slant. The quarter-sawed surface of such interlocking grain wood shows characteristic striped or ribbon figure. There is no actual variation in color of wood, the alternating light and dark bands are caused by the difference in light reflection of these alternating zones.

Crotch, burl and stump-wood figures result from twisted grain in these parts of the tree. A crotch is that part of the trunk that forks. Burls are large, abnormal swellings that are formed on the trunk and limbs of trees. Stump wood comes from the base of the tree above the roots. All may produce very striking and unpredictable designs as a result of the contorted orientation of the wood tissue as it originated from the cambium. The temptation is great to use such beautiful wood in gun stocks, but there are serious problems of warping and splitting.

The finest of all stock finishes is London dull oil. It is highly resistant to scratches and other misadventures and gives a remarkable depth of finish which no other substance can attain. Only custom-hewn stocks are finished in London dull oil. It is an expensive process; a great deal of hand-rubbing is involved, and this more than anything else raises the price. Standard models never sport wood thus richly treated.

Happily the gunsman who has a stock of handsome figure can do his own oil finishing.

To oil finish an old stock requires, first off, that the original finish must be removed. This old finish most times is ordinary varnish and may be removed by the application of a varnish remover. The old coating can also be cut away with bits of glass.

After the varnish has been eradicated, sand the stock with a fairly coarse sandpaper, this is to eliminate scratches, small dents and other blemishes. Should there be dents of such depth as to make it impractical or undesirable to sand them out, they may be raised by the following process:

Place a folded and dampened cloth over the dent and then apply a hot iron to the cloth. An electric iron for ironing laundry is just the thing. The steam that is generated will cause the grain to rise. If needed more water should be poured on the cloth, the iron should be kept quite hot but care must be exercised to see that it does not burn through the cloth and char the wood.

It sometimes happens that stocks have undesirable pinholes in them. These should be filled and there is nothing better that I have found than stick shellac. It may be secured from any paint store. Heat a putty knife or a hacksaw blade and while holding the stick shellac against the pinhole, apply the heated blade. It will cause the shellac to flow into the indentation. It is best to swab off the area with alcohol before commencing.

After the marks of all former violence have been sanded down, switch to the finest sandpaper obtainable and work on the wood until it is smooth and slick as glass. Finish with the finest grade of steel wool cutting very gently and slowly. Work around the pistol grip and other spots where the cutting must be across the grain so as not to cast up any burs.

Wet the stock and raise the grain. This is best done by going over the stock with a rag that has been dampened with water and then squeezed out. As soon as the stock is dampened, dry it before an open flame. Do not get the wood so close it will be scorched or charred but work closely enough to dry it rapidly. When it is dry use the finest steel wool to cut away those whiskers of grain that have been raised. Repeat the process at least twice more. Never bear down strongly with the steel wool, rub only until the wood feels smooth and slick and when, virtually, it is observed that the grain has been reduced to the common surface.

Go over the stock with a good wood filler. This preparation may be purchased in any first-rate paint store. Allow the filler to set and then cut off the excess with a very light treatment of finest texture steel wool.

Make up a mixture of two parts boiled linseed oil and one part turpentine. Put the linseed oil on the stove and as it slowly warms add the turpentine. Remember turpentine is inflammable, so use care during the mixing. After heating apply the mixture to the stock while it is still hot, and continue to swab on the finish until the wood will accept no more. Let the stock set for two days and then repeat the business.

Heat up the linseed-turpentine just as before and apply it very generously. Give the stock all it will take and then put it aside for a full week. After that rig a buffing wheel; this buffer may be mounted in a lathe, or in a portable drill, or other suitable device. Cover the wheel with a buffer of soft, woolen cloth. Buff the stock with a mixture of finely powdered pumice stone and water, feeding the pumice and water slowly into the revolving wheel. If you cannot rig a buffing wheel then make a buffing block. A block of wood about four inches in length by three inches in width will do nicely. Tack a section of felt to this block to form the pad. Wet the pad with the pumice-and-water mixture. Rub the stock with long, even and lightly applied strokes.

When finally the various parts of the stock have begun to blend together, commence to rub the wood by hand. Add a little linseed oil now and then as you rub.

After that it is a matter of persistence coupled with lots of patience The longer the stock is rubbed the more handsome it will become. It should be rubbed a quarter-hour daily for the succeeding 90 days, and longer if the finisher can summon the necessary enthusiasm.

Unless the wood begins to take on an undesirable dark color, it is advisable to moisten the palm with a few drops of linseed oil each day before commencing the rubbing stint. If it appears that the stock is growing too dark, the oil should be discontinued. Use care when performing the daily treatment that your hands are not sweaty; the salt in the perspiration will do harm to your work.

The very finest gunstock finish done in oil. The standard factory gun comes with a varnished stock. This varnish is quickly applied and is much cheaper than a genuine oil finish. You can finish your stock in oil quite cheaply—but there is considerable work involved. All you need is a pint of raw linseed oil, some lacquer remover, sandpaper, paint brush, toothbrush, a piece of sheepskin—and lots of patience.

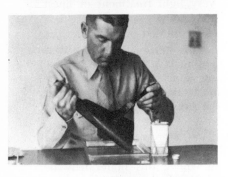

A stock cannot be satisfactorily refinished while attached to the action. Dismount it and remove buttplate. The old finish, almost invariably varnish, must be taken off. This is most expeditiously done with a liberal application of ordinary paint remover. A can at the local paint store will cost fifty cents. Permit the stock to dry thoroughly after the paint-remover treatment.

Heat up a teakettle of boiling water and liberally douse the stock, pouring on the water slowly and deliberately. This is necessary to raise the grain, the hot water causes this grain to stand out more quickly. Unless a stock is finished in this manner, there is danger during subsequent usage afield that rain on the stock will cause the grain to swell, thus ruining the appearance.

After the stock has been thoroughly wetted, force-dry it by exposure to the flame of the gasoline camp stove, or hold before an electric heater. Use care that the wood does not come in contact with the flame; to do so will char it.

Utilizing a fine grade of sandpaper, cut the upraised grain down to the stock. Use great care around the checkering that borders are not mutilated. Be equally careful around all corners. Sandpaper should be applied with the grain—never across it.

After the first wetting with boiling water and the preliminary sanding, the stock must be wetted and sanded again and again. Ordinarily not less than six applications will suffice. You must keep on until the grain will no longer rise. Operator is here wetting stock with a sponge and hot water.

It is conducive to time-saving to dry the stock artifically after each wetting. However, if time is not of the essence, the stock may be thoroughly wetted and then set aside for 24 to 36 hours and thereafter sanded lightly to cut off the "whiskers."

When the grain will no longer rise despite repeated wettings, the stock is ready to receive the final sandings in preparation for the application of the linseed oil. Use only the finest grades of sandpaper obtainable and apply gently, working always with the grain of the wood.

Warm a pint of raw linseed oil until it is unpleasant to the touch. Warm the stock before an electric heater until it likewise is uncomfortable to the hand. Then apply the heated oil with a piece of clean sheepskin. Be generous, continue to offer the linseed oil until the stock will accept no more. Set it away in a room with a temperature of 70 degrees F. for 24 hours. Then repeat the oil treatment.

The linseed oil is applied daily until the stock will accept no more. This usually takes some four to six applications. The wood is then ready to be rubbed down by hand. This is a process which may be concluded in a half-dozen sessions or may be extended over a long period. The longer the wood is hand rubbed the more beautiful it becomes. Place a drop or two of the linseed in the palm before commencing, rub always with the grain.

Some walnut is a bit on the blond side, and for this type a stain can be added in the form of burnt umber or other substance. This should be added to the oil. The resulting appearance will be much enhanced.

Standard model shotguns all have varnished stocks. The varnish may be applied quickly; and while it does not stand up nearly so well as oil, it still produces a very handsome finish provided the wood beneath the varnish is properly figured. The disadvantages of varnishes are that scratches, dents, and other misadventures show up, and over a period of a few years the varnish tends to chip off. On the credit side it should be pointed out, however, that a new coating can be quickly and easily applied, giving the stock a new weapon appearance.

To prepare a stock for varnishing the dull oil finishing process must be followed up to a certain point. That is, the old finish must be cut away; the stock needs to be sanded and smoothed up just

The most commonplace stock is improved by the oil finish. And stocks of first-water walnut are handsome beyond compare when oil-finished and hand rubbed. The oil finish makes a stock highly resistant to rain and the elements, and scratches and other misadventures inevitable in the hunting fields are never nearly so noticeable.

The linseed oil should be worked into the checkering with a toothbrush, otherwise it will not reach the bottom of the checkering cuts.

as painstakingly. Then the grain should be raised and steel wool applied until it will rise no more. Should it be necessary, wood filler can be applied after the grain is raised and sanded away.

The best method for applying varnish is to spray it on. This eliminates tell-tale brush marks and achieves a much more pleasing surface. After the first coat has dried, give it no less than 24 hours, then apply a second. Before adding the second coat of varnish, rub the stock down very, very lightly with the finest steel wool you can buy. You may want to add a third coat; and if you do, permit the stock to dry for another 24-30 hours. Give the wood the once-over lightly with the steel wool between the second and third coats.

Accept nothing but the best varnish on the market. The amount needed is trivial and for that reason use only top quality.

Don Newell, a paint and lacquer technician, has written in his book *Gunstock Finish and Care* (Samworth, $4.50), how to completely finish a gun stock in one hour! Newell uses infra-red heat lamps to hasten his various drying processes; and while I haven't tested his process, I am completely satisfied that it is probably just as successful as he claims.

This technician mounts a battery of three infra-red lamps along his work bench, each bulb pointed upward and ahead. He places his stock to be finished in a fixture which may be readily revolved.

He says you must use care never to shine the powerful beams into your eyes. Neither should you use sun glasses, for then a great deal of the detail will escape your attention.

Those items necessary before work is begun are:

    3 infra-red bulbs
    1 pint of clear lacquer
    1 pint of lacquer sanding sealer
    1 pint of water stain
    1 pkg of extremely fine steel wool
    10 sheets of waterproof sandpaper, 360 to 400 grit
    1 small, good quality paint brush

The first step is to remove the old finish just as described in the application of the London dull oil treatment. After that comes the scraping, sanding, and smoothing with steel wool exactly as done when applying oil. If the stock is somewhat light in color it may be advisable to stain it. The stain should be labeled "walnut" on the can; and as walnut comes in various shades, the operator must make sure he is buying the precise shade he wants.

The infra-red battery is permitted to play on the stock until it becomes uncomfortably hot. Use care to see the wood is not actually burned. When it is too hot to touch brush on the water stain. It will be noted that the water evaporates almost at once, leaving the coloring matter behind. Although it evaporates quickly there will be enough penetration to accomplish the desired purpose. Newell comments that sometimes unsightly marks of the brush will remain. These may be wiped out with a dampened rag. He states that in doing this oft-times the appearance of the grain will be enhanced by clever application of the rag, in places piling up a concentration of the stain, in others wiping it thin. A time of eight minutes suffices to do the stain job.

Due to the continuing play of the powerful lights the stock may be sanded at once. This should be done with extremely fine steel wool, and little pressure or force need be applied. After that the stock is ready for the filler.

Newell uses lacquer sanding sealer because he says it will dry faster and harder than shellac. The lights should not be closer than 10 or 12 inches so that there will not be any overheating. Apply the sealer very liberally, using a rag. As you finish both sides of the stock it will be noted that due to the heat the stock is completely dry. It takes about 15 minutes, says our expert, to apply three separate coats. Make sure the preceding coat is completely dry before applying a follower!

Place a square of 360-grit sandpaper in a pliable sanding block and level the dried film down to almost the bare wood. Use care to see you do not go through the filler and rip into the stain.

The stock is now ready for the lacquer. Apply the clear lacquer liberally, using a brush. The lights, just to remind you, are still burning. Heat continues to be applied but care must be exercised to see the wood is not gotten overly hot. Use the brush in long, sweeping strokes but do not work it unnecessarily, as unsightly brush marks may appear in the finish when it dries. A complete lacquer job will take about three minutes. Several coats may be applied if desired. Great care must be practiced to insure that the lacquer is dry before a following coat is slapped on.

When the lacquer is dry the finish must be sanded. The sanding block is rigged with a square of 400-grit sandpaper, a can of water is placed handy, and the sanding commences. First wet the sandpaper and then rub lightly, using long, sweeping strokes. Gradually a white film will appear on the surface. This film is created by abraded lacquer particles and water. It will dry very rapidly from the heat of the lamp battery. When the sanding has been completed use a coarse rag and rub the surface very energetically. The final finish will develop a handsome, glossy, high-polish surface; a delight to the eye of the most critical.

And according to Newell the entire process requires only 60 minutes!

Chapter 7

BEGINNER'S GUN: WHAT SHALL IT BE?

THERE COMES A TIME when the shooting father decides the son and heir had better be initiated into the mysteries of wing gunning. Maybe the boy is seven, possibly he is ten, more likely he has reached the age of twelve. Be that as it may, it is a pretty momentous milestone when father decides—and mother acquiesces—that Sonny is ready for his first shooting iron.

Papa, a shooting man himself, needs no advice as to the kind and caliber of ordnance to buy. He'll get Junior a 410, of course. A 410 is a very nice little gun. No kick. It will give the boy a lot of confidence because it won't hurt him. After a few seasons dad will graduate his aspiring young marksman to a 20 and ultimately he'll be shooting a 12. It is all very simple. First he starts the cub with a little gun, and as he gains skill and confidence he gradually brings him along, and lo! he has a full-fledged wing gunner on his hands.

So the 410 is duly purchased. Ordinarily the Old Man spends fifty-four-fifty every month for a case of fair-to-middlin' bourbon whisky and thinks nothing of it. But when it comes to laying the *dinero* on the line for a piece of shooting hardware for Johnny-boy, he gets pretty penurious and buys a cheap little bolt-action job. One of these shotguns with a rifle stock and a feel like swinging a fence railing.

The boy is happy though. It is his first gun, and maybe he is only ten and any gun looks like a prize.

Then commences some haphazard coaching on papa's part. After a box and a half of cartridges fired at tin cans and maybe a few hand-thrown targets, father pronounces him ready to go a-hunting.

Another box of 410 cartridges are purchased, and under the overly critical eye of the Old Man the game-questing begins. Several months and many dreary hours and as many monotonous miles later the season draws to a close.

What has the boy killed with his bolt-action 410? Well, he has killed two rabbits sitting under a patch of mesquite, one squirrel and two jaybirds. He has fired away several hundred of the pipsqueak shells at things a-wing but nothing falls. Is his interest as keen, his enthusiasm unabated, his zest for the redblooded sport

A proper choice of first gun insures a lifetime interest in shooting.

at passion pitch—just as it was when Poppy handed him that stinking little shotgun at season's beginning?

You're damned tootin' it ain't!

If the Old Man can get him out during the succeeding season he is going to be mighty lucky. Sonny has had all that nonsense he wants. Maybe in the beginning he had a lot of enthusiasm for hunting, but that ineffective little shotgun has cooled all of it.

The 410 is for the most expert of our wingshots. Only the very most skilled shotgunners can handle the tiny 11.50 mm., and then they have plenty of difficulty with it.

It is true the gun weighs only a trifle, a boy can lug it all day and never feel the weight; it is easy for him to bring it up and he swings it sharply. But the weight of metal it spews forth is wholly, totally inadequate. So small and so trifling is the charge, it requires not a poor fumbling tyro just breaking into the shotgun sport but a champion like an Alex Kerr to direct that charge.

Don't for godsake give a recruit a 410. And that goes not only for our young fry but for anyone who would become a smoothbore fan.

This advice is equally applicable to the 28. It is a slightly better performer than the 410, nevertheless it is too little a gun for the beginner. Both shotguns throw three quarters of an ounce of lead, a charge totally inadequate for the unskilled. In justice to the 28 it should be commented in passing that the manner in which it handles the three quarters of an ounce of metal is a credit to the 410.

The latter has a bore too narrow for this tonnage of lead, the shot column is too long in the case and even worse in the bore. A great deal of jamming and distortion occurs in the shell, and the number of pellets coming in contact with the forcing cone and the barrel is fantastic. As a result the pattern is adversely affected because a shot pellet with a flat side kills nothing. The 28 with a bore ranging some .014-inch larger does not mutilate the shot quite so badly. Even so it is not a sensible choice for the boy just getting under way as a wing gunner.

The beginner's gun is the 20.

Here, for the first time, we have sufficient shotload to do execution. The 20 bore kicks but not much. Loads can be had with one ounce of shot and only enough powder to blow your nose. And if this is still too painful, all that need be done is to attach the Cutts Compensator and thus eliminate something like 30% of the recoil. As for gun weight the 20 is available in standard models at 5¾ pounds. The new shooter who cannot swing a five-and-three-quarter-pound fieldpiece had better get a bow and arrow.

The 20 will kill game. It does poisonous execution in the hands of an expert and it encourages the novice. He does not grass his game at every shot but he connects with sufficient regularity to sustain his interest and encourage him to believe that he is learning. Unlike the half-pint guns, the 410 and the 28, the 20 runs through a gamut of loads. While the new marksman may commence with the one-ounce charge, he can, as his skill grows, increase the power of his cartridge until finally he is firing a full one-and-one-eighth ounces of lead. This was formerly the old 12-gauge standard load. Yes, the 20 is a versatile gun.

Good though the 20 may be as a first gun for the boy just breaking into the shotgun sport, a better gauge is the 12. There isn't anything the 20 will do that the 12 does not do better. And as for versatility, the larger weapon is the more flexible, the most versatile of the entire family. There are cartridges for the 12 no heavier than for the 20, and by the same token shells can be had that are more heavily loaded than for the standard 10 gauge.

Weight and recoil are against the 12 as a first gun, it will be argued. The 12 can be had in a weight of 6¼ pounds; and as for recoil, that can be compensated, thanks to Lyman.

Don't undergun your son. If you do, his lack of killing will dampen an enthusiasm kindled in the beginning but dangerously apt to snuff out due to the inadequate performance of the pony guns.

Shooters, whether tyros or old hands, do not like weighty fowling pieces. If they must swing a gun that tips the beam at upwards of eight pounds they bitch. At skeet this heft is of no moment, but it is quite another matter to follow the dogs on uplands game all day with a smoothbore that runs over 7½ pounds. Toward the shank end of the gunning most of the snap will be gone from the marksman. He's dragging, and it doesn't matter whether it is the football-playing sophomore home for the holidays or the Old Man himself. Hand a seasoned wingshot a strange shotgun and you may be certain one of his first comments will have to do with the weight.

The beginner here shoots a smooth-bored .22, an ineffectual and exasperating shooting iron, now disappeared.

He'll either attest that it seems light or feels like a quarter of Santa Gertrudis beef.

Despite the prejudices toward over-weighty fowling pieces it appears inevitable the poundages will go up. This is coming about in a rather obtuse manner. During the last few years we have developed a family of magnum shotloads; every gauge from 20 through 10 now has a super-duper Magnum loading. These busters kick like a rodeo steer. To shoot these new souped-up numbers in our present crop of scatter guns, practically all of 'em running six to eight pounds, is simply so punishing that shotgunners must sooner or later demand more weight to offset the beating they are taking.

An average man, weighing 165 pounds and standing 5' 10", to shoot the 12 Magnum load in comfort should have a gun weighing 9 lbs. Who in hell wants to lug a mortar of those proportions over six bogs and through a couple of sloughs?

The answer is two shotguns. The 12 for wildfowl and a second gun of somewhat smaller gauge and lessened poundage for uplands game. A quick run-down of the available hardware persuades that the 20 is the answer.

There will be those who will argue that the 20 is just as good as the 12 anyhow; and even more will rise to contend that most certainly it outshines the 16. Neither is true. The 20 gauge is not the 12, it isn't even up with the 16, but it is a mighty sweet uplands gun for all that.

Probably no one, speaking as a group, can better attest to the remarkable capabilities of the 20 that can skeet people. At uplands game distances, *i.e.* those at which we bust our skeet targets, the 20 performs quite as competently as the 12; the difference over a thousand targets won't tally more than 1% in favor of the bigger gun. This relative equality extends to 30 yards, beyond that the 12 edges ahead of the smaller weapon.

Unfortunately we aren't statistically minded enough. If the sportsman would simply pause long enough to get out his surveyor's chain and carefully measure the distance from gun muzzle to dead game on every bird brought to bag during the season he'd be astonished how many quail, doves, pheasants, and grouse are grassed at 30 yards and under. Mostly under. Those 40-yard, dead-in-the-air hits he makes are mostly over highballs in the evening.

The 20 will kill quite as efficiently as the 12 or the forgotten 16. And it accomplishes this mayhem with a minimum of strain on the part of the gunner. Watch the man who totes a 7¾-pound 12 all day and beside him the hombre with a 6½-pound 20. Other things being reasonably equal the latter will kill more birds after lunch and most certainly finish the shooting stint ever so much fresher come evening.

Standard target loads in the 12 gauge, the cartridge we use for both skeet and trap, are charged with 2¾ drams' equivalent of powder. That is also the standard powder charge for the 20 gauge. As to the shot, it amounts to 1⅛ ounces in the 12 and a full ounce in the 20. What is the difference then? A pipsqueak advantage in favor of the larger gun.

Of course in all honesty it goes a bit beyond the one-eighth ounce of lead. The 12 because of its bigger bore does not mutilate the numbers of pellets as does the 20, so there is an edge in favor of better pattern distribution and killing effect.

The 20 is ordnance for uplands game-taking. It is medicine—and proper medicine—for quail in all the species; for grouse, for partridge, and for woodcock and Jack the Snipe, for our mourning dove and our whitewings, for cottontail and squirrel. It is not a shotgun for wildfowling unless you consider those immature and slightly stupid early comers bound to squat among the decoys, or for jump shooting along slough or western drainage ditch. It is not, most assuredly, for geese, and I would hesitate to enter turkey cover with the little piece. It is too lacking in power for serious use with slugs on any species of our deer unless maybe those Florida Keys remnants reportedly only a size-and-a-half larger than a Texas Panhandle jackrabbit.

The 20, like the 12, has been included in the family of Magnum loads. The 20 standard Magnum (2¾-inch case) contains 1⅛ ounces of shot; the super 20 Magnum (3-inch case) holds 1¼ ounces. A switch from the garden-variety 1-ounce load to these atomic rounds changes 20-gauge gunning from fun to work. Deadly serious, punishing mayhem. You can shoot 'em but you are a liar if you say you like it!

The 20 is built to a general poundage of 6½ pounds. At this weight it is intended to be employed with 2½ to 2¾ drams' equivalent of propellant and ⅞ ounce to 1 ounce of shot. Stuff a 12-

A cabinet of double shotguns, a rare sight today. The double makes an excellent first gun for the just-getting-started tyro shooter.

gauge load, as the 1⅛- and 1¼-ounce bruisers are, into the 6½-pound gun and you are asking for a kick in the teeth—and you get it!

The solution is simple. The Magnum and super Magnum cartridges are going to stay with us. The longer they stick around the more shooters are going to bitch about how much recoil the big rounds develop. This will ultimately compel the manufacturers to step up the poundage of their 12-gauge guns. When this occurs the 12 will be pretty well relegated to wildfowling usage, for ducks and geese exclusively. No one is going to burden himself with a 9-pound fusee for taking quail. Turn to the 20; at its handy weight of 6-and-a-fraction pounds, it will be the answer.

The beginner should begin with the largest shotgun commensurate with his age and strength. The 12 is a good gun if he can take the recoil.

Chapter 8

THE OVER/UNDER SHOTGUN

THE MOST EXCITING SHOTGUN today is the over-and-under or superposed model. It is virtually unknown to the average wing-shot and for that reason he is intensely interested in it. And well he should be, for there is concrete evidence to indicate that better shooting can be done with the stacked-barrel model.

The over/under points more naturally, handles more surely and possesses a liveliness that is missing in all the others. I have been shooting the scattergun intensively the past 35 years. I've tried 'em all, the conventional doubles, the auto-loaders, the pump repeaters and the over-and-under. For me the latter is the only gun. I have eight of 'em and I'll probably possess another eight before I am through. I have kept close account of my killing against the cartridges expended this past decade and shell for bird the superposed delivers more game to bag.

Not only does it account for more game killed but it is a joy to handle; a beautiful, vibrant over/under shotgun is truly a glamor piece!

A shotgun is an extremely short-range proposition. It has got to be pointed in the hundredth part of a second and unless it falls dead on during that first mounting it is apt to miss. It is unlike the rifle which can be mounted rather leisurely and the aim corrected after the stock cradles at the shoulder. I sometimes think I have the trigger half gone before the butt really strikes my shoulder. At any rate the lead is taken as the gun comes up and if the gun does not fit me perfectly the shot is apt to be a miss.

The over/under performs as though it were a part of the gunner. It will fall dead on the mark and do it faster than any gun. It possesses this elusive yet highly essential quality because of its design.

A shotgun is pointed with the hands. If the hands are not in horizontal alignment, that is both in the same plane, the gun cannot be properly pointed and many times a miss will occur. The left or forward hand is the guiding element; the right, or rear, is the anchor. If the hands do not function in the same precise unison, with a coordination that is perfection itself, sloppy shooting results.

73

The still-popular Model 32 Remington O-U shotgun. Not made since World War II, this gun is much sought after by skeet shooters.

With many of our magazine squaw guns, both the automatics and the pump repeaters, the hands are not in similar horizontal plane at all. The left hand is compelled to clutch a fore-end only slightly smaller than Kate Smith's thigh and this drops it below the trigger hand. When this occurs the gun is continually pushed upward and the "pointing out" abilities of the weapon are adversely effected.

Fine double shotguns possess the "hands in line" factor and for that reason are excellent game killers. But I am not especially wedded to the side-by-side double, for it has a number of fundamental faults despite its good points. For one thing the fast wing-shot does not see the front sight; he is only aware of a blur at the muzzle. In effect what he is doing is using the last three or four inches of the business end as a front sight. When that front sight is. as broad as the two muzzles of the conventional shotgun it is just too wide for me. I simply cannot be precise with such a gun. Again we habitually fire the right barrel first. This causes the weapon to recoil in that direction due to the arrangement of the tubes and the support afforded by the gunner's shoulder. To recover from the first shot means the marksman must not only fight the shotgun back down but whip it to the left to compensate for the direction taken during recoil.

These are very elementary shortcomings in the double-barreled shotgun that will live with the weapon as long as it is made.

Once on a time all doubles had small and graceful fore-ends. These were little more than splinters of wood, and after shooting his way out of a hot corner the hunter would complain that his hand was burned. As a cure we went overboard for beavertail fore-ends. These great globs of wood hung beneath the tubes protect the shooters hands no matter how fast he may fire, but they also do harm to the good balance and handling qualities of the firearm. Just as occurs with the magazine repeaters the big beaver-tail throws the hands out of their vital alignment, and once this occurs the gun-and-gunner team perform in something less than top form.

The over/under has its tubes arranged in vertical bank. The

under barrel is invariably the more open bored and it is fired first. Because of the remarkable low position of this under tube it develops less apparent recoil than any gun of like gauge. This is due to the absence of the upward turning motion at the time the gun fires. So neatly does the shoulder absorb this recoil, due as I have said to the axis of the bore being in line with the support, the kick is remarkably mild. Because of this, the shooter does not have to fight his gun back into alignment and can get the second shot off much more quickly and effectively.

Virtue this may be, but it by no means ends the case for the over-and-under. Due to the arrangement of the tubes the forward hand wraps itself about the lower one. This is a most ideal arrangement. The higher the forward hand can carry about the barrel the more accurately the gun can be pointed. This, undeniably, accounts for the precision of the top-and-bottom model.

Not only do we see the hands retain their "in line" relationship but both are carried just as high as it is possible, due to the design of the shotgun. Therein lies the secret of the good shooting qualities of the glamor gun of the shotgun family.

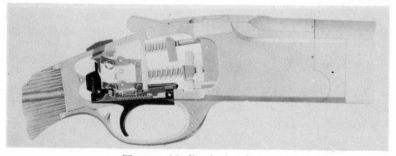

The new Marlin single trigger.

Pre-war Marlin over-under.

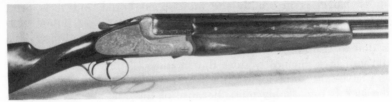

The handsome AYA Model 37 over-under shotgun as made by the firm
of Aguirre and Aranzabal in Eibar, Spain.

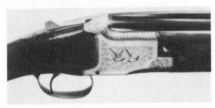

The Browning over-under in one of the highly ornamented grades.

I once conducted a long series of experiments to determine
which type of gun would deliver the shot charge to the center of
the target in the shortest time interval. I fired 25 shots with each
of three repeaters, two pump guns and an auto, and then set off
a full box of cartridges with each of three side-by-side doubles;
finally would up the shooting stint with an equal amount of firing
from three over/unders.

The time interval was an important factor and this I carefully
measured with the use of an electric timer which was activated
the instant the gun was moved from a low hunting carry. The
shooting distance was only 23 yards as I was simulating uplands
shooting. All the weapons were light, open-bored models.

The over/under not only won the speed-trial end of the tests
but placed the center of its shot charge nearer the middle of the
pattern sheet more consistently.

Time for the over/under based on the 75 shots and taken as an
average was 24/100th second; for the conventional double,
27/100th second; and for the 75 rounds with the 3 magazine shotguns was 32/100th second. This shooting required three weeks
and I fired only three-quarters of an hour each session, sometimes
commencing with one gun sometimes with another.

The ability of the over/under to get the shot off more quickly
and accurately is indication of its inherently perfect design.

Some over/unders from the standpoint of good design are better than others. I do not speak from the consideration of durability
or safety but from the standpoint of pointability. This factor hinges
in great part on the design of the receiver and more specifically

on the location of the locks. These locks, essentially, spell the difference. The over/under when it was first designed was locked up like the run-of-the-mill double gun, that is, the locks were placed on the underside of the lower barrel and took the form, generally, of two under-lugs. This was fine and made for a very strongly latched-up breech. But the fly in the ointment was that it also made a very deep action, vertically. This is objectionable. The receiver that has great depth simply will not shoot on a par with the shallow action. It is a matter again of positioning the hands too far below the axis of the bore.

The over/under with the most shallow action ever seen in this country is the old Remington Model 32 O/U. It was discontinued in 1942. This gun had a sliding-wedge cover that locked the barrel to the breech. There were no under bolts and for that reason the receiver was the most shallow it was possible to design. Remington ceased the manufacture of the Model 32 because it was a costly proposition. Shotgunners have been crying ever since. It is still eagerly sought in used models by wing gunners in the know and now fetches some astounding figures. Alex Kerr, one of the truly greats of the skeet world, has been a long-time user of the Model 32.

The most sturdy, probably, of all the over/under shotguns is the Merkel. It originated in Germany and has been copied by manufacturers all over Europe. Today, it is the action that is incorporated in the handsome AYA (Aguirre y Aranzabal Co, Eibar, Spain) over/under shotguns. Likewise it is seen on Ferlach-made superposed guns; and on some Italians. The Merkel-type action incorporates not one under-bolt but two, these arranged in line; as well the top barrel has extensions machined into it through which pass separate bolts. This is called the Kersten fastener. Either the underbits or the Kersten bolt would be sufficient to lock up the weapon, but you cannot convince a European gunsmith of that. "The customer will not accept your product," Agustin Aranzabal of the Spanish firm of AYA said to me, "unless it has a multiplicity of bolts on it." Unquestionably this has accounted for the popularity of the Merkel-type action.

The two under-bolts are machined as an integral part of the under-barrel. These bolts accept the locking lugs at an angle so that the locks bite deeper and deeper as the recesses wear away. It is an action that will never shoot loose. The Kersten fastener is in a great many respects very similar to the Greener crossbolt, except that instead of a single bolt passing through a single barrel extension, there are two.

While the Merkel type is the strongest of all superposed actions

The Browning superposed model in one of the finer grades.

it is open to criticism because of its depth. Those double lugs on the under-barrel give it a great deal of dimension vertically.

The English gunmakers have been in the business of building over/under shotguns for more than 40 years. Such firms as Purdey, Woodward, Westley Richards, Holland and Holland, and Boss all are manufacturers of very handsome barrel-over-barrel guns. While individual models differ somewhat, all have incorporated a type of action which has eliminated the under-bolt. These guns lock up by the utilization of lugs that are machined into the rear face of the barrels. These lugs enter the standing breech through openings that have been cut there. Such a design makes for the most shallow action.

This type of lock-up has gained scant favor on the Continent. It is accepted in England and the over/under enjoys popularity there, but your German, Spaniard, Frenchman, or Italian has scant praise for the system. He believes the two tiny lugs that serve as the major part of the lock will never keep the gun tight, and besides he believes it is dangerous!

Actually it is not, and the Woodward, H&H, or Westley Richards will handle any progressive burning load and continue to remain sound and tight for years.

The graceful lines of these superb shotguns is a joy to the shooting man's eye. The very ultimate has here been reached in providing a flat, shallow action that permits of the highest possible placement of the hands.

Unfortunately an English O/U from one of the better makers will cost upwards of twelve hundred bucks in Audley Square, London.

I was shooting live pigeon in Madrid with some Spanish *amigos* and chanced on a Browning 12 O/U in a Madrid *Armeria*. I examined the gun and noted the barrels were pitted beyond hopes of reclaiming them. I inquired the price and found I could possess the gun for the equivalent of forty bucks. I snapped it up.

I threw the stock away, it was one of the narrow comb, sharp-featured European abortions seen on many smoothbores before the war, and had a stock maker in Eibar, Pedro Arrazabalaga, fit a handsome piece of walnut to the weapon. Since the gun had two triggers and as I am partial to a single, I sent the action to John Val Browning at the Fabrique Nacionale plant in Herstal, and he had installed a single trigger. Then I carted the receiver up to Unceta, the pistol manufacturer in Guernica, in Northern Spain, and there had it engraved. After this the pitted and worthless barrels, together with the action, made an ocean crossing.

I shipped the gun to Ernie Simmons of Simmons Gun Specialties, Kansas City, and Ernie really did a job! He cut the 12 gauge tubes off just at the forward end of the chambers, bored out and enlarged the stubs and into these he fitted two 16-gauge barrels. These barrels came from Winchester Model 12 pump-gun assemblies. Once the tubes were in place, he completed the jointing, and to make the job complete added the Simmons raised ventilated rib.

The over/under is the only 16-gauge Browning extant. It weighs about 6¼ pounds and is a deadly executioner on bobwhites, doves, snipe, and other close-rising uplands species.

The over/under is tomorrow's shotgun. It is popular today; it will be increasingly so in the days ahead. The trend is to two-shot smoothbores, as evidenced by the Browning "Double" Automatic which has recently appeared. Curtailed game bags, shortened seasons, restricted hunting lands all impel a selection of a shotgun that provides more sport while surely accounting for the relatively few chances the sportsman gets. The over/under is the answer. Here is a gun that points more naturally, swings more surely, is lively and responsive in the hands of the marksman, and fills him with a fine pride of ownership.

Chapter 9

THE ALL-AROUND GUN, THE BIG 12

WHEN MY YOUNG CUB was six, Apache *amigos* urged me to teach him to shoot. I consulted the experts and they advised a 410. "Finest little gun. No kick. Give the lad confidence." Thus spake an *amigo*, ranking authority on squaw guns. So I got Bill a four-ten.

We went out to shoot it. I'd thoughtfully tied up a captive crow, haltering him, Apache style, by driving two stakes in the adobe soil about six inches apart and dallying a leg to either pailing. We walked up to the hapless *cuervo*, the boy toting the little double. I reached in my pocket and fetched out a cartridge. The shell in hand, I snapped open the blade of my jackknife and lopped off the overshot wad. The few dozen pellets bounced into my palm. To these I added a like quantity of rock salt and stirred the lead and condiment together.

"Pour these salted pellets on the bird's tail," I directed my off-spring, "that's the only way you'll ever take game with the 410." He laughed sprinkling the crow's tail. That done we walked over to the corral and I jammed the barrels through the heavy cedar palings and bent them into a permanent S.

The boy cried a little but the next year, when he was 7, I presented him with a 20 gauge, and when he turned 11, a 12 bore was among his gifts.

The perfect shotgun is the 12. If, man or boy, a gent isn't stud enough to shoot a 12 then he should take up ping-pong. The other gauges are makeshifts that do a killing job but never with the lethality of this remarkably versatile gauge.

Once we had 4 gauges, and 6 gauges, and an 8; 10 gauges and 12s. Too, there was a 14, and of course the 16. There was an 18 gauge, not very well known today, and of course the present 20. And there was a 24, and the 28, which is still around; and virtually unknown, a 32 gauge. And finally that unparalleled bird crippler—that most efficient wounder of game—the wholly ineffectual 410.

In recent years the list has been pared somewhat. Standard today are only the 10, 12, 16 and the 20, 28 and 410.

There has not been a new shotgun gauge since Prince Albert got his likeness on all those tobacco tins. And it isn't very likely

White-fronted goose taken in Mexico with the versatile 12-gauge gun.

we'll see a new gauge. The subject is pretty well exhausted, or so the designers would like us to believe. Every change of the moon we are confronted with a new rifle cartridge, but not so on the scattergunning side.

Maybe we don't need any new borings. Quite possibly we could eliminate a few and never miss 'em.

Take the 16. A forgotten gun. It used to be that the 16—a sort of bastard at the family picnic, objectively neither fish nor fowl—had a certain small following below the line euphemistically referred to as the property of a couple of hombres, Mason and Dixon. But not anymore. The popularity of the 16 is about on a par with death and taxes.

The 20 on the other hand remains a fairly popular shooting iron. However, there isn't anything you can do with the 20 that cannot be accomplished with twice the efficiency swinging a 12. If you want to argue the matter of weight I'll produce a 6-pound 12; the average 20, these days, runs 6½ pounds. And on the score of cartridge I'll find a 12-gauge cartridge that runs a mere 2 inches for length and poops out a trifling 1 ounce of shot.

That brings us down to the 28 gauge and also to that abominable little stinker, the 10.50 mm. The 28 handles three-quarters of an ounce of shot, and so too, allegedly, does the 410. Superficially it would appear one is as good as the other. Both spew out the same dosage, don't they? The more narrow bore of the 410 is a veritable grinding mill. When you funnel three-fourths of an ounce of soft, leaden pellets size 7½ (.09-inch) through a bore measuring only .410-inch, a fantastic number of the tiny spheres are hammered out of round. The pellets are jammed and crushed in the cartridge as the powder burns, are rubbed against the unyielding sides of the barrel, so that many are out of plumb by the time the load is free of the muzzle. These flat-sided pellets will not kill.

The 28 with the same charge—¾ ounce—does not mutilate the shot nearly so brutally. In the first place the bore runs a little more than one-half inch (.550) and this means there isn't so much jamming in the shell and fewer pellets come in contact with the barrel surfaces. This isn't intended to say the 28 is much shakes

The 12 is the long-odds choice of the majority of shotgunners.

as a shooting iron. It is stinking poor, too. It's another dread crippler, a toy and not a tool, a sad something dreamed up years agone by some head-shrinker who faultily believed he was so smoking hot with the 12 that he had to handicap himself by using a scatter gun that doesn't pack enough powder to blow your nose and scarcely enough shot to poison jaybirds.

Breath was blown into the 28 corpse by the skeetmen. For some obscure reason they elected to write the bastard into their shooting program. It has clung to the outskirts of the shotgun herd ever since. The numbers of 28-gauge guns sold to other than skeet gunners throughout the year wouldn't, if the profits were skimmed and tallied, keep a Plott hound in regular vittles.

The 410, on the other hand, has a certain following. It, too, was incorporated in the skeet program, and if it could just be confined there it would be perfectly ducky, serving to exasperate perfectly sane clay-target men who otherwise enjoy their favorite sport. But the gun is carried into the game fields, and then it is the greatest boon to those dog kennels that specialize in breeding the retriever types. For every bird cleanly grassed the 410 will account for four others that the spaniel must painstakingly nose out.

Deception is practiced where the 410 is concerned. It is sold with a 3-inch case and the shell is alleged to contain three-quarters of an ounce of shot. It does not. A full three-quarters ounce of lead has never been fitted inside a 410 cartridge. This is chicanery and deludes the average naive gunner into believing he has more load than is actually present.

Among other loadings there is a single ball, a slug, for the pipsqueak that weighs one-fifth ounce. Now slugs are loaded in all the gauges and are intended, very specifically, for deer slaying. Patently a hunk of soft metal scaling only one-fifth ounce simply will not cut the mustard as serious deer medicine. What is it loaded for then? Apparently for no other purpose than to complete the family of shotgun slug loads.

Smallbore shotguns handle big shot poorly. This fault extends to the 20, which is sort of an intermediate gauge. Shot larger than 6 in the 20 pattern sketchily. This fault is exaggerated in the 28 and 410. There simply isn't space in the restricted confines of the tube to permit the passage of the big pellets. These jam and batter each other frightfully. This means that the pygmies—the 28 and 410—are limited to shot sizes, 7½s, 8s and 9s. True, both cartridges are loaded with 4s and 6s, but just pattern 'em sometime!

What is the worth of a shotgun(s) limited to one or two shot sizes and those so small as to preclude anything save restricted gunning on our smallest uplands game?

The reader may leap to the conclusion, judging from these comments of mine, that I am somewhat prejudiced against the dinky, two-bit smallbores. If he has gotten this impression, I am delighted to know that the salvo hasn't missed the mark. Had I my way, I'd bundle the two pea-shooters into the first moon rocket and get them out of the picture once and for all.

As for the 16 and 20, I hold no such antipathy toward the pair. Both are useable, performing shotguns. Neither will equal the versatility of the 12 but each has its exponents.

Scatterguns are made in single-barrel one-shot, double-barrel, and repeating types. To enlarge on this a bit, the repeaters are further differentiated by pump-action, self-loading, and bolt-action

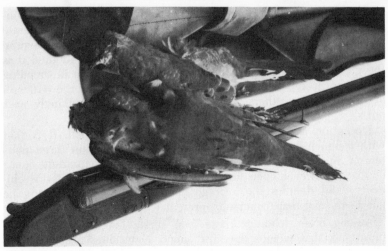

The 12 here accounts for the fast-flying dove.

magazine types. The doubles are of two designs; the first, and more conventional, the side-by-side double barrel; and, secondly, the over-and-under or superposed model.

The single-barrel, one-shot, like ham and eggs, needs no elaboration. Of the several shotguns, however, it is by far the older. It is about as interesting, and as useable, as the long bow. The sportsman who, preforce, must confine his shotgunning to a single barrel earns my heartiest sympathy. He only gets into the soup course of a seven-point gourmet's delight. I'd as soon hold a jackass in the rain without a coat as to hunt with a one-round, single-barrel shotgun.

Next to the single the double is by far the oldest. It has been under constant manufacture these past two centuries. The over-/under is of the same vintage, essentially. Double shotguns, both flintlock and percussion, are to be found in half the museums on the Continent. These weapons, oft-times upwards of a hundred years in being, are finest examples of good balance and grace of line. Gunsmiths, at the behest of their shooting clientele, learned a long time ago how to build balance and goodness into the double shotgun.

The johnny-come-lately is the repeater. Whether pump-action, automatic, or bolt-operated, it is the newcomer on the scene. These magazine arms were designed to slaughter wildfowl during those golden days when Buffalo Bill roamed the Orpheum circuit, when women stayed to-hell out of the *bistros,* and a shooting man could gun down a Studebaker wagonload of mallards in a morning and peddle the fowl, all neatly plucked, iced and barreled, to the Parker

House the day following. That was the Diamond Jim Brady era of the repeating scattergun.

It is now gone, gone forevermore, but the aroma lingers on in the shape of a coterie of magazine cornshellers.

To say the pump repeater or the auto-loader is not an efficient killer would be utterly asinine. But to contend it is a pleasure to shoot would be distortion. None of the breed have any particular

The new Winchester Model 50 is offered only in 12 gauge. Indication of the popularity of the flexible cartridge.

balance about them. That a marksman kills with the piece is simply an indication of the adaptability of the human to the machine.

How can a weapon possess balance and a responsive aliveness when the waterline is adorned with a collection of tubing, pump handles, operating rods, bolts, nuts, stops, springs, and cartridges —a veritable plumber's nightmare? How, may I ask, can the gunner be expected to swing with his target, fire, and then shuffle a pump handle which starts with the abruptness of atomic reaction, and after three inches of travel is even more rudely halted—halted to have the direction of movement changed by 180-degrees? How is a smooth swing possible and the second and third shots triggered off effectively with an arrangement like that?

The automatic has no moving pump handle. With every shot the balance shifts rearward, however. With every shot the gunner is kicked twice; first when the cartridge explodes, which is generally referred to as primary recoil; and a micro-second later by the slamming action of the breech mechanism as it closes. This is secondary recoil. You get slammed coming and going, your full money's worth, as it were.

The best of the shotguns is the double. So subtly is the weapon designed, so flawlessly does it balance that the marksman swings the piece to attain proper lead even as he brings the gun to shoulder. On the instant that it falls into the cradle formed between cheek and shoulder, it fires, explodes directly in the path of the hurtling target. Only a gun perfectly designed for its user is capable of such performance.

A shotgun, like a forkfull of June peas, has got to be well balanced to hit the mark. It, like a golf club, must perform a-wing. Rifles are fired at immobile targets more often than not. This isn't true of the smoothbore. Speculating about a shotgun as it stands in the rack is about as idle as admiring a jet fighter on the ramp. You cannot tell a whoop about either until you set 'em a-moving. The double, whether side-by-side or over/under, once snapped into motion will outperform all others by reason of better basic design, balance, weight distribution, fit, and feel.

The acquisition of a double-barrel shotgun is no open sesame to full game bags. Until they develop built-in radar the gunner will still have to do his part.

The double when selected in the 12 gauge unquestionably offers the ideal combination. If the perfect boring can be said to have been found, it is in this number. Shotgun weight ranges from poundages actually lighter than the standard 20 to weights that are sufficient to compensate for the new Magnum cartridges. And as for loads, these are quite as varied as the gun weights. In this country we load nothing lighter than a 2¾ dram equivalent load behind 1⅛ ounces of shot. In England, however, a 12 gauge cartridge has long been available which holds only 1 ounce of shot. On the other end are our Magnum 3-inch loadings of 1⅞ ounces of shot; and in the standard case length of 2¾ inches, are the 1½-ounce bruisers.

What probably is of more utility, however, than these speciality loads is the vast miscellany of intermediate 12-gauge cartridges. Those that we find so extremely lethal on every bird that flies. The standard 12-gauge load for many years was 3¼ drams equivalent of power and 1⅛ ounces of shot. With this combination everything was killed in North America from sandhill cranes to rice birds. More lately, we have decided this load is only fit for a 16 and we've humped the standard 12 loading to 3¾ drams of powder and 1¼ ounces of shot. This is considerably hotter, and maybe pouring in that additional propellant has helped the sale of muzzle brakes. The ordinary 12 with this load has a hefty kick, and while it is okay for wildfowl is defintely on the heavy side for uplands flyers.

A favorite catridge of mine is 3¼ drams of powder and 1¼ ounces of shot. This load, a real duzy, probably strikes the ideal balance in the average 12-gauge gun. It performs well in all of 'em. It is mild as to recoil and patterns with a regularity that is pleasing indeed. If I had to live with one gun and one catridge the rest of my days, I'd just settle on a good double-barrel twelve and 3¼ dram, 1¼-ounce catridge.

Chapter 10

THE CONTINENTAL SCATTER GUN

OUR KNOWLEDGE of European shotguns is a sketchy thing. As a result of the war we gained some knowledge of them, our GIs fetching guns home by the thousands. Unfortunately a great many of these weapons were obsolete types and not a few were actually dangerous. The impression gained from these souvenir shooting irons was generally not a good one.

Since the war a great many Continental shotguns have been imported by a coterie of arms importers. For the most part these arms represent good ordnance. The old legend about the pot-metal booby trap simply does not hold today. Current models are built of good alloyed steel, are well made, carefully fitted, designed along lines that are acceptable to us, and, withal, are appealing hardware.

It is a familiar cliché of our gun-writing hacks to say that Continental smoothbores are "hand made" and in the same breath claim our shotguns are "machine made." Both statements are open to question. A weapon to be handmade would imply a very minimum of machining operations. The action, as an example, after forging would have to be shaped and inletted, completely fitted and finished by the use of hand tools.

On the other side a machine-made gun would indicate that the weapon during manufacture was set up in a series of fixtures and passed from one machine to the other, never touched by hand, until, like doughnuts, it issued forth at the far end ready to fire.

European shooting irons are not handmade; neither is the American counterpart machine made.

I have spent a good many days in some of the largest—and what must be some of the smallest—firearms plants in Western Europe and I know from personal observation that literally hundreds of machining operations go into the fabrication of the Continental scatter gun. By the same token it is the long hours of hand labor, performed tediously and painstakingly with the file, that makes such guns as the Winchester Model 21 so costly here at home.

A shotgun, whether built here or on the Continent, must have a lot of hand-fitting and finishing go into it. The European craftsman does more of this kind of work than does his American counterpart.

He is paid much less, so it is good economy to permit him to devote additional hours to the hand-finishing. As a result the Continental smootbore is notable for a better joining of metal to metal and metal to wood, is more handsomely engraved, more artistically checkered, and by any standards is a more richly turned piece. It is correct to label such an arm hand finished but certainly far from the mark to say it is "hand made."

The contention has been voiced again and again that European shotguns are so individualized as to make it impossible to produce

Agustin Aranzabal, gun maker and a great live-bird devotee. He has won every worthwhile pigeon championship.

them in quantity; and besides the interchangeability of barrels and minor assemblies is out of the question. There is strong justification for these statements, but we dare not set ourselves up as paragons on this score. I have yet to see one of our so-called "production line" smoothbores that does not usually require the services of a skilled gun-tinker to fit even a minor part!

That continental scatter guns are too light of weight is another charge oft repeated. Especially is this stigma attached to English models. It is quite true that some ridiculously light guns are made; however this leaves the story only half told. If you wish you may buy a 12 in England today that conforms in every weight particular to our own, *i.e.* 6¾ to 8¼ pounds. Or if you happen to be a hog for punishment you can get a 10- or 12-gauge Magnum from Spain or Belgium that will run in the 11-12-pound class.

We have hooted at the inability of the Continental gun to digest

our express and magnum wildfowl loads. European flyweight 12s
simply will not stand the racket with these cartridges, so say the
boys. Granted a 6-pound 12 is not going to remain tight if we
pour some of our so-called standard magnum 1½-ounce loads
through it for a season or two. But a man would be an idiot to so
misuse a light uplands gun. The English featherweights are built

The largest arms-making firm in Spain, Aguirre and Aranzabal, Eibar.

for grouse and quail and moderate charges of powder and shot are
indicated.

We too build some feathery 12s, and any hombre loco enough to
shoot express loads in such a flimsy will very soon find that his
gun is on the highroad to the bow-wows. The end result is the
same whether the gun bear English or US trade markings. Keep
the Continental lightweight stuffed with the fodder for which it is
intended and it will stand up as long as any.

Complaints are registered that current imports sport more locks
than a New England bank vault. For the past half-century we have
locked up our shotguns with never more than one, or sometimes two
bolts. Some Continental powder-burners are latched with as many
as five. This is entirely needless as American gunmakers have long
since proved. Nothing new has been developed in shotgun mechanisms for the past 40 years in Europe, with one exception, and
that may scarcely be credited to the Europeans. The new "Double"
Automatic Browning shotgun is a radically new design. However,
it is the brainchild of Val Browning of Ogden, Utah, and while
American in origin a great deal of the spadework was accomplished
on this short-recoil, self-loader in the great plant of the Fabrique
Nacionale d'Armes de Guerre, Herstal, Belgium.

But as for double shotgun actions, they are as unchanged as morals in Macao. When the swing was made back in the late 90s from black powder to smokeless, with its increased breech pressures, many innovations to shotgun actions were made. All these alterations were intended to provide greater locking strengths. The result was a multiplicity of locking bolts, most of which have been retained to this day.

As this is written we import from Belgium, Austria, Italy, Spain, Germany, Finland, and England. Suppose we take a look at these guns to see how the current crop shapes up.

AYA. This is the trade name of the firm, Aguirre y Aranzabal, Eibar, Spain. The company is the largest in this thriving Basque city, one of the most famous gun-building centers in the world. Eibar is situated in Guipuzcoa Province. It is a dozen miles from the Bay of Biscay and 40 miles from the French border.

In Eibar you will find some 62 different firms all engaged in the ancient trade of arms-making. Some of these houses produce upwards of 15,000 weapons yearly, others turn out no more than a twentieth part of this total.

The city is literally one big arsenal; the industry is banded together in a guild, and among the little fellows there is much interchange of effort. Some small manufacturers do nothing save fit and finish actions, others make stocks, still others are solely engravers, while others are specialists in boring barrels. The alcalde (mayor), Don Esteban Orbea, is himself a gunmaker. He is descended from a line of gunsmiths that reaches back 600 years. Today, among other activities, he manufactures more empty, primed shotshells than any firm in Spain.

The AYA shotgun, unlike many made in Spain, is the product of a new company. The firm of Agustin Aranzabal and Nemesio Aguirre was organized after the Spanish Civil War which ended in 1939. Today it is the largest and most firmly established of any. Last year more than 17,000 side-by-side and over-and-under scatter guns flowed from its assembly lines.

A total of 22 models are in production. These shotguns run the scale of the gauges from the worthless little 9 mm. to the Magnum 10, and are made in single barrel, double barrel and over/under. There is no production of repeaters.

Single-barrel models are limited to five different weapons. They all are cheap numbers costing from about $12 to $32, and are for export to such places as Pakistan, India, South America, and Egypt.

Among the side-by-side doubles are eight models which range from a very few dollars to prices slightly above one hundred bucks. These AYA are soundly and strongly made of alloyed steel, are proved in the Government Proof House, and are reliable and good shooting; but are not generally equipped with such refinements as ejectors, single triggers, fine stocks, and other trimmings.

Above this group is a select little coterie of five very fine side-by-side doubles. These represent the very cream. A representative arm among these five is the Model 53B. This gun in consideration of its price and with regard to the quality of the piece probably is the best buy in a side-by-side double shotgun anywhere today.

Finally the AYA line is completed by the inclusion of four models of over-and-under shotgun. Before we discuss the barrel-over-barrel models, let us take a long look at the conventional shotguns.

Throughout the world, and especially in Europe, the Purdey shotgun has a reputation for being the best. This lofty stature is based on good design, long life, and excellent shooting qualities, and is a fame gained over more than a century of steady usage. When Agustin Aranzabal looked about for a shotgun design to follow, he and his partner Aguirre decided they could not improve on the Purdey. The resulting AYA closely resembles the famous English smoothbore: the bolting mechanism is an exact copy. However the ejectors are Holland by type, and two different easy-opening mechanisms are sometimes incorporated; neither follows the Purdey.

It should be pointed out that all the patent rights on Purdey shotguns have long since expired so that the decision to manufacture a more or less faithful copy of the celebrated fowling piece did not imply any infringement—quite the contrary. It was an acknowledgment of the goodness of the Purdey design.

Once the partners had settled on the Purdey they went to work. Today some 350 highly skilled Basque gun-craftsmen are turning out the AYA conception of the world-famed Purdey shotgun. Unless the examiner searches for the name it is impossible to tell an AYA from a Purdey.

The AYA employs barrels of chrome nickel steel, barrels that are drop forged and twice proof-tested by the Government with blue pills overloaded thirty-three and one-third percent. Actions are likewise of alloyed steel and are proofed along with the tubes.

The locks, sideplate by type, are a joy to behold. These locks are made and finished with the care lavished on a mariner's chronometer and are gold-plated to eliminate the nuisance of rusting. The engraving is handsomely executed. In this detail the AYA varies from the English scroll common to the Purdey. The engraving conforms more especially to our tastes, it is replete with hunting scenes, game in flight, dogs in action, and the like. Finally the quality of the wood in the stock is a distinct improvement over the English counterpart. Wood in the AYA shotgun is the finest walnut found in any shotgun today. It is superb; grown, cut, and cured in Spain. I have yet to see anything including genuine Circassian that

Finest of the over-under shotguns made on the Continent today is the Model 37 AYA. This shotgun is made in 20, 16, and 12 gauges and utilizes the rugged and extremely reliable Merkel-type action. Made by Aguirre and Aranzabal Co., Eibar.

can compare with it for sheer elegance and beauty of grain.

The AYA today sells for about one-fourth the cost of the Purdey. How is it possible to build a smoothbore, in every particular the equal of the famed Purdey and do it for only 25% of the cost of the latter weapon? The answer is that the Basque mechanic after four years in a gun-craftsman apprentice school is paid as a finished journeyman about $2.50 for a full eight hours work. After eight or ten years he may draw as high as $5.00 daily. This is the answer.

The Count of Teba, several times winner of the live-bird championship of the world, shoots an AYA. Billy Perdue, Mobile, Ala., top-flighter who was the live-bird king of Europe during '52, is another owner. Homer Clark, East Alton, Ill., twice live-bird champ, owns several of the guns. Warren Page, Guns Editor of *Field and Stream,* is an enthusiastic booster for the fine Spanish shotgun. Frank Steinhart, live-bird title holder of Central America and president of the Cuba Pigeon Shooting Association, is another consistent shooter of the AYA. His wife, Olga, champion in her own right, fires only the Spanish weapon. The list is a long and imposing one. The shotgun has probably no better or more consistent booster than the company's President, Sr. Aranzabal. He has won every championship in Spain, and currently is the trap champion of the Peninsula.

The over/under shotguns made by the firm are close copies of the sturdy German Merkel. The four models are available in gauges from 20 to 12, with selective auto ejectors, single triggers, finest walnut, handsome engraving, good weight, and excellent balance. I have been shooting the Model 37 Super, most costly of the quartet, for the past six years. During that time, as an average figure, I have burned up a case of shells every month. Right now my AYA is as tight and as sound as the day it left the factory. The Aguirre y Aranzabal shotguns are sold in the U.S. by the firm, Firearms International, Washington, D. C.

Firearms International also acts as import agents for the mail-order firm, Sears, Roebuck, and import an AYA which is an excellent value. This shotgun sells for a moderate figure, and is equipped with a sturdy single trigger and selective auto ejectors. In my opinion the AYA shotgun offers more gun value for dollar expended than any firearm manufactured in Europe today.

The increasing interest in the super Magnum 10 gauge, the big walloper that fires the 3½-inch casing and a full 2 ounces of shot, has seen the AYA Company equal to the occasion. The firm has under export to the Firearms International a boxlock 10 with 32-inch full-choke barrels, double triggers, and non-automatic ejectors, and ranging around the 10½-pound weight. This is an extremely sturdy and yet well-balanced and fast-handling goose gun. The weapon has a nicely designed semi-beavertail fore-end and a full-sized, well-rounded comb which, together with a slotted recoil pad, dampens recoil until it is not unpleasant at all.

There is also a deluxe model of this super 10, a handsome wild-fowler's piece that is as pretty as a shotgun ever gets to be. This AYA is built with sideplate locks, a single trigger, and selective auto ejectors. It is stocked with a magnificent piece of Spanish walnut, checkered at 26-lines-to-the-inch, and engraved as only the master engravers of Eibar can do! Barrels run the same 32 inches but are chromed inside, full-choke, and chambered for the Roman Candle shell. So cleverly has this great gun been built the ten-and-a-half pounds feel like no more than eight; it swings and stops, points and settles like an uplands gun. Here, truely, is the *crème de la crème* of the long-range Magnum shotguns.

BERETTA. J. L. Galef and Son, New York City, are the importers of the Beretta shotgun, which is retailed by authorized dealers throughout the country. The shotgun is in two types; the conventional side-by-side double, and the over-and-under. The parallel gun is made in both boxlock and sideplate; the over/under is made only in sideplate lock.

The firm of Pietro Beretta of Brescia, Italy, has been manufacturing firearms since 1680. Despite the fact that shotguns have been made even longer than pistols by this famous old Italian guns firm, the name Beretta is better known in America for the latter arm. The Italian Government adopted a Beretta 9 mm. automatic pistol in 1915. The weapon has been continued in manufacture ever since. During the last war the Beretta sub-machine gun was among the best. I had one in Africa, and later in Sicily, and I carried it in preference to our own. It was very well made, sure functioning, and featured two triggers, a handy innovation. With the double triggers the shooter could instantly shift from semi-auto to full automatic fire.

The side-by-side shotgun is available in all the gauges from 28 to 12. In 12 bore it weighs from 6¾ to 7¾ pounds, and utilizes a lock-up that is very similar to the Greener, *i.e.* two underbolts, a dolls-head extension rib with tapered wedge-bite and the customary crossbolt. The safety, unlike the Greener, is located on the upper tang. This is an extremely sturdy action.

Cesare Merlo, winner of the world's clay target championship at Caracas, Venezuela, in 1954. He shot a Breda Auto-loader. T h e r e were no U. S. entries.

The Beretta Company chrome the interior of all barrels, and on the more costly guns of the line, chrome hammers, sears, and other parts of the lock. This is a highly commendable practice; not only does it eliminate the nuisance of rust but very materially improves, insofar as the barrels are concerned, the patterning goodness of the guns.

The Beretta over/under is made in 12 gauge only. The Model 200 has chrome-lined barrels, and the action is similarly treated; there is a slightly cheaper version of the O/U, the Model 100, that lacks the chrome treatment. The Company, in the production of the barrels, forge a stub into which the barrel-tubes are inserted. The stub has the underbolts forged as an integral part; this eliminates the hazard of shooting this important portion of the lock loose, a not uncommon happening with shotguns sporting brazed-on lugs.

The Beretta over/under employs a lock-up that closely follows the better English models. The faces of the barrels are forged and machined so that the locking lugs are an integral part. These lugs—

there are two of them—pass into the walls of the standing breech. Slots are milled into the standing breech and these openings provide the latches for the barrel lugs. This type of action from the standpoint of perfect design comes nearer the ideal than anything yet developed for the barrel-on-barrel shotgun.

Regrettably the Beretta shotguns are not offered with single trigger.

BERNARDELLI. Shotguns bearing this name are manufactured by V. Bernardelli, Brescia, Italy; importer, Stoeger Arms Corporation, 507 Fifth Ave., NYC. Bernardelli shotguns are conventional double guns, differing one from the other in finish and ornamentation. The action is a copy of the Purdey, sometimes in sideplate and others in boxlock. Gauges range from 20 to 12. The cheapest model is without ejectors and all models are two-trigger. The Model Roma No. 6 has automatic selective ejectors and a chromed barrel.

A year or so ago the Bernardelli Company offered an auto-loading shotgun on this side of the Atlantic. It has now disappeared from view but is, I understand, still sold in Europe, South America, Egypt, Pakistan, and other way stations. This is one of very few repeaters made in Europe. Interestingly, of the five auto-loading shotguns (no pump repeaters are in manufacture) now in production, three are made in Italy; the Bernardelli, Franchi, and the Breda.

The Bernardelli is a departure from any semi-auto shotgun on the market today. It is a straight blow-back gun. The Brownings, both the new "Double" auto and the older number, utilize short recoil in the case of the new gun and long recoil in the case of the original; and so too do the Remington M48, the Breda, and the Franchi. The Bernardelli functions just like a .22 blow-back rifle.

To accomplish this an extremely elongated receiver is used. The cartridges are contained in a detachable box magazine ahead of the trigger guard. The breechblock return spring as well as a buffer is located in this ungainly receiver. The gun is offered in 20, 16 and 12 gauges and weighs 6½ pounds.

It goes without saying that a blow-back action is the most simple of any to design and manufacture. John Browning looked into the matter a half-century back. While simple of design and construction the straight recoiling system in the major shotgun gauges develops many headaches. The movement of the bolt, unless it is a ponderous piece, is far too brusque, and this gives rise to broken extractors and deformed ejectors. The bolt itself is quickly battered and frequently develops cracks. The same is true of the buffer mechanism. Not infrequently the receiver develops cracks at those points of greatest stress.

The stock where it meets the force of the recoil may split unless

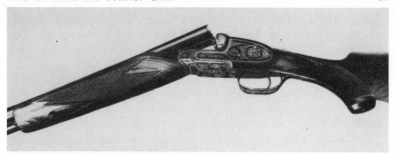

The AYA Model 53 side-by-side double shotgun. This weapon is widely used by live-bird shooters throughout the Continent.

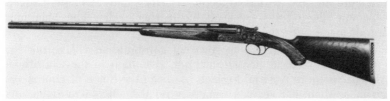

The Model 51 AYA side-by-side double, equipped with raised ventilated rib and single trigger.

it is quite heavy, the weight of 6½ pounds in this Italian gun indicates the stock is on the feathery side.

BREDA. This auto-loading shotgun is the product of the largest arms-making firm in Italy, the Ernesto Breda Company. During the war the Breda machine gun was a standard arm of the Italian soldiery. What is not so generally known is that the Breda Company also made airplanes, rail cars, locomotives, farm tractors, and machine tools. The Breda shotgun is a slightly modified copy of the original Browning. It is long-recoil operated, just like the old Browning, and has a similar tubular magazine and an identical forestock. The receiver differs somewhat; it has a light sheet-stock cover which acts as dust shield, and which when removed exposes the entire action to view.

The gun has a chrome-lined barrel, an excellent feature which could well be copied by American gunmakers. The bolt is also chromed, and the weapon has double extractors. The first safety on the Breda was perched atop the tang, but more recently the safety has been placed on the side of the receiver and takes the shape of a swinging lever. A series of choke tubes are available which are screwed into position. These tubes provide a variation in choke but are not so constructed as to afford any recoil reduction. The gun weighs 7 pounds, 8 ounces, empty, is a 5-shot, and has a novel feature about the magazine which permits the cartridges to be spilled from the tube without working 'em through the action. Importer, Continental Arms Corp., New York.

CENTAURE. This is a plainly finished, Belgian-made double shotgun, imported by Continental. Liege is the center of shotgun manufacture in Belgium, and the reputation of firearms from there is excellent. The Centaure is graced by a Greener-type action, one of the strongest made, and is proof-tested by the Belgian Government. The shotgun is made in 20, 16 and 12 gauges, weighs 7 pounds, with 26-, 28-, or 30-inch barrels, is chambered for the 2¾-inch shell in every case, and is a two-trigger, non-ejector model.

Continental Arms also imports more finely turned doubles, one of which is the so-called Supra Deluxe Model 5. This shotgun, like the Centaure, is a boxlock; but is a decided improvement over the Centaure in that it has selective ejectors and a single trigger. Magnum 12s and 10s are available in this model. The Magnums are all made with two triggers.

FERLACH. Ferlach is an Austrian gun-building village not too far from the historic city of Salzburg. It is high in the Carinthian Alps of Southern Austria. Ferlach has been the home of gunmakers for more than 400 years. In many ways this village resembles its Spanish counterpart Eibar. Ferlach, like Eibar, has a gun-building guild and there is much interchange of effort. Some firms produce only gun-frames, others fashion barrels, while still others are specialists in finishing, fitting, and engraving.

There is a line of side-by-side doubles under importation. The double referred to as the Constant Companion is a boxlock, built on the Greener action. It is made in 20, 16 and 12 guages, weighs 6¾ pounds in the larger gauge, is equipped with auto ejectors, has two triggers, and is engraved in that high-relief, game-scene style of the old German school. The stock is selected walnut and sports a cheekpiece.

There is also a Ferlach over/under. Gauges run 20, 16 and 12. The Merkel type of action is used, a single trigger is available for extra money. The trigger is a copy of the Blitz, a system which positions the entire assembly on the trigger plate itself. The gun has automatic, selective ejectors. The stock is handsome walnut and supports a well-designed cheekpiece. Delivery time runs four to six months; a payment of 50% of the price must be laid down at the time the order is placed and cancellations are *verboten!*

Elmer Keith, writer of the excellent book *Shotguns* and ranking firearms authority, wrote me that he tried two Ferlach guns. One was a side-by-side, the other an over/under. On one of the guns he found a badly machined and faulty chamber and on the other noted some deep tool scars in the bore. It has been an ancient plaint with us that the European shotgun invariably looks like a million bucks on the outside, but brother! beware the interior! Far too often in the past these complaints have not been without

The AYA Model 400E, sold in the U. S. by Firearms International Co. This shotgun is equipped with single selective trigger and selective ejectors. Moderately priced.

justification. It would appear from Keith's experiences that Ferlach 'smiths haven't entirely overcome these questionable practices.

FRANCHI. This is an Italian self-loading shotgun imported by Stoeger. It is made in 20 and 12 gauges. Weight in 12 gauge is claimed to be 6¼ pounds, weighed on the local butcher's scales the weight came to 7 pounds 1½ ounces in 12 gauge. The gun is a very faithful copy of the original Browning. There is an alloyed receiver and chrome-lined barrel; the shell capacity is four cartridges.

FRANCOTTE. The Francotte shotgun is made in Liege. It is imported by Abercrombie and Fitch. Both side-by-side and over/under models are common to the line. These are expensive shotguns built with all the goodness of materials, skill of manufacture, and soundness of design that characterizes the Purdey of England and the Winchester 21 of America.

Francottes are built in all the gauges, within any reasonable weight limits, in any barrel lengths, single triggers, if desired, finest walnut, and handsome engraving; in short, they are very deluxe arms sure to combine all that is desirable in a double-barreled shotgun.

The firm is a small one and output is limited. Few if any models are held in stock for outright sale; a lead time of six months is needed and it is customary to make a 50% down payment at the time the order is placed.

GRIEFELT. This is a little-known German-assembled over/under shotgun. It is a more or less faithful copy of the original Merkel shotgun. The name Griefelt rings no bell from the days before World War II. The Griefelt is chambered for all the common gauges, is made with a single trigger and auto selective ejectors, has a raised ventilated rib, and is plentiously engraved.

IMPERIAL CROWN. This over-and-under is imported by Continental Arms from Belgium. It comes in two grades: the Imperial Crown is the finer of the two, costing upwards of five hundred dollars; the Royal Crown is the less costly of the pair. Shotguns are made up on the Merkel type of action; that is with Kersten fastener and Greener crossbolt, unquestionably the strongest of the several superposed locking systems. It is made in every gauge from 410 to 10 gauge Magnum. Ejectors are Holland by type, and a single trigger and raised ventilated ribs are extras—for a price.

An interesting and novel innovation with this Belgian scatterbore is that various sets of barrels may be purchased for the one receiver, thus providing the gunner with all gauges from 410 to 12. This is a feature which has a certain appeal to the competitive skeet shooter. Ernie Simmons of Kansas City offers the same combinations for the Browning superposed 12.

JANSSEN. This line of shotguns includes six models in side-by-side plus two over/unders. The shotguns are manufactured by the Janssen Fils & Co., Belgium. Importer is Firearms International. With one exception, the Model 70902, all are boxlocks.

SARASQUETA. Shotguns carrying this name are made by the firm, Victor Sarasqueta, Eibar, Spain. Importer is Stoeger Arms Corporation. The Sarasqueta Company is one of the oldest, if not the oldest in Eibar. The head of the firm is young Victor Sarasqueta, who, in addition to his gun building, is an enthusiastic and skilled live-bird and trap shot. He is a past Spanish trap champion and has a room filled with trophies from the Iberian live-bird and trap wars.

As a result of a comparatively recent visit paid by Alex Stoeger to Sarasqueta, a shotgun design was evolved between the pair which they believe will appeal to American sportsmen. One of the new smoothbores is the Zephyr. It is the least expensive of the several models currently under importation. It is without ejectors, has two triggers, and is quite plainly finished. Of infinitely more interest, especially to wildfowlers, are two Magnum doubles. One is chambered for the 12-gauge 3-inch Magnum cartridge and the other is for the 10-gauge 3½-inch Magnum cartridge.

These are two very well-built and soundly engineered howitzers!

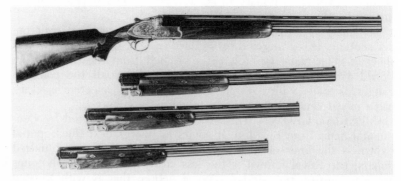

Continental Arms Corporation, New York, offers the Imperial Crown over-under shotgun with four sets of barrels. The shooter may fire the 12, 20, 28, and 410 gauge. Made up especially for skeet marksmen.

I am especially wedded to the big 10, which chambers a shell like unto a Nike missile. The 10, when first I saw it in the Eibar plant of Sarasqueta, was too light. Since then the poundage has been stepped up to about 11 pounds and at this weight the big gun is comfortable to fire.

Sarasqueta also makes a very close copy of the Woodward over/under shotgun. At present production has been halted, temporarily, I presume, due to trouble with primer ignition. Due to the shallowness of the receiver the firing pins must strike at acute angles. This has caused misfires and considerable bellyaching on the part of owners. I am very well acquainted with Spanish-loaded shotshells, and realizing the poor standards maintained during the fabrication of these loads, I have a suspicion that most of the trouble lies here.

SAUER. Before the war the firm of J. P. Sauer and Sohn, Suhl, Germany, were manufacturers of some of the finest shotguns in Europe. Since the war the original plant has been converted into a "people's" factory by the Soviets. Sauer escaped to Ulm in the US Zone just before the Muscovites entered Suhl. He has since commenced the manufacture of his famous shotgun. It is said a nucleus of his old mechanics have gotten out of Suhl and joined him in this new venture. Importer is Stoeger.

SIMSON. The Simson shotgun, like the Sauer, was a product of the arms center of Suhl. The plant was converted by the Soviets to their uses and it is known that shotguns are being made. Whether the Simson is now, in fact, made on this side of the Curtain or is an export isn't known.

UGARTECHEA. This is a shotgun imported in the U.S. and made by the Eibar firm, Casa Ugartechea. It is an over/under, with boxlock and the Merkel-type action. There are two variations; a plainly finished model and a much more nicely finished arm. While there are more than 60 arms makers in Eibar, there are no more than a half-dozen who are really outstanding. Among these is the Ugartechea Company. Casa Ugartechea is a small outfit with a limited output. Actually they are only fitters and finishers. The over/under receiver which they make up comes in semi-finished state from Aguirre y Aranzabal. The barrels, semi-finished, are provided by Patricio Echeverria of Legaspia. This in no manner adversely affects the final product. Quite the contrary.

VALMET. This is a Finish shotgun imported by Firearms International. It is an interesting scatter gun, for it is modeled very closely after the fine Remington Model 32 over/under. The weapon is made up in 12 gauge and in 16. In the former it weighs 6½ pounds, a neat heft and sure to make it fast-handling. There is a single trigger but unfortunately no auto, selective ejectors.

Chapter 11

THE ENGLISH CONTRIBUTION

THE W. W. GREENER ARMS COMPANY was founded in 1829. Present location is at St. Mary's Row, Birmingham, England; there are showrooms and a sales office at 40 Pall Mall, London.

Greener shotguns are made in two styles today. The first is a single model of side-by-side boxlock double made in all the standard gauges; the second is a single-barrel called the General Purpose Gun. Unlike most of the better known English shotguns the Greener is moderately priced.

*Whereas the Purdey costs $1008, the Greener sells for but $215.60. As might be expected, this much less expensive gun does not carry the fine appointments of the Purdey. Nevertheless the goodness of the steel and the mechanical soundness of the Greener is quite on a par with its more costly fellow.

The Greener—there is the one model of double, as I have said— is known as the Empire Gun. There are variations of the basic arm; for example the Deluxe Empire is offered for an additional twenty-eight bucks (ten pounds); or the purchaser may select the model known simply as the Empire for $170. This economy package has no automatic ejectors.

The Greener is a boxlock. Few English or Continental shotguns are so made. The Greener box boasts only four parts and is one of the most simple made today; the firing pin is integral with the hammer, and the manner in which the sear is cammed out of the tumbler notch is simplicity itself. The action incorporates both underbolting and the famous crossbolt which has taken its name from the original Greener. There is no more sturdy breeching system.

The Empire gun weighs from 7¼ to 7¾ pounds, the variations depending on gauge and barrel length. The stock is French walnut and may be specified as half-pistol or straight grip; and while the standard length of pull is 14½ inches, any length of pull may be specified when ordering. The shotgun is not available with single trigger; standard trigger pulls are adjusted between 4½ and 5½

_____

* Based on the current exchange of one British Pound worth $2.80 U. S. dollars.

102

pounds. Standard chambers are cut to 2¾ inches; in the case of the Magnum 12, chambers of 3 inches may be specified.

The Empire, in common with all Greeners, has the safety on the left side of the frame. For the hunter who snaps a safety off after the game is a-wing this is an abominable location. On the other hand for the shooter who uses a safety sparingly this location is ideal. Personally I approve the location.

For a modest additional amount the Empire model can be supplied with a specially selected French walnut stock, a beavertail fore-end, recoil pad, and a horn cap for the pistol grip. Available, too, are flat raised ribs, or file-cut ribs, a conversion job on the safety so that it works automatically (perish the thought!), and sling swivels. A solid gold or silver monogram engraved with your initials completes the extras.

To dwell on the gun-worthiness of a Greener is a great deal like questioning the sturdiness of the Winchester rifle or the Smith and Wesson sixshooter. The Greener is in a class with these immortals. It is not a show piece, but more nearly falls into a class with those US-made smoothbores which are long on performance and short on ornamentation. This latest Greener, the Empire Gun, was designed not so much, I suspect, to please home trade as to appeal to those shooting men in the outlying areas of the Commonwealth where absolute reliability is of cardinal importance. The gun, from butt to muzzle, has been designed and made so that it will function for a long time with a minimum of maintenance. Ample margins of strength have been built into action and barrels with a view to providing an arm that will stand up to hard service over a lifetime of usage. Greeners are sold by Abercrombie and Fitch. Lag time varies from five to nine months after order is placed.

The firm of Holland and Holland may perhaps be better known for their big-game rifles than their scatter guns, good though the latter are acknowledged to be. Holland shooting irons are produced at 906 Harrow Road, London, N. W. 10. Sales offices and show rooms are at 98 New Bond St., London, W. 1. There is a shooting school maintained by the company at Ducks Hill Road, Northwood, Middlesex. The U.S. representative of H&H is Abercrombie and Fitch.

The H&H shotgun in parallel type is made in a number of models, each varying only slightly in finish, grade and kind. There is also an over-and-under, made at present only in 12 gauge.

Holland shotguns are sideplate locks. The Holland lock takes the form of what is known as the back action, a system which provides a stronger receiver than is to be found on such smoothbores as the Purdey, Boss, and others. These latter are equipped with the bar-action sidelock. In passing, however, it should be noted that very probably the bar action of the Purdey provides a little better trigger pull. The correct angle between hammer notch and sear is perfectly achieved in this action.

A popular model among the various Hollands, at least among English sportsmen, is the Centenary model. This double is bored for the 20-, 16-, and 12-gauge cartridges, and on order may be chambered for the 2-inch, 12-gauge load. This pipsqueak holds only 1 ounce of shot! Weight of the gun is less than 6 pounds.

The Holland and Holland incorporates the Southgate ejectors, a venerable and time-tried system that was invented by a gunsmith named Beesley in 1893.

It is standard practice on the Holland to install what is known as an "easy opener" or "self-opener" system. This mechanism takes the form of two spring-actuated studs which extend through the flats of the watertable. When the piece is closed the studs are forced downward, the weapon locking against the spring force of the two devices. When the gun is unlatched the force of the springs causes it to open snappily. Complaints have been made that the cuts in the watertable weaken the action, and that the self-opener mechanism, simple though it is, complicates the action. Actually the stresses on the action at the forward end of the watertable are small indeed; and as for the few extra parts added to the action, they do little to complicate what is essentially a very simple machine.

The cheapest of the Holland side-by-side guns sells for $420. This is the Dominion Hammerless Ejector Model. This gun does not have the self-opener feature and is a two-trigger number. At the other extreme is the Model de Luxe Self-Opening Hammerless Ejector, selling for $980.

This finest Holland and Holland is regularly furnished with two triggers; a single trigger increases the cost.

The H&H "Under and Over" gun, as they refer to it, is one of the best superposed shotguns to be found anywhere today. A really superb job has been done on the design of the gun frame and the arrangement of the locking bolts. The gun is especially outstanding for the fact that an action was achieved which is admirable for its lack of depth. Instead of locking up with the conventional underlugs, or with a crossbolt, or a sliding over-cover, or other device likely to deepen the receiver, Holland instead attached locks to the sides of the barrels and bolted these locks into the face of the standing breech.

By successfully accomplishing this engineering chore, Holland permits the shooter's hands to be more closely aligned to the axis of the barrels, reduces the apparent recoil due to the height of the barrels, dampens the turning motion of the tubes, realizes a

A rare bird, a peafowl, killed in southeastern Asia. The shotgun an ancient English Greener.

more natural pointing piece, and finally achieves a superposed gun second to none for beauty and grace of line.

The over/under may be specified with any barrel length, any choke, any stock dimensions, and with any reasonable amount of engraving. A more or less standard model shapes up generally as follows: Barrels, 28 inches, of highest quality Vickers steel. Prooftested. Fitted with flat hand-matted rib, silver bead front sight, any combination of chokes, to the customer's specifications. Locks are finest quality sideplate with Holland special detachable feature, may be removed for cleaning, oiling, or repair without tools. Double triggers are adjusted at 3¾ pounds first, and 4½ pounds second. A single trigger is available at added cost. Chambers are all standard, 2¾-inch. The action is special reinforced body of narrowest (from top to bottom) possible design and incorporating new locking features giving great strength and rigidity. The opening and closing is smooth and easy. Automatic, selective ejectors. The stock is selected, long seasoned, best quality French walnut of choice figure, with or without pistol grip. Gold inletted crest plate. Engraving by London's best craftsmen with fine scroll rosette design. Silver bright finish may be provided if the customer so desires. Weight from 7¼ to 7½ pounds, average weight runs 7 pounds 6 ounces. Cost $1176. FOB, London. Delivery time is around six months, may run longer.

The Woodward shotgun was formerly made by James Woodward and Sons; recently, however, the firm has been absorbed by the

Purdey Co. The Woodward over-and-under shotgun continues of
production. Orders may be addressed to Abercrombie and Fitch,
who are Purdey agents in the U.S. The James Purdey and Sons,
Ltd., is located at 57-58 South Audley St., London, W. L.; the factory is situated at Irongate Wharf Road, Praed St., Paddington.
Plant manager is C. H. Lawrence; General Manager, T. D. S.
Purdey, great-grandson of the founder, James Purdey. George III
was the English sovereign when James Purdey built his first
shooting iron.

The Woodward barrel-atop-barrel model is a dead ringer for
two of its rivals, the Boss and the Holland. The differences between
the three are small indeed and by the same token the goodness of
all of them is beyond question. The Woodward, third member of
this elite family, is like the others a shallow-frame gun. It, like the
Boss and the H&H, does not lock up by the use of underbolts but
has the locks on the sides of the tubes. The bolting is accomplished
into the face of the standing breech.

I cannot see how it would be possible to design an over/under
action with less depth. This type of frame, vertically squatty to
extreme degree, assures the weapon of an extraordinary degree of
pointability, a natural shooter that follows eye and hand more by
instinct than conscious effort.

The Purdey-built Woodward is made in 20, 16 and 12 gauges.
The 20, with 26-inch barrels, weighs an even 6 pounds; with 28-inch
tubes there is an increase of 4 ounces in weight. In 16, barrels are
made 26, 27 and 28 inches, any boring, weight 6 pounds 2 ounces
with 26-inch tubes; and 6 pounds 6 ounces with 28-inch. The 12
comes with 26-, 28- or 30-inch barrels and weighs 7¼ pounds with
26-inch barrels; 7½ pounds with 30-inch. Any stock dimensions are
provided, with or without pistol grip. The fore-end will be built
to any conventional pattern.

A raised ventilated rib, plain elevated swept-out, plain, or
matted rib are among the choices open to the customer. The shotgun in keeping with practically all English models comes with two
triggers, if the purchaser insists he can get a single trigger at considerable additional cost. Engraving is the customary English
scroll, executed by some of London's most skilled craftsmen.

Cost is $1330 on South Audley Street, delivery time not less than
ten months. A down payment of 33 1/3% of the price must accom-
pany the order.

The true Purdey—we have been discussing a Woodward up until
now—has been under continuous production since the times of the
American Revolution. "From George III to George VI" is the proud
boast. The firm is privileged to carry on its letterhead and in its
advertising the Warrant of Kingly Appointment; and while this

doesn't mean much to the average American, it carries considerable weight with your royalty-conscious European.

Mere appointment to the king has not been the only basis for the renown enjoyed by the Purdey gun. It is freely acknowledged the best shotgun in the world. And while many will probably not agree, the record speaks for itself.

The Purdey has always been an extremely costly gun; the unswerving policy of the owners has ever been to build the best firearm human skill could achieve and to hell with the expense.

Production today is low, at least measured by our in-series methods. In truth it has never been more than a trickle. Today you wait from six months to a year to receive your Purdey, never during the past could you expect a gun much quicker.

You do not find Purdey shotguns on the shelf when you go to buy. In Abercrombie and Fitch today, the American agents, you will encounter Purdeys but they are all used guns. New ones there will be none. By restricting the output, plus the employment of the finest gun-craftsmen, together with lofty prices, the Purdey has acquired a stature in the minds and the esteem of shooting men which no other shotgun even remotely approaches.

The company today makes but one side-by-side double. This model is known as the Hammerless Ejector Game Gun and sells for $1008. In South Audley St. If you want a single trigger that will be another $112. A special engraving job likewise hikes the figure by another $112.

An extra set of barrels will cost $225. The shotgun is ordinarily provided with a straight grip. If you insist on a pistol grip, that is $14. A recoil pad is another $14. It is readily evident that the Purdey is a costly bauble, especially in view of the fact that import duties, shipping costs, the dealer's profit, and other "bites" are not indicated in these prices.

The Hammerless Ejector Game gun is made in 20, 16 and 12 bores. Chambers are regularly made for the 2¾-inch cartridge in all gauges, and may be had in 2⅝- or 2-inch in 12; or 2⁹⁄₁₆ in 16; or 2½-inch in 20, if desired. The 20 bore with 26-inch barrels (or 27 or 28 inches if you like) weighs 5 pounds 9 ounces; the 16, available with 26-, 27-, or 28-inch tubes, weighs an even 6 pounds with the 27-inch barrels. The 12, made up with 26-, 27-, or 28-inch (longer if wanted) weighs 6¾ pounds with the 28-inch set. These specifications indicate the more or less standard guns. In passing it should be noted that weight runs slightly less if the 2½-inch chamber is specified. It should be emphasized that the Purdey is a strictly custom-turned gun and any reasonable variations are possible.

The action, heart of this ordnance gem, and widely copied

around the world, utilizes the bar-action sidelock. Bolting arrangement includes double underbits and an extension rib that actually
is only a stub. This stub is located above the ejectors and does not
interfere with the rapid reloading of the piece. This extension rib
locks up into the face of the standing breech.

Purdey also employs sideclips—as a matter of fact the company
is the originators of these devices. These clips are extensions on
the outer lumps of the frame and are made to form a snug contact
with angled surfaces on the barrel-breeches. The bar-action sidelock is designed to afford a working angle between the hammer
notch and the sear which is perfection itself. The trigger pull
never changes and is probably the sweetest found on any scatter
gun.

The firm of Boss and Co. is located at 41 Albemarle St., London,
W.1, and is owned by the Robertson and Rennie families. The
firm owns a shooting grounds at Barnet By-Pass, Rowley Green,
Herts, where the usual concealed traps permit of every kind of
practice.

This is a small company with a limited production. A Boss
shotgun is not commenced until the order is received, delivery time
runs better than six months. The U.S. representative is Abercrombie and Fitch.

Two shotguns are under production. The first is a side-by-side
double, any gauge, which sells for $840 in Picadilly. If you would
have a single trigger, add another $98. The second gun is an
over-and-under and for it the price is higher, $1176. fob, London.
The single trigger, as on the conventional double, is $98.

Boss shotguns are unsurpassed in the field of deluxe smoothbores. There simply are none better. It has been the long-standing
policy of this superior little firm to spare neither time nor effort
to manufacture the best shotgun. Output is low because the policy
has not been to attain a large production but instead to make a
modest number of really superior firearms.

The result is an expensive shotgun that is as nearly perfect as
human skill can make it. Boss guns, both the conventional double
and the O/U, employ sidelocks. Unlike some other English gun
builders their guns feature a single trigger. While other makers
will provide a one-trigger gun it has always seemed to me that
they were never too happy about it.

Some English single triggers have not been such howling suc-
cesses. Not like, for instance, the splendid single on the Winchester
M21 and the Browning over/under. In justice to Boss let it be said
that they make a good trigger and they know it.

The Boss over-and-under is especially worthy of note. It is a design that was developed forty years ago and from the theoretical standpoint, at least, has no superior.

The perfect over/under shotgun should have an action that does not extend below the bottom barrel. Such a receiver, if it could be achieved, would place the hands in closest proximity to the barrels and would make possible better and more natural alignment of the weapon. In order to produce a receiver with the least possible depth, also a forestock which would locate the forward hand just as close to the barrels as possible, the company designed locking bolts which are not located below but are on the sides of the gun-tubes. They also developed ejectors which lie alongside the barrels. This largely eliminated the pregnant look so common to all superposed scatterbarrels. The result is the most sleek and streamlined over/under in the book!

The Lang shotgun comes from the firm of Stephen Grant and Joseph Lang, Ltd., 7 & 8 Bury St., St. James, London S.W. 1. The Lang shotgun has been made since 1821; the Grant, from the year 1866. Combined with Grant and Lang are a number of other gun makers, some well known, others of little renown. These are Charles Lancaster Co., a firm dating back almost as distantly as that of Lang, to the year 1826. There is, as well, Frederick Beesley, who was the inventor of the Southgate ejector, and besides this and other shotgun developments, made fine guns. Harrison and Hussey, as well as the Watson Bros., complete the association.

The Harrison and Hussey Company was organized directly after World War I, and despite the unfortunate fact that both owners died within a dozen years after organization, the firm continues to manufacture a very high-class shotgun. Watson Bros. for more than 60 years were located in old Bond Street and Pall Mall, and made a specialty of building small bores.

It was Joseph Lang who developed the first of the English doubles to handle the 12-gauge 2-inch shell. This peewee contains only ⅞ of an ounce of shot, driven by an equivalent squib of powder. The gun weighs but 5½ pounds, barrel lengths are 25½ inches, and it is claimed that killing range and power leave nothing to be desired!

This freakish gun and load have left the English gunmakers open to a good deal of criticism. American writers have condemned all British-built doubles simply because this 2-inch cartridge had a certain popularity in the Tight Little Isle. Granted this feather-weight probably isn't worth shucks, there remain many fine English shotguns, and among them are those more standardized models from the benches of Grant and Lang.

Lang once made an over/under, but production has been halted. There are at the moment seven different models of Grant and Lang side-by-sides. Prices vary from $196 for a third grade, non-ejector up to $785 for the best sideplate lock in 16 and 12 gauges. The Beesley in 16 only is priced generally in the range of the Grant and Langs.

An interesting practice of this combined firm is that they accept used guns in trade for new ones. A current listing of used models on hand shows Lancasters, Watsons, and Beesleys as well as Grant and Langs. The company also makes double express rifles to include calibers from .280 to .577. Shotshell cartridges are sold but I am uncertain whether the shells are loaded on the premises or are manufactured under contract and simply carry the Grant and Lang name.

The firm of Westley Richards and Co., Ltd., is located at 23 Conduit St., London, W. 1. The manufacturing plant is in Birmingham, at Grange Road, Bournbrook. There is a third installation also in Birmingham, at 24 Bennett's Hill. The Westley Richards Co., like James Purdey, was established during the reign of George III (whose troops were given a drubbing by an upstart Yankee named Washington), and to this day proudly call attention to the fact that double-barreled pistols were made by the firm in 1812-14 for use by the Royal English Cavalry against the Americans!

Westley Richards Co. has contributed immensely to the advancement of the shotgun as a modern sporting arm. It was they who patented the top lever, a system which remains virtually unchanged to this day. Before the perfection of the top lever, the Lefauchaux under lever was employed. It was a weak and faulty system.

The company also developed the rib-extension bolting arrangement, the extension rib varies in design, size and shape but broadly speaking is a sort of flat-shaped stud which is an integral piece with the barrel-ends and extends into and locks up with the standing breech. It provides the top lock for the action and serves, most sturdily, to bolt and close the firearm.

Westley Richards are the developers of the Anson and Deeley action. Anson was a gunsmith with the company and Deeley was managing director. Their action was the first practical hammerless and it introduced among other improvements the universal practice of cocking the hammers by utilizing the turning movement of the barrels. The Anson and Deeley action is practically the only type made today.

Westley Richards developed a fore-end ejector, and to this day we haven't been able to design another that does not utilize the forestock to contain this essential mechanism. In 1899 the company came along with something quite revolutionary in a detachable lock. This lock is of original type and more than a half-century of use proves its goodness. Instead of bolting to the sides of the receiver, as do almost all conventional sideplate locks, the Westley Richards utilizes a hinged floor plate, which when unlatched swings downward carrying the hammers and sears into view. The locks may be inspected daily if desired.

The locks permit of a considerably stronger receiver due to the retention of more steel in the frame, and the total absence of pins and screws not only contributes to an added strength but also very measurably enhances the beauty of the piece. Spare locks can be purchased at the time the gun is ordered; but it is difficult to foresee, bearing in mind the strength and goodness of the Westley Richards shotguns, when they would be needed.

The firm also makes a selective single trigger, a trigger developed in 1901 and little changed to this day. Cost is $130.

Today the company manufactures three shotguns with the box-lock. This is somewhat unusual in Englind where boxlocks are usually looked upon as inferior to the sideplate. The firm also makes four models of sideplate scatter guns.

The boxlock is stronger than the sideplate lock. It has more strength for the reason that less metal is removed to install hammers, sears, firing pins, etc. A shotgun boasting this style of action has a much stronger joint between frame and stock. This is due solely to the manner in which the wood and steel are joined, a great deal more wood being retained. In fitting the stock to a shotgun with a sideplate lock a great deal of the wood must be whittled away to make room for the action.

All American side-by-side and over/under shotguns today are made with boxlocks. The last remaining sideplate, the L. C. Smith, has fallen by the wayside. The boxlock is easier and more simply made; also it is designed for the use of coil springs, a type which ordinarily possesses a longer life expectancy than the flat kind used in the sidelocks.

As to the disadvantages, the boxlock does not offer as much surface for engraving and ornamentation as does the sideplate. Neither is it so easy to disassemble for cleaning, and replacement of parts is a damnable nuisance. These are its major faults.

Westley Richards regularily provides three types of lock-ups. The oldest, and by far the best known, employs underbolting together with the famous extension dolls-head with wedge-bite. This is the original action and is known as the "C" model. It is one of the most sturdy ever built. It is recommended by the company for guns that will handle magnum loads and for competition shooting.

A second action is similar to the Purdey. It is underbolted; but instead of employing the customary dolls-head extension, a concealed barrel extension is fitted just above the ejectors. In this position it provides a third locking surface but in no way interferes with the rapid reloading of the piece. This gun is triple bolted, as may be realized, and is referred to as the "B" model. It will also withstand heavy loads and long, intensive usage.

Still a third action is regularily manufactured. This is the "A" model. It is for 20- and 16-gauge guns, essentially; and should it be ordered in a 12, it should be chambered for the 2⅝-inch cartridge. This action has only underbolts. In the U.S. our very best double, the splendid Winchester Model 21, is underbolted. We fire our heaviest loads in it. In England this simple lock-up is considered insufficient to withstand express and magnum loads. The Winchester, in common with others of our double guns, has been proved with our hottest loads; all of which persuades me to conclude that the Westley Richards, if built with sufficient weight in the "A" model, would withstand any modern shotshell.

The "C" model is what is referred to as "Best Quality" and sells for $882 in Conduit St., London. This action, as I've just said, is the most strongly locked up of any; and while it is intended for the 2¾-inch cartridges, it may also be had for the 2⅝-inch-long case. Weight starts at 6¾ pounds, when chambered for the standard 12 gauge; 6 pounds when specified for the 2⅝-inch.

Barrels may be selected of any length and bored to any chokes. A flat-top, dead-level rib is fitted unless the buyer specifies otherwise. The ventilated raised rib is fitted for an additional $30. Barrels are polished and blackened by hand to the highest finish. The stock will be made to any measurements; it is of specially selected French walnut of finest figure. It is oil finished and is checkered by hand. A gold crestplate is inletted. Straight or half-pistol grip may be had as desired. A Monte Carlo comb together with a beavertail fore-end may be had. Cost of the Monte Carlo is unknown but the over-fatted forestock runs $28. A rubber recoil pad, if ordered, is $14.

The action has the detachable locks which have been mentioned. These locks, while enclosed in a receiver of box type, do not employ coil springs as we do in our box actions, but are of the flat type. An extra set of locks cost $130. If a single trigger is deemed necessary that's an additional $130. Engraving is finest English scroll. If the shooter has any special desires in the matter of ornamentation, it can be accomplished at added expense.

Besides the three models of boxlock, there are, as I have said, four sideplate guns made. The most expensive of these costs the same as the "C" model Best Quality boxlock, namely, $882. This gun is equal in quality, good looks, fit, and balance to its fellow.

The company also turns out a non-ejector sideplate model which sells for $255.

Extra sets of barrels for either the "C" model Best Quality box-lock or the similar model with sideplate lock may be had for $235 the pair.

The Westley Richards Co. is the largest manufacturer of custom-turned shotguns and rifles in England. Unlike many of the smaller gunmakers the firm does not contract for the manufacture of various pieces and assemblies outside the plant. The weapon is commenced, machined, fitted, engraved, and made ready to the last detail within the walls of the Birmingham home base.

The Westley Richards is an expensive firearm. At the same time it is extremely well made, durable and beautiful. I doubt if a more handsome gun exists. The sportsman who buys a Westley Richards can expect to fire it 10,000 shots every year during his shooting lifetime, and then pass it along to his son, who may reasonably anticipate that he will need no other during his hunting span. This English-built smoothbore is just that well and sturdily built.

Chapter 12

SIX BARRELS FOR THE PRICE OF ONE

I WOULD NOT THINK of hunting seriously with a repeating scattergun that was not decorated with a changeable muzzle choke.

It is not so much the handiness of the gadget while you are in the field after quail or doves, grouse or the webfeet, as it is the fact that from season's beginning until its end, you shoot only one weapon. There is an old adage, "Beware the man with the single gun." The gunner who possesses only one smoothbore, and shoots it plentiously, invariably is a cracking good marksman. Much better than his fellow who owns an armory.

The repeating smoothbore—either pump or auto-loader—sporting a muzzle device is medicine for anything with wings.

I have read any number of fanciful tales in which the gun writer could visualize the huntsman busy in a snipe marsh, his adjustable choke opened up to its widest for the close-rising long-bills. Then along would come a flight of puddle ducks determined to alight in the nearby slough. The sportsman would simply give a quick adjustment to his handy gadget and instantly cope with the 40-yard targets. This was imaginative but not necessarily true. I have been using the whole family of quick-change chokes for the last 20 years and can never remember when I made a quick switch from one choke to another because the brand of game changed.

What really happens is that the choke is set for the game of the day and it won't be varied more than one degree throughout the shoot. When you go to hunt ring-necks you seldom jump any ivory-billed woodpeckers. I do find that I may attach a spreader tube for early-season bobwhites, and as the day progresses, find I need a wee bit more constriction and switch from the very open tube to a second and tighter choke, aimed at giving me a more killing spread at a trifle longer distance.

The same is true when hunting wildfowl; it is seldom in blind or on pass when the full choke setting isn't left undisturbed throughout the course of the shoot.

The major advantage of the muzzle appurtenance is the business of shooting only one gun. This is seldom appreciated as much as it should be. A repeater with a 28-inch barrel, measured from breech to the very mouth of the choke accessory, in 12 gauge, is competent to handle anything from skeet to Canada honkers. The shooter who lives with his one gun gets to know a familiarity with that weapon which makes him deadly accurate. The fit and swing of the piece become so sure as to be, virtually, as positive as the pointing of a finger. And it doesn't matter whether he is gunning for grouse, or pheasant, for quail or white-wing. The shotgunner who clings to the double barrel, in a sense, enjoys the advantage of a single gun. He can make do with his two barrels, the one invariably bored and choked for close-rising targets, the second much more tightly constricted and intended for the long range. Regardless of how thoughtfully he may have had those two tubes bored, however, he needs must strike a compromise. He may use his gun throughout the season and enjoy a modicum of good shooting, but at best his equipment is not perfect.

The user of the single barrel, pump, or automatic who does not attach a patented schnozzle is indeed behind the 8-ball. He has, in effect, no choice at all. The manufacturers tell us that more full-choke guns, in single-tube model, are sold than all others put together. This means the buyer has a weapon that is suited to only our widest flying game; wildfowl, for the major part.

Smarter gun men elect to shoot the modified choke in their pump or auto. This is infinitely wiser, for the modified boring is a compromise and a pretty good one at that. It will do, after a fashion, on quail and grouse, and serves maybe better on ring-neck and

From l. to r.: the Poly Choke, Cutts Compensator, Weaver Choke.

The Pachmayr Power Pac, one of the best of the muzzle-variable chokes.

mallard. But it is still a give-and-take sort of proposition, not really correct for much that flies.

All the vari-chokes worth their salt have a built-in recoil eliminator. The 12-gauge cartridge, in a gun of conventional weight, churns up something better than 20 foot-pounds of free recoil. This is considerable; and if you compound the punishment by whanging out maybe a hundred rounds in a morning, as many skeet and trap men do, it adds up to a sizeable beating.

Recoil isn't very well understood. All the gunner realizes is that he soaks up a sharp blow to face and shoulder. Actually when the powder ignites several phenomena take place in atomic-chain succession. While the gases are afire, a happening which runs into a millisecond or two, the pressures set up work in all directions. Not only is force exerted against the base of the shot charge, but against the sidewalls of cartridge case and chamber walls as well. Naturally this same force is slamming rearward, too. This is the first and certainly the most ponderous evidences of recoil. In big-bore guns this initial reaction tallys some 75% of the entire phenomena.

The gases as they drive up the bore, propelling the wadding and the pellet charge with a savagery scarcely imaginable, are continually changing their center of mass. This job of accelerating the shot and wadding induce a secondary reaction. This recoil is small and insignificant in the sum total, it may amount to some 8-12% of the entire sensation.

The final and third wave of recoil phenomena occurs on the instant when the white-hot gases, driven at extreme velocities—and violent stuff indeed—meet the outer atmosphere. The reaction thus occasioned is called muzzle blast. The shock wave set up by this violent meeting of the propellant gases and the free atmosphere accounts for another 10-12% of the kick.

Actually the recoil as it strikes the shoulder and cheek comes in a series of waves. It goes without saying that so far as the shooter is concerned he is aware of nothing save the sum total of the three.

Carefully controlled tests of a number of the better known

muzzle brakes on a standard recoil pendulum indicate that with heavy 12-gauge loads and the FC tubes (or settings), the Cutts Compensator (Lyman) and the Pachmayr Power-Pac will show a reduction in swing of 31%. The J. C. Higgins "Chokemaster" was not tested but I'd hazard it is just as effective. It is a device of essentially the same type as the Power-Pac, therefore results can be expected to be closely similar.

The Ventilated Poly Choke showed a reduction in swing of 14%; the Weaver Choke was the same. The Shooting Master device and the Herter Vari-Choke are untested but it is reasonable to assume that the capabilities of these accessories will closely approximate those of the Poly and the Weaver. Compensator surfaces are very much the same on all four.

Experiments indicate that when light field loads are fired through the more open tubes of the Cutts or the PowerPac that the amount of kick that is eliminated is much smaller—only 20%. These findings are equally true with those devices which provide less compensated bearing, the Poly, Weaver, Herter, and the others. Rduction with some is as low as 6%.

My tests of the variable-choke-compensator equipment show that the things will give the patterns that are claimed for them. Lyman's Cutts Comp comes complete with an array of six choke tubes. These tubes range from the Spreader which is even larger than full cylinder (.729-inch is cylinder for the 12 gauge) to an Xtra Full Choke, with a diameter of .680-inch. In between are tubes that will give Full Choke (.690"), Modified (.705"), Improved Cylinder (.725") and finally this open babby with a measurement of .755-inch. With a variety of loads these tubes will spray out the patterns that are expected of them. Weaver also lists six tubes with his gadget.

More lately the Lyman Co. has produced a second version of the Cutts invention, this is a Compensator which has the choking apparatus as an integral piece. It is located ahead of the ventilated cage and is adjusted by simply giving it a ⅓ turn. Instead of six variations as on the original model (which, of course continues in manufacture), the improved version only has settings for improved cylinder, modified and full choke. Today, the manufacturers only offer their standard, unadorned barrels in these three chokes. The new Lyman has the advantage of having the whole device in one piece.

The Poly Choke has six primary settings and three alternate settings between the main stops. This, according to the advertising propaganda, gives the gunner nine different chokes and presumably nine different patterns. This is malarkey. A perfectly normal shotgun, shooting the best cartridges, will oftimes vary as much as

15% between shots. This means that a gun with a Poly screwed up to full choke may produce a pattern that is no better than improved cylinder. To claim that patterns can be controlled to the extent that you can get differences of 2% to 3% by a twist of the choking collar is strictly for the birds!

The vari-chokes when used on a 12-gauge gun are perfectly sound, completely satisfactory. When the same device is hung on the business end of the 16 gauge it is almost as reliable as when mounted on the 12. However, when a 20 is equipped with a quick-change choke it is spotty indeed as to performance. You can set it for modified patterns and get everything from 35% to 70% and never be sure what is coming out next. The amount of recoil reduction that is secured is likewise of little moment. There is some elimination of the kick but it doesn't amount to shucks.

The accessories on the 28 gauge and the 410 are quite inefficient. You seldom see them on anything save skeet guns and I suppose then they give the user a certain amount of confidence. He generally has no idea how badly that confidence is misplaced.

Chapter 13

IS THE 16 A FORGOTTEN GUN?

THE 16, RUNNING LIGHTER than the average 12, throwing patterns on a par with the best of the big guns, capable of ranging out with all but the heaviest 12s, beautifully balanced, fast handling, with less recoil and lighter fodder to pocket tote, has plenty of stuff on the ball.

The 16 runs a gamut of loads which makes it possible to fire the standard 20 or run up the scale to heavy 12-gauge loadings. It would appear from this that the gun was an especially happy sort of all-purpose shooting iron. Despite this undeniable versatility it seems to be slipping from the picture. Once we had a 14 gauge and a 32 gauge; both have long since gone the way of nickel beer. Is the 16 destined to follow? Certainly the manufacturers aren't building as many 16-bore guns today as they were ten or twenty years ago.

On the Continent the 16 is the most popular gauge. Certainly that is not true here.

The 16 has been enhanced this past twelve months by the addition of the magnum cartridge. This walloper provides the intermediate with a shell that by weight of powder and charge of shot places it in a class with the 12-gauge heavyweights. The 16 magnum loading runs 3½ drams equivalent of powder and 1¼ ounces of lead. The standard 12, by comparison, hits only 3¼ drams equivalent of propellant and 1¼ ounces of shot.

The Ithaca Company make a pump 16 that can be had as light as 6 pounds; an average gun of this bore will go a bit heavier, from 6¾ to 7¼ pounds. In comparison the usual 12 scales 7¼ to 8½ pounds. The 16 is essentially an uplands shotgun and any study of those currently made will indicate this. Lessened weight and pleasant recoil are two prime virtues of the weapon.

If, now that you look back over the season just ended, you feel that you have slowed up a wee bit, that when game broke cover you were a long time getting on; if after a three- or four-hour tramp the old fowling piece seemed to weigh like thoughts of next year's income tax, then may I suggest you give some consideration to a switch to the lighter sixteen.

119

The Model 12 Winchester is pattern tested.

The 16 Ithaca double. It is a splendid performer on quail.

You may say it's all true the 16 is lighter, faster to swing and point; but what of its power? What about those times when a few ducks are to be shot, or the wildly rising chinks, that offer 40-50-yard shots? How then does the 16 stack up against the 12?

Yesterday I spent the day patterning a full-choke 16 and a full-choke 12. I used the standard 1⅛-ounce load in the 16, and the same shot charge in the 12, 1⅛ ounces shot, but with a powder charge running ⅛ dram heavier in the bigger gun. The shot was size 7½, ideal for uplands work, too small for wildfowl. The 16 that I used weighs 7½ pounds, the 12 tipped the beam at 8 pounds 10 ounces. The 16 was a sweet handling, smooth-working double; the 12 was a big automatic.

I commenced my pattern tests at 40 yards, ranged out to 50 and 55 yards before I was completed:

Gauge	No. of Shots Fired	Distance	% Pellets in 30" Circle
12 ga. 1⅛ oz.	5	40 yds.	72%
16 ga. 1⅛ oz.	5	40 yds.	77%
12 ga. 1⅛ oz.	5	50 yds.	41%
16 ga. 1⅛ oz.	5	50 yds.	64%
12 ga. 1⅛ oz.	5	55 yds.	32%
16 ga. 1⅛ oz.	5	55 yds.	51%

While I did no test firing at 30 yards—usual uplands killing range —it is apparent from the results at 40 yards that things would have been pretty nearly equal at that distance. But look at what happened at 50 yards. The 16 placed an average of 250 pellets inside the 30-inch circle; best the 12 could do using the same shot load was 161 pellets. That's quite a difference.

At 55 yards, admittedly too far to shoot the light 7½ shot, the 16 chalked up an average of 50%, which means an average of 199 pellets in the 30-inch; while the 12 made 32% or 125 pellets inside. Obviously the 1⅛-ounce load is better ballistically in the narrower bore of the 16. Some reason for this is apparent when you consider that the 16 gauge has a muzzle velocity of 1366 feet per second,

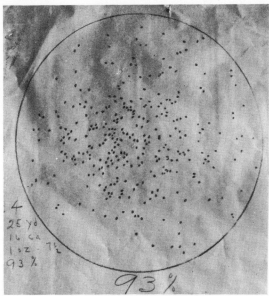

The 16 at 25 yards, FC barrel.

The 16 performs well on all uplands species.

and a remaining velocity at 40 yards of 747 feet per second, with an attendant energy per pellet of 1.56 foot-pounds at 40 yards. The 12-gauge 1⅛-ounce standard load starts at 1280 feet per second and at 40 yards has dwindled to 668 feet per second, with a per pellet energy blow of 1.50 foot-pounds.

That should be your answer to the lack of power in the 16!

Not only did the 16 shoot better and more uniform patterns than the 12 but it has a higher velocity and greater striking energy.

Now don't get me wrong. I'm not proving the 16 is a better gun than the 12. The best all-around shotgun in the world is the 12 gauge. All I'd need have done to shoot circles around my 16 would be to change to larger shot, say 4s, or fill the magazine with the 12-gauge magnum loads. But comparing the two guns, using similar shot charges and almost similar powder weights, the 16 showed that it is ample artillery for any kind of uplands species and plenty potent enough for wildfowl out to all practical ranges.

The original load for the 16 was 1 ounce of shot; and there was once a time when you could get seven-eighths ounce of shot! The 1-ounce loading is put up by all the makers today. Why this is, I do not understand, for the almost-standard hunting load of the 20 gauge is one ounce of shot. The 16-gauge shooter who persists in sticking with the 1 ounce might as well discard his heavier gun for the 20. There are other disadvantages to the use of the light and largely ineffectual 1-ounce shot, as well. Yesterday, I tried the 1-ounce load against the 1⅛ ounce in 3 different 16-bore guns.

Gun	No. of Shots	Load	Distance	% Pellets in 30″ Circle
Ithaca #4 16	10	1 oz.	30 yds.	82%
As above	10	1⅛ oz.	30 yds.	91%
As above	10	1 oz.	40 yds.	47%
As above	10	1⅛ oz.	40 yds.	79%
Johnson Skeeter, 16	10	1 oz.	30 yds.	80%
As above	10	1⅛ oz.	30 yds.	92%
As above	10	1 oz.	40 yds.	36%
As above	10	1⅛ oz.	40 yds.	65%
Ithaca #5 16	10	1 oz.	30 yds.	73%
As above	10	1⅛ oz.	30 yds.	89%
As above	10	1 oz.	40 yds.	62%
As above	10	1⅛ oz.	40 yds.	69%

It is apparent from these test firings that the load to use in the 16 is the 1⅛-ounce load in the 2¾-inch cartridge. The 1-ounce load is ballistically inferior to the heavier charge and I wouldn't be surprised if all the arms makers do not bore their weapons for the better balanced load.

It is regrettable that 16-gauge guns are to be found with two chamber lengths, 2⁹⁄₁₆-inch and 2¾-inch. Those gunners who possess older 16s are almost sure to have guns chambered for the short case. When they attempt to use the longer and better cartridge, it extends into the forcing cone and upon opening forces itself into the barrel, thus causing a lot of jamming and mutilation of pellets. Instead of normal patterns a sketchy spread results. If the gun has sufficient metal about the forcing cone and breech end of the barrel the chamber can be lengthened to the standard dimension of 2¾ inches. This should be done.

So I say if it is a proposition with you of wanting a lighter weapon, a gun you can catch your game with more quickly, a piece to permit a faster and easier swing, and a gun that will not be a burden after hours of tramping, select the 16. Using our newest and heaviest maximum charges it will shoot very, very close to the 12, will, most assuredly, bring in just as much game at the end of day, punish you less, and what's more important, probably, restore a lot of your wing-gunning confidence.

Chapter 14

IS THERE A 100-YARD DUCK GUN?

WHAT IS THE LONGEST yardage at which a 12 gauge stuffed with the heaviest magnum cartridges will rake down migratory fowl? How far will the more powerful magnum 10, with its Roman Candle case, transfix the winging Canada?

Is it 100 yards for the bigger bore, 80 for the smaller? Or will the 10 reach to 120 yards, as some contend, and the 12 kill regularly at 90-100 yards?

It isn't difficult to get the answers. Go ask the nearest shotgunner and he'll tell you. He may say 70 yards. Or 85 yards. Or 120 yards. If maybe you opine that he is just guessing, then go to the library and dig through the tomes that have been written. Or write one of the gun hacks who poses as an authority. The Man in the Duck Blind will give you his version of maximum killing yardages; the books another; the gun writers still a third.

I determined to establish some workable data; and pondering how best this information could be gathered, it appealed to me that the only accurate figures would have to come from actual killing over yardages that were carefully measured and staked from the blind. This determined, I then considered the four-ducks-per day bag limit and the chore it is to always be sure of placing yourself in front of sufficient webfeet to get a daily whack at even this insignificant number.

Obviously what I would have to do would be to commence in Manitoba and work my way, delightfully and fulsomely, down the Mississippi flyway to the Gulf. Nor could I pause there. The game I'd kill most surely would not be sufficient to say with certainty that the magnum was a 100-yard duck killer, or an 120-yard piece. No. Most certainly I could not pause at the Gulf. I'd have to work my way through pond and marsh on across Mexico, into the Banana Republics and thence into South America. Perhaps six months later I'd finally gun my way to that shotgunner's seventh heaven of wildfowling delight, the Tierra del Fuego, hard above Cape Horn.

In this manner and always careful to stake out my yardages, I felt reasonably sure I'd return home with a hatful of usable data.

124

The only hitch in this otherwise elegant scheme was that I could not devote the time to the experiment. The researcher must ever bow to such mundane things as time, finances, unsympathetic bosses, and the like. Obviously if I was to assemble the facts for or against the 100-yard shotgun, I'd have to hit on other tests basically just as sound but maybe a mite less grandiose.

Cancelling my flight plans to Manitoba, I set to pondering what it takes to kill a goose, and a duck, and even a snipe. Nobody knows. My old man, unquestionably our greatest shotgun authority, said that it took five pellets to stop an old Canada's clock and these have got to nick him in a vital spot and possess sufficient English to penetrate. Each of these pellets has got to develop three foot-pounds of energy at the target. This, as we can see, is an aggregate blow of 15 foot-pounds.

As for ducks, a much smaller bird, the pellet hits must tally a minimum of four, and each has got to deliver 1.5 foot-pounds of blow. A total force of 6 foot-pounds. Game like snipe, doves, bob-

The author (left) and Harold C. Russell, Director of Sales, Federal Cartridge Co., on a goose-shooting foray in Mexico.

white quail, need 3 pellets as a minimum with a total force of 3 foot-pounds.

These figures are assumptions. Major Askins, my father, died when he was 86 and hunted until a few months of his death. He shot game from the time he was able to walk until he cashed in his chips. Something around 75 years in the game fields. His figures are calculations but until someone can come up with a better rule-of-thumb, I shall accept them.

Just how far will a shotgun carry and place 5 pellets on a target the size of an old honker? The goose has a vital area about 12 inches in length by 6 inches in height when he passes at right angles. This does not take into consideration his wings, head and neck. Many geese are downed with lucky hits in these body areas. For the sake of my experiment I chose to disregard these luck shots and determined to count only hits in the solid body regions. The 6″ x 12″ vital area figures out to 72 square inches. The patterning circle we habitually use to check choke percentages is a 30-inch circle, a circle containing 707 square inches. Slap the 6″ x 12″ rectangle upon the 30-inch circle and what do you see?

At 40 yards a full-choke gun firing the new 1½-ounce load of No. 2 shot will put an average of 8.4 pellets into the bird. Returning to our formula of 5 pellets needed to connect and a total blow of 15 pounds, we find our goose would be killed. Not only has he been pierced by more than enough shot but the accumulative blow amounts to 57.96 foot-pounds. The No. 2 shot at the muzzle has a per-pellet energy of 18.7 foot-pounds; at 40 yards this has fallen off to 6.90 foot-pounds. Mighty dead gander!

But what about 50, 60, 70 and even 100 yards? What happens then?

At 50 yards with the same load, tried on 10 targets, average shows 6.72 hits falling within the 72-square-inch outline. No. 2s at this yardage deliver 5.5 foot-pounds per pellet. The blow, 36.96 pounds.

At 60 yards hits averaged 4.5 and energy per No. 2 pellet runs 4.12 foot-pounds. The blow, 18.54 pounds. At 65 yards—still short of the 70 so glibly bandied about—hits worked out to barely 3.36 and total energy only 12 foot-pounds. This is not only shy on the required numbers of leaden missiles but the blow is too puny to dump a goose.

The story with the big magnum 10, the old bruiser that burps out a full two ounces of shot whooped along by 5¼ drams equivalent of powder, is somewhat more rosy. At 65 yards this gun for an average of 10 patterns placed 6.1 pellets in the 6″ x 12″ square, for an average blow of 21.77 pounds. *Bueno* for geese on the score of both numbers of pellets and striking force.

Trying the new 12-gauge magnum load in Mexico.

At 70 yards the margin is not quite so good. Hits for 5 rounds averaged 4.9, energy per pellet, 3.25 foot-pounds; total blow, 15.92 foot-pounds. It can be seen that the gun has just barely scraped under the wire as a goose killer. What we need, just to reiterate once again, is 5 shot in the bird for a total blow of 15 foot-pounds. We've just barely got it here.

Did I test the big 10 at 80 yards? Nope. At 80 yards the No. 2 pellet, best of all shot sizes for goose-taking, has a pipsqueak energy of only 2.25 foot-pounds. Even had I been so fortunate as to have gotten the requisite 5 pellets into the 6″ x 12″ rectangle—a trick I couldn't accomplish a full 10 yards shorter—the sum total blow would only have aggregated 11.25 pounds.

A 10-gauge magnum to be an 80-yard goose gun would have to pattern, I calculate, 95% at 40 yards. The best I've gotten out of some half-dozen I have tested is from 83-87%. The gun that will pattern for 10 shots or more, at 95% at 40 yards just ain't being built these days. Carried further the 10 would have to crack 80% at 50 yards; 65% at 60 yards, 50% at 70 yards, and a full 40% at 80 yards. The best of them can muster about 25-30% at 70 yards and not all of 'em will do that.

Where is this cock-and-bull saga about 100-yard wildfowling?

To shoot at a square of paper 4' x 4' and once the shot is fired inscribe a neat 30-inch circle takes advantage of the best concentration of shot. Thereafter the experimenter slaps his 6" x 12" rectangle over the heaviest part of the pattern. This kind of skullduggery gives the gun and load every advantage. An advantage that does not shape up very big when you attempt to supplant that big, immobile sheet of pattern paper for a whistling honker drifting by at something around 85 feet per second. Not only must you judge his distance to a neat fraction but all in the same instant calculate a lead which at 40 yards is theoretically 10.4 feet and in actuality something around 5 to 6 feet.

A not unimportant part of the equation is this matter of shot stringing. The shot load does not reach the target like a ball from a rifle. It goes like a kite-tail in the wind. The pellets that are mutilated in the cartridge, in the cone, up the barrel, and through the choke, lag behind and cause what we refer to as shot-stringing. A shot string from a big 12 or the larger 10, will have a total length of approximately 12 feet at 40 yards. A rough rule for calculating the length of the string is to say that for every 10 feet of range there will be 12 inches of elongation of the shot load. With shot stretched out from head to rear a full 12 feet at 40 yards, at twice that distance it is quite safe to assume that the string would have more than double its length, and more probably close to 30 feet.

All these tag-along pellets finally reach the pattern sheet and register thereon. The fact that it took some of them a lot longer

Ducks—but killed at much less than 100 yards. Recent advertisements to the contrary, ducks are not killed at such ranges.

to reach the mark than others doesn't register on the paper, except that the stragglers invariably hit on the outer perimeter of the target.

On a winging goose these late-comers do little damage. The poppycock that if a gunner over-lead his bird the tail end of the shot string will catch the target is pretty well exploded. These trailing pellets are damaged and out-of-round and don't have the oomph needed to penetrate a tough old Canada. These are the shots you hear rattle off his pinions.

My tests should not be accepted too literally. Actually all figures are on the optimistic side. If the same firing could have been done on live game neither the guns nor the loads would have turned in such rosy performance.

Finished with the pattern sheet and the 72-square-inch rectangle of the goose, I turned to the silhouette of a duck in flight. This duck outline measured 12" x 18" and included the head, neck and wings, the latter outstretched. Pellet hits were counted regardless of where they fell.

I commenced firing at this cut-out with the most popular duck load in the book, a 12 crammed with 1¼ ounces and 3¾ drams equivalent of powder. The shots were 2s. Five rounds at the bird at 60 yards showed an average of 4.6 hits per cartridge. Energy, 4.12 foot-pounds. Result, an average of 18.95 pounds, more than three times the blow needed to murder the mallard.

At 70 yards with the same load and same number of trials, a grand total of 19 pellets hit the mark. Energy per pellet is 3.25 foot-pounds. Average blow per shot, 12.35 foot-pounds.

I then switched to the new standard magnum load of 1½ ounces, this time charged with No. 4 and not No. 2 shot—a better medicine for ducks—and secured an average of 7.8 hits per round. This at 60 yards. Pellet energy for the No. 4 shot at 60 yards is 2.20 foot-pounds. The load showed a reserve of power for mallard and canvasback, 17.16 foot-pounds for each of the 5 shots.

I then switched back to 2s and at 70 yards got an average per shot of 4.2 hits in the silhouette. Energy in this larger pellet is 3.25 foot-pounds. Final tally 13.65 foot-pounds. Twice as much as we calculate we need to kill ducks.

At 80 yards the 12 magnum and 1½-ounces No. 2, resulted in 14 pellets striking the mark out of the 5 shots. This is an average of 2.8 hits with an energy per pellet of only 2.25 pounds. The puny blow of 6.3 pounds might kill the duck but it is doubtful. By our formula he has been struck the 6-pound blow but he hasn't been ventilated with the requisite 4 pellets. These are the unfortunate fowl that set their wings and glide into the tules to suffer miserably and finally die.

The big 10 magnum came into the picture. At 70 yards with No. 2s I poked 47 pellets into the duck with the 5 shots. This is an average of 9.4 pellets per blast, with a final figure of 16.57 foot-pounds per cartridge. This would not only kill ducks but geese as well.

With No. 4s at a yardage of 80, I got 33 hits, an average of 6.6 hits per shot, and figures out to a blow of 9.76 foot-pounds. Still potent enough for ducks. Switching to 2s, really the only stuff to use seriously at the extreme ranges, I got 19 hits with 5 shots. The No. 2 pellet at 80 yards has a force of 2.25 foot-pounds. A little calculation shows that each shot only indicates an average of 3.8 pellets into the mark for an energy of 8.55 foot pounds. This would probably kill the duck, but my hunch is that he would only be crippled and would have to be hunted down and a finishing shot delivered.

Doc Cummings, chief cockalorum of Remington's ballistic laboratories, says that a charge of No. 2 will drift 23 inches at 50 yards in a 30-mph cross-wind. The good man of science doesn't go on to conjecture what the drift would be at 80 yards but I'd unhesitatingly estimate that at a minimum it would easily be twice 23 inches or in the neighborhood of 4 feet. A moment's cogitation on this factor will persuade the most sanguine that he's going to have to be pretty cute about figuring windage to slap his shot charge on a web-foot at 80 yards. Say, for instance, that the bird is flying directly away from the gun and there is a 30-mile cross-wind. The shot charge would be drifted 4 feet, which would be sufficient to cause a complete miss. At 80 yards a normal lead in a dead calm would be something around 15-24 feet. If this lead were further compounded by the drift of the shot in a 20- or 30-mile wind, not really such a gale on a good ducking day, a feller would have to keep his slide rule around his neck to make the necessary corrections.

Still another angle to this extra-long-range shotgunning is the decidedly two-bit distances which the shot will travel. Wallace Coxe, who has just retired after a couple of centuries as the chief guru in the DuPont ballistics laboratories, says that a 10-gauge gun elevated to 40 degrees will poop out its charge of No. 2s to a maximum distance of only 330 yards or 990 feet. This means at 80 yards (240 feet) that the fall of the shot is between 3 and 4 feet.

Slapping the charge on a bouncy old gander at 80 yards then simmers down to a simple little deduction about his speed—he generally churns up something around 60 mph—the drift of the shot which amounts to 4 feet in a 30-mile breeze, plus the fall of the shot charge which is 40 inches or in that neighborhood. The equation appeals to me as being just the stuff for one of these gun directors which we use on the 90 mm AA gun. Certainly the hombre in the blind is going to have to have a touch of Einstein about him if he can come up with an answer during those split seconds when the game is in range.

This chapter purported, according to its title, to be an opus on the 100-yard duck gun. There ain't no such animal. There is just barely an 80-yard gun and I'd not have much confidence in it. Tales about duck killing at 100 yards are shaggy dog stories best saved for the psychoanalyst's couch. Not only will the shotgun fail to hold its charge together to any such distance as 100 yards but even if it could the pellets have shed so much energy as to scarcely punch through a wet paper bag.

Chapter 15
OPERATION AUTO-FIRE

THE AMERICAN SHOTGUNNER likes a repeater. Whether he puts more of his money on the pump or has a predilection for the auto-loader, I frankly do not know. I have a suspicion his allegiance is pretty evenly drawn. It is worth noting, however, that this last pair of years has shown a marked flurry of activity 'mongst the makers of the self-loaders, but nary a bit of new pumpgun hardware has appeared.

The manufacturers are in the game for the *dinero,* so if new models are any indication, the boys who build 'em must feel the self-stuttering jobs have more market oomph.

Lately Remington has come along with a startling new auto-loader, the Model 58, a gun that cooks with gas, *i.e.* gas-operated, a development which ultimately will retire their Model 11-48 auto. Winchester has a new model, the 50, a revolutionary short-recoil shotgun that utilizes a floating chamber. Browning led the pack in the shift from long recoil to short when the interesting new Browning Double (2-shot) Automatic made its bow. Then there is the Sears, Roebuck "J. C. Higgins" gas-functioned 12, the first of the gas-powered scatterguns.

Finally we have still the older Browning-type long-recoil autos, the Savage M755 and the Browning Auto-5. Lastly there are the two importations: the Franchi, fetched from Italy by Stoeger; and the Breda, also an Italian arm imported and sold by Ted Tonkin of the Continental Arms Corporation.

This figures out to nine different models, a field sufficiently broad as to make the choice no minor chore.

The about-to-buy gunner is confronted with the perplexing equation of long recoil *vs.* short, a matter basically of whether he is going to be conservative and stick with the original Browning action—a design that has been around for a half-century, and is about as time-tried and thoroughly proven as New England ethics —or is he going modern and so swing to short recoil. Guns like the Remington 11-48, Savage M755, Browning Auto-5, the Franchi, and the Breda are long recoiling. The Winchester and Browning Double Auto are short-recoilers.

To further complicate the selection the gunner must also decide

whether he is going in for gas operation, as exemplified by the
J. C. Higgins and the new Remington M58; lastly, shall he buy
a domestic breed or cast his lot with the furriners.

The wingshot is prone to buy a new shotgun based on the way
it points and comes up. Looks are important with him too, but he
just naturally assumes that the performance of the weapon is going
to be top flight. American shooting irons have been made to such
quality standards for such a long time that operational goodness
is taken for granted. But even if the average sportsman is going to
blow himself to a new scattergun, it will take some energetic
scouring and beating of the bushes to lay hands on all of the
six relatively new automatics. The Franchi, for example, is peddled
only through the Stoeger catalog; the Breda is a mail-order
proposition, too.

I then decided to give the current crop of self-acting scatterguns
a comprehensive field test. As a preliminary it was arbitrarily decided that the older automatics had been around so long little
would be gained by putting them over the jumps. This eliminated
the Remington M48, the Savage M755, and the Browning Auto-5.
This left to be test-fired the Breda, Browning DA Auto, Franchi,
J. C. Higgins, and the Winchester. The Remington M58, might
well have been included but it has been tested and is reported
elsewhere in this book.

Covered with desert sand.

Before we describe the actual firing, which was long and arduous, suppose we parade each horse comprising the stable and take a long hard look at the entries.

BREDA AUTOLOADER—12 gauge

Manufacturer's Data		*Author's Findings*
Action type:	Long recoil	....
Weight:	7 lbs. 4 oz.	7 lbs. 8 oz. empty
Length, overall:	Not given	47½ inches
Length, barrel:	28 inches	27 3/32 inches
Boring:	Extra full choke (An attached choke-tube)	.669-inch
Length, receiver:	Not given	8 17/32 inches
Stock:	14" x 1½" x 2⅝"	14⅜" x 1⅝" x 2½"
Trigger pull:	Not given	3 lbs. 14 oz.—creepy
Shell capacity:	5	5
Price:	$169.50	

Comment: Gun fired 652 shots with Western, Remington, Federal loads; trap, skeet, and standard (1⅛ oz.) magnum, slug, and 3-inch magnum loads. Shot 100 trap loads in 12 minutes, perfect performance. Recoil pronounced, developed typical vibration of all long-recoiling weapons. Fired 25 shots in 3 minutes, standard (1½ oz.) magnum loads; 1st round failed to eject, 16th round failed to feed. Slug load performance ok. Tested with 3-inch magnum loads, frequent failures to feed (gun is chambered for standard 2¾-inch cases and 3-inch should not be used! Fired for test purposes only). Fired 25 shots with weapon upside down, live rounds frequently tumbled out the ejection port. Fired 25 shots gun on left side, ejection port upward, malfunctions were frequent,

The test panel looks them over.

Firing for familiarization.

gun would not always reload 2nd and 3rd rounds. Gun fired 25 shots with ejection port downward, malfunctions numerous, live rounds fell through ejection port.

Average of 25 patterns at 40 yards, 30-inch circle, 67.7%. Weapon is equipped with a screwed-on choke tube, length 3⁷⁄₁₆ inches, inside diameter, .679-inch to within ¹⁄₁₆-inch of muzzle where measurement is .669-inch. Normal full choke in U.S.-made shotguns is .690-inch to .698-inch. This tube is extra full choke (XFC) and instead of producing very tight patterns is over-choked, thus accounting for the 25 patterns which only averaged 67.7%—little better than improved-modified performance.

Cold-soaked at minus 30F for 48 hours, gun fired 25 shots without a hitch. Thrown on the desert and covered with sand it fired exactly once, and that was the round that was in the chamber before burial. Tossed into a tub of muddy water it stopped after two shots. Washed under a hose it fired continuously after the stream was played on the action for two minutes. Bore was wiped out at conclusion of the test firing (652 rounds) with a dry patch and examined for lead deposits and fouling. It was badly leaded.

The Breda has a handsome blued finish. There is an equally appealing Italian walnut stock and fore-end. Moving parts are chromed, and double extractors insure more positive extraction. The safety is a swinging lever on the side of the receiver. The action is positioned in an open-top receiver. A dust cover, riding in longitudinal channels, provides a top for the receiver. This cover, made of light sheet stock, is easily removed once the barrel is disassembled from the action. Once the cover is out of the way the entire action is open to inspection.

BROWNING DOUBLE AUTOMATIC—12 gauge

	Manufacturer's Data	*Author's Findings*
Action type:	Short recoil	. . . .
Weight:	6 lbs. 12 oz.	6 lbs. 11½ oz.
Length, overall:	Not given	46 13/16 inches
Length, barrel:	28 inches	27 9/16 inches
Boring:	Full choke	.694-inch (FC)
Length, receiver:	Not given	6⅞ inches
Stock:	14¼" x 1⅝" x 2½"	14⅜" x 1⅝" x 2½"
Trigger pull:	Not given	4 lbs. 11 oz.—clean breaking
Shell capacity:	2	2
Price:	$133.00	

Comment: Gun fired 650 shots. Same brands and same types of ammunition used in this weapon as fired in the Breda. Fired 100 trap loads in 13 minutes, perfect performance. Recoil is noticeable due to the lightness of this arm. Fired 25 shots in 3.5 minutes, using standard magnum (1½ oz.) loads, 3 failures of bolt to lock open

100 shots in 12 minutes!

on last shot, otherwise perfect performance. Slug load performance perfect; weapon found to be extraordinarily accurate with slugs. Tested with 3-inch magnum loads, got occasional jams (gun is chambered for the 2¾-inch standard 12 gauge. This firing was for test purposes only). 25 shots with gun held upside down, firing from hip, no malfunctions. 25 shots, weapon held with ejection port upward, perfect performance. 25 shots with ejection port downward, perfect functioning.

Average of 25 patterns at 40 yards, 30-inch circle, 71.2%.

Cold-soaked for 48 hours at 30 degrees below zero F, 25 shots perked without sign of failure. Buried in caliche dust, much finer than desert sand, weapon fired twice. Dunked into a tank of muddy water gun ran through 12 shots without a miss and would have gone on indefinitely. Washed for two minutes under a stream of water, performance was entirely normal. Upon the conclusion of all firing (650 rounds) bore was wiped clean with a series of dry patches and inspected with a bore-scope. Lead deposits were insignificant.

The Browning Double Automatic is finished in either grey, green, black, or brown alloyed receivers, and it may be had, of course, in the conventional blued steel receiver. There is no magazine, one round is carried in the chamber, the second on the shell carrier. Reloading is especially fast may be done with either left or right hand. This is the most compact of all our auto-loaders.

FRANCHI AUTOLOADER—12 gauge

	Manufacturer's Data	Author's Findings
Action type:	Long recoil	....
Weight:	6 lbs. 4 oz.	7 lbs. 1½ oz.
Length, overall:	Not given	47 15/16 inches
Length, barrel:	28 inches	28 inches
Boring:	Modified	.718-inch (Quarter choke)
Length, receiver:	Not given	7 11/16 inches
Stock:	14" x 1½" x 2⅝"	14 7/16" x 1¾" x 2⅜"
Trigger pull:	Not given	4 lbs. 12 oz.—clean breaking
Shell capacity:	4	4
Price:	$157.50	

Comment: Gun fired 656 shots. Cartridges included all makes and types fired in Breda and Browning. Fired 100 trap loads in 12 minutes, shooting from the hip. Eighth round failed to chamber, 19th round (last in magazine) popped out of ejection port, 25th round locked in magazine and would not feed out, 27th round would not chamber, 34th round released from magazine while carrier was lifting, dropped on ground, 42nd and 45th rounds

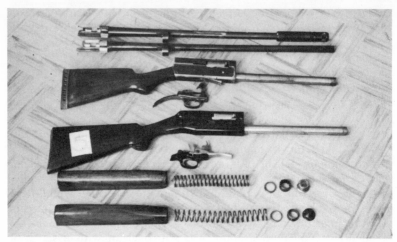

A comparison of the old Browning Auto and the Italian-made Franchi. The Browning is above.

released from magazine out of time and caused malfunctions. 25 shots with gun upside down, normal performance. 25 shots with ejection port upward, one malfunction. 25 shots with ejection port downward, many failures (11).

Twenty-five shots with standard magnum (1½ oz.) loads, 8th round failed to chamber, 11th round failed to eject, 12th round not held by magazine cut-off, 13th round would not eject cleanly, caught by breechbolt in ejection port, 18th round failed to load.

Slug load performance, normal. Gun shoots 12 inches high, 6 inches to right.

Tested with 3-inch magnum loads, many jams resulted (weapon is chambered for 2¾-inch cartridges, the 3-inch magnum tried for test purposes only).

Average of 25 patterns at 40 yards, 30-inch circle, 47.3%. This is improved cylinder performance. The barrel, stamped "modified," should produce shot percentages from 58% to 64%.

Cold-soaked for two days and nights at a constant temperature of −30F, the Franchi was sluggish and jammed 4 times during the firing of 10 rounds. It was slowly warmed to 70 degrees then completely torn down and washed in solvent, dried, and again subjected to the cold room for 48 hours. 25 shots resulted in 3 minor malfunctions. Buried in the desert sand together with all other weapons in the test, it fired once, this the round in the chamber. Dropped with other test hardware in a tank of muddy water it fired once and jammed in recoil. Breechbolt and barrel would not cam apart. Washed under a ⅜-inch jet of clear water for 2 minutes did not eliminate the mud.

At the end of the test (656 rounds) the bore was wiped out with dry patches and examined through a bore-scope for signs of lead fouling. The Franchi showed minor traces only, the chrome-lined barrel undoubtedly accounting for this freedom from lead deposits.

This shotgun is a very close adaptation of the original Browning. It has an alloyed receiver which accounts for its light weight. When the test was about half over it was noted that the stock had split on both sides of the small of the grip. Recoil is unpleasant. The gun is offered by Stoeger Arms Corporation with any of the current crop of recoil elimination devices which the buyer happens to like. It would be much more pleasant to fire, especially where a hundred or more shots are to be pooped off, with a Cutts or PowerPac muzzle brake in place.

J. C. HIGGINS AUTOLOADER—12 guage

	Manufacturer's Data	Author's Findings
Action type:	Gas	. . . .
Weight:	7 lbs. 12 oz.	8 lbs. 5 oz.
Length, overall:	Not given	46 3/16 inches
Length, barrel:	26 inches	26⅜ inches
Boring:	Variable, Chokemaster	See below
Length, receiver:	Not given	7 7/16 inches
Stock:	14″ x 1⅜″ x 2¼″	14¼″ x 1⅝″ x 2½″
Trigger pull:	Not given	4 lbs. 3 oz.—clean breaking
Shell capacity:	5	5
Price:	$89.95	

Comment: Fired 648 shots. Same makes and loads shot in other test weapons. Fired 100 trap loads in 12 minutes, all shooting from the hip. It's been alleged that this gun, due to its gas operation, must have a solid support at butt to get the necessary resistance to function—not true! On a run of 100 rounds of trap loads, 8th

The new gas-operated Remington Model 58 gets an amputation job.

and 89th rounds doubled—2 shots with one pull of the trigger—the 94th round failed to feed. Fired 25 shots using standard magnum (1¼ oz.) loads, 7th round failed to feed, 24th would not feed out of magazine due to failure of magazine cut-off. 75 rounds fired, 25 with gun upside down, 25 with ejection port upward, 25 with it down, and all together but 3 malfunctions occurred.

Slug-load accuracy was poor. It is suspected the slug gets off course during passage through the ventilated cage of the Choke-master, striking the choke collar as it passes through the muzzle of the device, and never regains a true course.

Tested with 3-inch magnum shells, only 2 jams developed during 25 shots. Obviously the Higgins could be modified to handle the long cases with little difficulty.

Average of 25 patterns at 40 yards, 30-inch circle, 67.7%. This with Chokemaster set at XFC (Extra Full Choke). An additional 25 targets with the choke gadget set to FC (Full Choke) produced an average of 71.6%. I was convinced the XFC setting over-choked the gun, so I dropped a plug into the device and the reading indicated a measurement of .718-inch. This is a quarter choke. The adjusting collar was then moved to FC and a reading of .724-inch (improved cylinder) was indicated. The modified setting was then miked and it read .728-inch. Full cylinder boring for the 12 gauge is .729-inch. This variable choke device was the most surprising I have ever investigated.

Cold-soaked for 48 hours at minus 30F the Higgins never missed a stutter. Buried on the desert it fired 5 shots, all that were in

Operation Auto-Fire didn't spare the fodder!

barrel and magazine. Dropped into a tank of muddy water, which was under constant agitation, it fired once. Obviously the water and mud had gotten into the gas-ports. Washed for 2 minutes under a jet of water it then functioned okay.

At the end of the firing (648 rounds) the bore was inspected, after passing 3 patches through it, for evidence of leading. The gun showed the least lead of any.

Having fired and tested 3 of the J. C. Higgins during the summer of 1955, I find this latest and 4th gun a very much improved version. Performance is completely satisfactory. The Chokemaster eliminates such a considerable percentage of the recoil as to make the weapon a pleasure to shoot. It is an excellent skeet gun, the eight-pounds-plus once set into motion is well-nigh impossible to stop, thus insuring a good follow-through.

WINCHESTER MODEL 50 AUTOLOADER—12 guage

	Manufacturer's Data	*Author's Findings*
Action type:	Short recoil	. . . .
Weight:	7 lbs. 12 oz.	8 lbs. 6½ oz.
Length, overall:	Not given	49 9/16 inches
Length, barrel:	30 inches	30 inches
Boring:	FC (Full Choke)	.695 inch
Length, receiver:	Not given	7 11/16 inches
Stock:	14" x 1½" x 2½"	14" x 1 7/16" x 2¼"
Trigger pull:	Not given	4 lbs. 12 oz.—creepy
Shell capacity:	3	3
Price:	$120.50	

Comment: Fired 664 shots. Trap, skeet, standard magnum, slug and 3-inch magnum loads fired. Federal, Remington, Western cartridges. Fired 100 trap loads in 12 minutes, perfect performance, all shooting from the hip. Tried 25 shots with piece upside down, normal performance. 25 shots with ejection port downward, one failure to load. 25 shots with ejection port upward, no malfunctions.

Twenty-five shots with standard magnum 12-gauge loads, one failure to load on 3rd round, second failure to load on 17th round. Screw holding forestock loosened every 25-35 shots.

Handled slug loads perfectly, shooting 14 inches high at 50 yards. Groups well.

Fired 25 magnum 3-inch loads with poor performance. Loaded singly the empty was ejected cleanly, but with additional cartridges in the magazine, performance was spotty. The Model 50 is chambered for the standard 2¾-inch 12-gauge cartridge and should not be expected to handle the 3-inch magnum load. This firing was for test purposes only.

The sand test was too much for the Italian Franchi.

Average of 25 patterns at 40 yards, 30-inch circle, 76.6%. Gun possesses a swaged choke, measuring .695-inch, at the very muzzle. Choke begins approximately 1½ inches behind the muzzle and maintains what appears to be an even taper to the very gun-mouth.

Given the arctic treatment in the cold room for 48 hours at the customary minus 30F, the Winchester thereafter galloped through 25 hulls without a pause. Buried in the sand along with the other test shotguns, it was unearthed and stopped after firing only one round, the cartridge placed in the chamber before interment. Examination showed the fine caliche dust had gotten between the floating chamber and the barrel proper. Dunked into a pot of agitated water and mud it was hauled out and again fired a sum total of one round. Washed by hosing down for 2 minutes it fired only the round in the chamber and refused to reload.

With all 664 shells expended the bore was cleaned and inspected. It was badly leaded, the deposit commenced at the forcing cone and extended to the muzzle.

During my test firing of the crop of new autoloaders, I had more than a little suspicion that I might possibly be living too close to the brutes and might be arriving at conclusions that wouldn't necessarily reflect in the eyes and in the opinion of Mr.

John Averageshot. This decided, I cast about and found within my own outfit a group of typical sportsmen.

These fellows, five in all, were not experts. But they all most decidedly represented Mr. Wingshot. The sum total of their hunting years ranged up to a full three-quarters of a century and yet none were old men.

This 5-man panel consisted of senior noncoms of mine. All save one had hunted on three continents, North America, Europe and Asia. The last had added a fourth, Australia.

I arbitrarily gave each a test number: My No. 1 hailed from Pennsylvania had shot and hunted for 20 years. No. 2 was a comparative recruit with only four years of rabbit shooting under his belt; he came from Chicago. No. 3 was an Ohio boy with 15 years' experience. No. 4 was a West Texan with some 20 years of hunting to look back upon, a shooting go-around that had taken him from his native sage to the Black Forest of Germany, thence to Korean rice paddies, and a lengthy sojourn in the Australian bush. Finally, No. 5 had been banging away for 14 years around South Carolina.

Clearing a jam.

Guns were all loaded before being covered with sand.

Before the firing began I painted out the manufacturers' names on the shotguns and assigned each weapon an identifying number which was pasted to the buttstock. My panel was instructed not to attempt to identify the weapons but simply to judge each on its appearance, operation and general performance.

Each member of the group—we were on an extended field problem and so were miles from any distractions—was permitted to examine the guns as long as he desired. He was urged to try the balance, get the feel of the piece, see how it pointed and how it swung, try the trigger pull, examine the finish, test the safety, load and unload, and finally shoot all he liked.

This each did.

Since every man had to handle each weapon over and over again it can be appreciated that this was a very time-consuming chore. However in the accomplishment of the tests I had in mind it was vital that each panel member be completely familiar with all the hardware.

The test teed off with the following essential questions:

No. 1—Question: Which gun do you think is heaviest?

Answer: Four cited the Winchester (8 lbs. 6½ oz.). One put the finger on the J. C. Higgins (8 lbs. 5 oz.).

No. 2—Question: Which shotgun do you believe is lightest?

Answer: All unerringly selected the Browning Double Automatic, weighing 6 lbs. 11½ oz.

No. 3—Question: Which gun is the best looking?

Answer: Three of the panel selected the Browning. The Breda got a single vote, as did the Franchi.

No. 4—Question: Which gun is the homeliest?

Answer: Unanimously the crowd curled its lip at the matronly Josephine Clementine (J. C., that is) Higgins.

No. 5—Question: Which gun has the best balance?

Answer: No. 1 man said the Browning. Nos. 2 and 5 selected the Breda. Nos. 3 and 4 decided they liked the imported Franchi best.

No. 6—Question: Which gun has the poorest balance?

Answer: Two said the Browning, two said the Higgins, and one voted the Winchester most lacking.

No. 7—Question: Which pistol grip do you like best?

Answer: Three of my testers voted for the Browning, two gave the Franchi their support.

No. 8—Question: Which forestock do you like best?

Answer: 3 for the Franchi, 1 for the Winchester, and 1 in favor of the Browning.

No. 9—Question: Which stock finish do you like best?

Answer: Four decided the Breda was the most appealing, the 5th liked the Winchester.

No. 10—Question: Do you like the accessory muzzle choke devices?

This test was too tough. Sand stopped all the guns.

A highly ornamented Breda auto-loader. The Breda is Italian made.

Answer: Three were in favor of them, two were opposed.

No. 11—Question: Of the two choke accessories we have here (Chokemaster on the Higgins and the simple, screwed-on choke tube of the Breda) which do you like best?

Answer: All 5 went for the Chokemaster.

No. 12—Question: Which gun kicks the most?

Answer: Four said the Browning, one said the Breda.

No. 13—Question: Which gun recoils the least?

Answer: J. C. Higgins, said all 5.

No. 14—Question: Which gun is easiest to load?

Answer: Four said the Browning, one picked the Winchester.

No. 15—Question: Which gun is most difficult to load?

Answer: Three picked the Franchi, one selected the Breda, the 5th said the Higgins.

No. 16—Question: Which safety do you like best?

Answer: All 5 panel members voted for the crossbolt (as found on the Winchester, Higgins, and Franchi).

No. 17—Question: Is the stock of the proper dimensions on the Winchester?

Answer: All 5 opined it was.

No. 18—Question: Is the stock of the proper dimensions on the Browning?

Answer: One man said it was too short, the others gave it their approval.

No. 19—Question: Is the stock of the proper dimensions on the Higgins?

Answer: Everyone answered affirmatively.

No. 20—Question: Is the stock of the proper dimensions on the Breda?

Answer: Four approved, one disapproved.

No. 21—Question: Is the stock of the proper dimensions on the Franchi?

Answer: Four called it too long, the 5th said it would do.

No. 22—Question: Should the bolt-release button be on the right side (as found on the Winchester and Breda) or left side (Higgins and Franchi) or beneath the gun (as on the Browning)?

Answer: Unanimous agreement that the bolt release should be on the right side of the receiver.

No. 23—Question: Which gun do you like best?

Answer: Three said the Winchester, two cast their votes for the Franchi.

No. 24—Question: Which gun do you believe you could shoot best and account for the most game?

Answer: Three selected the Winchester, two again went for the Franchi.

No. 25—Question: In consideration of your answers to Nos. 23 and 24, and keeping the price in mind, which of the guns would you buy?

Answer: Four selected the Winchester and one decided on the J. C. Higgins.

Chapter 16

IT TAKES GUTS TO BUILD A 2-SHOT AUTO*

TO OFFER THE AMERICAN shooting public an automatic shot-gun that only holds two shells takes a lot of guts. The Browning Arms Co. have done that very thing. And not, mind you, a 5-shot or even a 3-shot self-loader with a plug in the magazine but an honest-to-god autoloader without any magazine at all!

This shooting iron is called the Browning double automatic.

The gun is the result of the inventive genius of Val Browning, son of the greatest firearms inventor the world has ever known. Old Man John delivered up the first and damned near the only successful automatic shotgun a round half-century back. But the old bucko wasn't perfect. When he whamped up his corn-sheller he put one of the most hideous shoulders on the stern end that has ever graced a piece of ordnance. And to add insult to injury he built the gun on the long-recoiling principle. It remains for son Val, an inventor in his own right, to eliminate not only the un-sightly receiver but the long-recoil system as well.

The new "double automatic" is as streamlined as la Monroe, as smooth handling as a good Purdey, and it only shoots twice.

When John Browning came along with the first self-loading 12 gauge there were duck limits of 25 birds per day, but nobody noticed; there were bobwhite restrictions too, but the game ward-ens had to cover seven counties and were never near. A head count of all the shooting men in the country totaled less than a million by count of licenses sold, and of this number at least three-quarters were crying for a gun that would hold more than two shells. The grand old Mormon from Ogden gave it to 'em.

This was back at the turn of the century and Browning had for years been selling all his rifle inventions to the Winchester Repeat-ing Arms Co. He offered T. G. Bennett, president of the big red "W" his automatic shotgun and it was accepted with alacrity. However, investigation disclosed that the lock-up infringed the Brochardt patent, so Browning was asked to modify the link.

---

* Reprinted from GUNS Magazine.

148

I tested the two guns, one the standard weight and the other the lightweight, with every known load—squib reloads, skeet and trap loads, standard duck and magnum loads. The guns digest 'em all without any changes or alterations.

Meanwhile the patent firm of Seymour and Earl, who represented Winchester for many years, were busy sewing up the patent rights. The link was easily corrected by the remarkable inventor, and between 1900-1902 three patents were granted. These patents were applied for by Seymour and Earl but always in the name of John Moses Browning. More about that later.

The gun, after long and exhaustive tests at Winchester, was pronounced a success. It shot through rain, snow, sleet, mud, and sand. It worked best without a drop of oil and it would digest every shell known to man. It was a tough old bruiser and responded best to mistreatment and neglect. It held five shots and ambitious wildfowlers soon discovered you could put an extension on the magazine which gave 'em nine quick blasts. Of course this latter piece of brilliance was no child of either Browning or Winchester, but it was tried. The balance, let it be noted, was horrible. Anyway, the old musket was everything Winchester hoped it would be.

Bennett offered Browning his usual deal, a straight and outright payment for all the patent rights. Up to that time Winchesters had bought all the Browning lever-action, pump-action and other rifles and were then deeply in the manufacture of the splendid Model 1897 repeating slide-action shotgun. In every case Browning had sold all his rights. This time he balked. "Give me," history records

The Double Automatic in Indo-China.

him saying, "a fair royalty on every gun made and I'll talk turkey."
Thomas Gray Bennett, undoubtedly the most astute *jefe* Winchester ever had, wouldn't budge. "We have always bought your patents outright," he is said to have told the great Browning, "and that's our offer for the automatic."

Winchester has been living down that one ever since. John Browning by that time was known as the leading firearms inventor. Whereas during his early years of association with Winchester, he had been getting started, his many developments in the machine gun, rifle, shotgun, and auto pistol fields had established him as an inventor due anything but cavalier treatment. John went over to see the rival camp, the Remington folks.

Marcellus Hartley by that time had gained control of the Remington Company; and while Browning had never had any truck with the UMC people, he felt the time was ripe. As he waited to see Hartley—it was right after the lunch hour—word was passed out that the financier had dropped dead while eating. The Ogden genius gathered up his powder burner, hied him away to the water front and three weeks later was demonstrating his shotgun to the big wheels in Fabrique Nationale d'Armes de Guerre, Liege, Belgium. The weapon, with the exception of time out for a couple of international shooting affrays, one in 1914-18, and another a bit later, has been made since by FN. In 1905, license rights were purchased by the Remington Arms Company to make the automatic. They discontinued the manufacture in 1948. When the patent ran out others commenced to copy the Browning gun. It can be found today in every country in the world.

Let's backtrack a bit:

Certain Winchester would buy the Browning gun, the patent lawyers for the Company wrote the patent application, descriptions and relevant data so painstakingly that when the deal fell through it only required 10 years for T. C. Johnson, Winchester's designer, to come up with a new auto-loading smoothbore—and it was a failure!

Because the 12-gauge cartridge has got a lot of oomph, Browning decided he had better tie barrel and breechblock together until the shotload got out of the barrel. This he did, the tube and the bolt remaining locked together through almost three inches of recoil. After all this travel the two are cammed apart and the barrel returns to battery, while the bolt returns a bit slower, picking up a new live shell as it moves along. All this banging and bouncing around of the gun's innards don't exactly please the shooter. There is a helluva lot of vibration, springs squeak and sing, steel bangs on steel, the forestock shudders, and when finally all the ruckus quiets down the marksman can fire again. He can shoot provided he has schooled himself to look over the huge and unspeakably ugly shoulder at the buttocks end of the receiver. Old John really hung a duzy on that gun of his here!

The new double automatic by son Val licked these two objectionable features.

The receiver is now sleekly rounded at back and the recoiling system has been modernized. The objectionable 90-degree shoulder has disappeared from the receiver and now it is rounded and flowing. The self-loading system is bent to the short-recoil principle. Instead of barrel and breechbolt traveling together through some

The Double Automatic in Twentyweight Model is just the medicine for snipe and all uplands species.

three inches of movement, the two are now locked in union for something less than a half-inch. Then the lock is cammed out of position, the barrel moves forward into full battery, and the breech-block is free to extract and eject the spent shell and subsequently chamber the live round. It sounds simple but it took eight years to perfect and a quarter of a million test rounds to prove.

Val Browning, like his Pop before him, was faced with the same problem. You cannot open the 12-gauge breech too quickly. If you do there is a considerable gas escape that is hot and dangerous and you soon beat up your bolt, bust the extractor, ruin the ejector and play hell generally. Old John beat the game with the long-recoil, Val accomplished the trick more efficiently by compelling his shooting iron to work against two sets of powerful springs.

In the forestock, where ordinarily the shells are contained, he located an extremely powerful coiled spring. Behind the breech-block, reached through an inertia weight, he placed two more springs, one coiled within the other. When the gun fires the gases must build up sufficient pressure to set the barrel and breechbolt into backward motion. The two are strongly locked together and both are held against the action of the expanding powders. Slowly and grudgingly the steel accepts motion. All the time the shotload is being forced down the barrel. As the barrel-and-breechblock assembly recoil the two sets of springs are compressed. When at last the camming action occurs and the bond is broken the shot has passed the muzzle. A neat bit of engineering was accomplished here, for as the barrel moves forward and backward it is cushioned and pillowed by spring action; likewise the bolt through the effect of the inertia block and the double springs is softened as to action.

Because the gun has no magazine the second round lies on the shell carrier all the time. As the bolt starts forward, the carrier is cammed upward, the lift isn't dependent on springs, it is wholly mechanical and is the strongest and most effective feed system of any repeating shotgun. You can bet your whole pile of white chips that this new double automatic will never give any feed troubles!

A port has been cut in the left side of the receiver to admit the shells. This port permits the cartridge to be laid directly on the shell carrier. If the bolt is locked back, the business of charging round No. 1 will release the bolt, and as it moves forward the carrier rises and the cartridge is driven into the chamber. The second shell can then be loaded. The fact that the gun has a round on the carrier is at all times evident, the most of the shell can be seen through the loading port at a glance. This is the fastest repeater to load of 'em all. A cartridge can be slammed into the gun with either hand. I am a southpaw and I believe the loading is a trifle easier for me; but it is a question. At any rate loading is

The original Browning auto-loader has been around for 50-odd years, and is still quite popular.

like chain lightning. Val Browning contends that a third shell can be rammed into the gun while the birds are still a-wing but I dunno. I ain't thet fas' mahself, suh.

Something I do not like about the loading port is that it leaves a gaping hole in the side of the receiver which is an open invitation to dirt, snow, twigs, grass and other trash. The action is too open. To compound the crime, the carrier at the bottom of the receiver is cut away, and by this design leaves the action susceptible to the entry of foreign matter. To test the effect of sand in the action, I scooped up a cartridge box full and dumped it into the loading port. I then turned the gun wrong side up and let as much filter out as would. The gun fired until the 7th shot, on that round it chambered the cartridge but would not extract the empty after firing. Three minutes' cleaning had the weapon back in action.

A thumb-nail sketch of the Browning shapes up like this: Chamber, 12 gauge (no intention to offer the new auto in other gauge at this time) 2¾-inch, will not accept the 3-inch magnum cartridge; capacity and loads, two-shot, digests light, medium, skeet, high velocity and 2¾-inch standard magnum loads without any changes, adjustments or other modification of the recoil. Stock, full pistol grip, French walnut; dimensions, 14¼ by 1⅝ by 2¼. It is interesting to note a 1⅝X drop at heel 2¼ inches. The standard model shoots low for me; the lightweight model is a better fit and does not. The gun needs a raised rib badly, and Browning realizes this as they offer a variety of ribs with both models. One of these ribs is a raised, "recessed" job. The recess consists of a groove or channel cut the length of the rib. Due to the low shooting propensity of the standard gun I have, a rib will have to be attached by an honest-to-god mechanic, else the gun will shoot lower than ever. Recommend the Browning factory or some first rate technician like Simmons of Kansas City. Fore-end, French walnut, checkered. The ugliest part of the gun, very European looking, has two bolts running through the wood that detract from the appearance, front end is simply chopped off. The forestock is hinged at front and has a latch at rear which permits the stock to drop downward, thus withdrawing the barrel lock. This lock is a bar of steel which abuts against a shoulder on the barrel breech. Barrel may be removed in three or four seconds, another installed just as quickly. Barrels, plain, matted, or with raised recessed rib; 26, 28, or 30 inches, any standard choke. Receiver: Choice of blued steel or new special light alloy with gray, black, red, or brown finishes. The standard weight (7¾ pounds) has the blued steel receiver; the lightweight (6¾ lbs.) and twenty-weight (6 lbs.) have aluminum-alloyed receivers. The actions are partially engraved with an English scroll of beautiful appearance. The work is done by hand and obviously the engraver is an artist. Safety, simple block directly behind the trigger and positioned in the guard. May be operated by either a left hander or a right, with gloves or without. This safety does not block the hammer but only acts as a stop against the trigger. Safeties on all our repeating shotguns are based on the same principle; this one should be as good as the others.

During my first tests, I pumped an entire case (500) of shells through the Browning in a period of two days. Part of the shooting was done with the standard (7¾ lbs.) model and the remainder with the lightweight (6¾ lbs.). I have hammered out a dozen rounds of skeet and patterned both weapons through exhaustive tests at all ranges from 20 yards up to the standard 40 paces. One of my guns is bored full choke and regularly shoots 80%, the other is modified and shoots full choke more than half the time. I have fired field loads, skeet loads, express loads and magnum charges through both guns, neither has ever faltered or hitched once. I ground the standard gun to a halt when I poured a box of sand into the action, but when the gun is clean it never bobbles. I have turned 'em upside down, on their sides, fired the two cushioned in the palm of my hand, placed the stock in my belly, against my forehead, and otherwise tested for both sure functioning and strength of recoil. The kick of this new Browning is unbelievably soft. The jar and shock have been so smoothed out and delivered in such a prolonged sequence as to seem very appreciably lighter.

It is a sweet thing to shoot this double automatic! The receiver is the shortest on any repeating shotgun; as a result the trigger is set 'way forward. It can be reached comfortably by a man with long fingers, but for the gent with a small hand and short fingers it is a stretch. It makes him reach up on the small of the stock too far.

The repeating shotgun is being legislated out of the picture. It is going to disappear as sure as death and taxes. Several states and the Dominion of Canada have barred the automatic already. It used to be that the repeater, whether pump or auto, could be crammed with five or six hulls, but that was yesterday. Today the gun can hold only three shells. Tomorrow game departments, conservation groups and others will pressure our legislators to reduce capacities to only two shots. Brownings, with all the sagacity and foresight that has made them one of our greatest arms manufacturers, have foreseen this trend and the double automatic is their answer.

Chapter 17
THE J. C. HIGGINS

SEARS, ROEBUCK are now making firearms. It has been a gradual evolution first commenced by peddling Stevens and Savage ordance under a Sears pseudonym and later by the acquisition of a controlling interest in the High Standard Arms Co. Along with the venture into gun manufacture has came the practice of calling their sporting goods the "J. C. Higgins" line. This *hombre*, Higgins, has his monicker tacked on everything. To the uninitiated it would appear that John Clarence, or whatever those initials stand for, must be a rootin' tootin' going-hell-for-leather outdoorsman. He lends his name to tennis racquets, golf clubs, fishing tackle, boats, skis, shooting irons, and a thousand other sports items.

As time has gone on I have grown increasingly curious about old John Clarence. Finally I asked some of my *amigos* at Sears to give me a rundown on this redoubtable if somewhat nebulous character. I figured he must be a seventh vice-president in charge of sporting goods at least. The gobbledegook I got for an answer would do credit to a page straight from this year's Congressional Record. Higgins ain't no vice-president, he ain't in charge of sporting goods; as a matter of fact he ain't in charge of nothing, he ain't—but that's another story.

Suffice right here to state that John Clarence is not John Clarence at all. Those initials stand for Josephine Clementine; for you see, J. C. Higgins is a female.

I know this to be a fact, for the gal is in a family way. And if you don't believe it just take a gander at the latest Higgins silhouette. There amidships, right between the poopdeck and the waterline, is a bulge unmistakable and damning.

The evidence of this blessed-event-in-the-offing is revealed in a brand new Sears product, the latest to bear the name J. C. Higgins; and it makes out a bad case for Josephine Clementine, I'll tell you! The belly line looks worse than the last time Farouk made *Life* magazine.

This latest is a shooting iron, a shotgun, an automatic; and if it were human and famous, Winchell would be braying to the heavens that here was grist for his mill. For the gun is as neat and trim as a Briggs Cunningham racer—until it comes to the mid-

156

Testing two of the early J. C. Higgins gas-operated shotguns. Gun on the right with shortened barrel would not function with tube cut to 20 inches.

section. Here it bulges, sags, protrudes, distends, swells, and just looks like hell generally.

The offending member is the forestock.

Maybe there is some excuse for the late-pregnancy appearance of the forward stock, since it houses the gas-operating system; but despite the somewhat revolutionary mechanism contained within, I still hold that this fore-end is as ugly as a jackass eating cockleburs.

It took High Standard, who make some of the finest auto pistols, five long years to conceive and birth this Sears offspring. One of the engineers up at New Haven, home base for High Standard, took a long, hard look at the kraut Gew '41-M auto-rifle right after World War II and decided the gas system could be adapted to a shotgun.

This gas system, briefly, is based on the employment of a collar-like piston and not the more conventional solid-head job. This collar receives the blow of the gases and due to its shape provides greater surface upon which the gases may impinge. Necessarily this somewhat novel type of piston must work upon a guide rod; in turn this provides a second advantage, for this guide eliminates torque to both the piston and the operating rod.

The new "J. C. Higgins" hardware has a gas system designed along essentially similar lines. The gas piston is a collar-like piece which is fitted very snugly over the tubular shell magazine. Gas is vented from the barrel through three ports, lying parallel to each

The Model 60 auto-loader will handle all 12-gauge loads without any adjustments.

other and at right angles to the bore, approximately a dozen inches ahead of the chamber. This gas is jetted into a conventional gas cylinder and there impinges on the oddly shaped piston. The piston presents a double-shoulder surface. The gas flows from the upper shoulder to the lower, and in effect produces a movement of the piston which is not so harsh and violent, especially during the first stages of its travel.

Hitched to the lower end of the piston is the operating rod which transmits the movement to the bolt slide. This slide is loosely hinged to the breechbolt and has been purposely given five-tenths of an inch (approximately) of free travel before it commences to unlock the bolt. This false travel is necessary to give time to get the shotload out of the bore and permit pressures to subside; also the paper case has got to be given an interval to contract, else the extractor will tear the head off the case.

As the piston moves along the magazine tube which acts both as a guide and a gas seal, it compresses the operating spring which is wound about the tubing. Once the breechblock has reached the limit of its travel and ejection of the empty has occurred, the spring must then provide the energy to move the breechblock back into battery, chambering the live round as it comes forward. The gas cylinder, piston, operating rod, return buffer spring, and the operating spring are all contained in the bulbous fore-end. The fore-end is metal lined and fits so tightly it is shimmed with rubber to snug it the more. A small and unobtrusive vent at the rear is utilized to permit the escape of residual gases. Thinking the operation of the gun might depend on trapping a portion of the gases inside this cover, I removed it to see if in truth the weapon would malfunction. It would not. The performance was just as certain with the forestock tossed under a bush as when in place on the shotgun. Why precisely it has been so carefully fitted even to the extent of adding rubber stripping, I do not quite *sabe*.

The Josephine Clementine—called the Model 60—is remarkably free of parts. It has only 67 pieces altogether. There are fewer parts in this shotgun than any other auto-loading scattergun on the market. The weapon is a non-takedown. This is both a blessing and a curse. A repeater, whether pump action or self-loader, shoots loose after a few years if it is one of the demountable kind. I have had trombone jobs that finally got so the barrel wagged like a Llewelyn's tail. This mail-order prize will never do that. It will remain rigid and strong through all its life. The gas system dictated that it be built thus. When it comes to cleaning one of these non-take-apart numbers, it is a nuisance, especially when the cleaning patch has got to pass through a variable choke gadget to reach the bore.

The receiver—heart of any firearm—is the most handsome feature of the Model 60. It is sleek, rakish, flowing, and sufficiently long to place the trigger far enough back where the gunner with short arms and stubby fingers will have no trouble reaching it. Too, it is not so abruptly curved that difficulty is experienced in looking over the rump end; and finally it carries a highly polished and most appealing blue job. This lustre gives the weapon a rich and attractive appearance that adds immeasurably to its good looks.

There are no screws in the receiver. The trigger group is held in place by a couple of pins, pins that may be pushed out with a brass drift.

The stock is American walnut, not pretty, not homely. Measurements of the stock are entirely standard, *i.e.* 14″ x 1½″ x 2½″. The fore-end due to its ponderous size places the forward and all important guiding hand too far below the axis of the bore. There is no shotgun on the market today with a forestock quite as deep as this Sears. Not only does it violate the well-established "hands-in-line" concept (the left is lower than the right) but it locates the forward hand so far below the bore that over-shooting is sure to result. One of the primary reasons the over/under shotgun points and handles so well is because the forward hand literally surrounds the barrels. This is as it should be, the higher the hand the better the piece will point. Conversely the farther below the barrel the hand is situated the poorer will be the handling qualities of the gun.

It is popular today to use a dural receiver, or at least sub-assemblies within the standard alloyed steel receiver of this light alloy. High Standard didn't deign to consider any lightening of the new gun. The Model 60 hefts a good 8¾ pounds, and if your fancy runs to the delux version, it hefts more. The barrel is 28 inches and it has been made unnecessarily heavy. An inch and three-quarters are lopped off this tube when the Chokemaster is attached. By a switch to a dural receiver, a weight-trimming operation on the barrel, plus a redesign job on the 7-months-gone receiver, they could have trimmed an easy three-quarters of a pound from the howitzer and it would have materially increased its popularity.

How does the first gas-powered shotgun behave when cranked up?

It digests any 12-gauge load crammed into it. It doesn't matter if you fill the magazine with two of the heaviest magnum loads and follow these with a couple of the 2¾-dram peewees, Josephine Clementine assimilates 'em without pain or strain. And best part is that when the type of cartridge changes from heaviest to lightest you don't have to punch any buttons, adjust any rings, twirl any wheels—just pull the trigger.

Equally versatile is the performance of the gun with various makes of ammo—Remington, Peters, Federal, Western or Win-

The author clearing a jam while test-firing the new Sears gas-operating "J. C. Higgins" shotgun.

The new "J. C. Higgins" Model 60 Automatic 12-gauge shotgun, built by the High Standard Manufacturing Co. for Sears, Roebuck, the mail-order firm. This is a somewhat revolutionary firearm, the first shotgun to be functioned by gas.

Three ports in the barrel are utilized to divert the propellant powder gases. A very small portion of these gases impinge on a piston which in turn functions the action. Gun will handle field, standard, express, and magnum cartridges of 12 gauge without any adjustments.

chester, it makes no difference. The gun will accept 'em all.

The full choke barrel (70%) shot modified patterns with Federal skeet and Peters field loads at 40 yards. It shot full choke with Remington Express and Western Super-X; and with Winchester, Remington, and Federal standard magnum loads ran from 80 to 85% at the regulation distance. It is a closely bored barrel and developed no signs of patchiness or any tendency to blow patterns during any of the firing.

The first gun I received was function fired 200 shots during a single afternoon. It developed ejection trouble due principally to faulty performance of the shell carrier. The carrier was out of time and would rise and impede the ejection of the spent case. Seven days later the company had another gun in my hands. I ripped the shell carrier out of it and placed the thing in the first gun. I then fired it 198 shots and caught 10 jams, all of them caused by failure of the weapon to eject cleanly. The ejector on the Model 60 is of the plunger type. It passes completely through the breechblock, and when the block reaches the very end of its travel the protruding end of the ejector rod slams into the receiver bulkhead. This contact pushes it forward and the nose comes in force against the rim of the cartridge. The blow it strikes should spin the empty out of the gun and send it for a dozen feet at least. Instead of doing this the cases fall at the shooter's feet. Obviously the answer is to get more gas pressure so that the bolt comes back like the devil was after it. Then the ejector would really wallop that case and send it whistling.

I fired the second gun shipped me 303 shots in 53 minutes. It smoked. Three jams occurred, all due to weak ejection. I found the hotter Josephine Clementine got the better she perked. Oil oozed from the forestock and the empties when ejected glistened as though they had been buttered. The oily appearance was due to the wax cooking out of the paper. Despite the fact that the cartridge remained in the chamber for only an instant the weapon was so hot it instantly rendered the paraffin liquid.

I had been told the gun would malfunction unless it was fired from the shoulder, this substantial support necessary to give some resistance to the gas. This, I found was poppycock. I did most of my shooting by firing from the hip. With this flimsy support the gun was free to recoil all it liked and it clattered beautifully. I had also been told it would rip the head off the case if the stock was backed up against a tree. I tried that too and found this was another old wives' tale.

It functioned okay when I stood it on a firing stand and triggered off five shots at high noon; likewise, I dropped the muzzle to six o'clock and knocked out another five shots. It will not perform satisfactorily if rolled over on its back, and jams are frequent if fired on the left side or on the right.

I rolled three magazines of cartridges in the Texas sand and crammed 'em into the gun without any cleaning. These sand-encrusted loads never missed a turn. I followed these dirty ones with clean shells; the sand left in the gun caused no trouble.

I scooped up a generous handful of dirt, gravel and sand and with the bolt locked back, poured it into the action. I followed this by turning the gun upside down and then on either side, I let the loose soil trickle down the barrel so that the chamber had a liberal dosing. I then dumped out all the sand that was loose and loaded up. I jacked 15 rounds through the gun. It worked as if it had been oiled. I did not bother to clean it after this treatment but went ahead and fired about 100 additional rounds.

Josephine isn't going to be popular with the Army and her appeal to prison guards, industrial peoples with guard problems, the Police, and like groups is going to be small. She won't perk when her business end is shortened to 20 inches, standard dimension for buckshot-throwing guard weapons.

I whacked 8 inches off the muzzle end and she stopped like a union man at the five-o'clock whistle. The gas ports are approximately 12 inches ahead of the shell chamber, a certain amount of barrel tube must extend beyond these ports to maintain pressures while the piston is doing its stuff. When I lopped the barrel off to 20 inches, I reduced it below critical length.

Sears, always slightly more decorous than a gaggle of Boston Back Bay dowagers, can take heart from the fact that their shootting iron isn't going to enjoy any marked popularity with bank robbers and gangsters, it ain't worth a tinker's hoot when chopped off to what this gentry considers good business lengths.

Chapter 18

THE NEW REMINGTON COOKS WITH GAS

DEVOTEES of the blast-furnace kind of shooting iron, the auto-loader, will give up with some lusty *olés* when they see the latest Remington offspring. This is a self-winding piece of ordnance, to be known as the Model 58, and a gas cooker. Remington's engineering brains poked a couple of wee holes through the barrel-tube about midway of the schnozzle end, and through the ports thus machined catch and leak off enough of the white-hot powder gases to set the action a-clatter. It is the second gas-operated scattergun to arrive on the American scene.

The 58 joins a new and growing family. Directly after World War II the Remington Arms Company jolted the U.S. gun-making fraternity by a radical departure from custom. They commenced to build hunting arms that were not intended to last like the wonderful one-hoss shay but were supposed to take care of the average guy who by an industry-sparked Gallup poll was found to shoot only two measly boxes of shells per rabbit season.

It all started in 1948 when the outfit cashiered the old Model 11 automatic shotgun. The 11 had been around for nigh onto fifty years, and, while like sex, it was good, it was outmoded. The old coffee-mill was retired in favor of what was first called the Model 48 automatic and since has come to be dubbed the 11-48. This was a slicked up, all-the-corners-knocked-off, hunting shotgun that got away from many of the things shooting men objected to in the original Remington. Weight was pared by a full pound; the cordially hated shoulder at the buttocks end of the action, the single most objectionable feature of the older gun, was rounded and streamlined; the balance was improved; the gun was given an aliveness never before approached in a self-operator; and the American shooting clan was given its introduction to the Remington New Deal.

The new 11-48 was peculiar for two things; stampings and a basic receiver which since '48 has not varied through (1) a pump-action repeating shotgun the Model 870; (2) a pump-action high-powered rifle Model 760; (3) a gas-operated highpowered rifle Model 740; (4) and now the gas-powered auto-loading shotgun Model 58.

Desert "cotton-top" quail, a prime favorite with your Western gunner.

The trigger-assembly group, the breechbolt, pins, springs, stops, and many lesser bits and pieces are essentially alike; and this is true of the entire new family of Remington weapons. It is a most commendable design and engineering accomplishment, and what's probably the best part of the story is that it has lowered the prices of UMC hardware below that of everyone save Sears.

To get back to the 58 gun. The 11-48 was good but it was a long recoil proposition, the barrel and the breechblock were locked together at the time the round fired and remained tied tightly until the full recoil occurred. This included slamming three inches rearward and then a like distance back to battery. The gunner, as can be imagined, was pretty well shook up over all these gymnastics. The Model 58 got away from this. It is designed with a barrel that does not move a peg. Nothing recoils save the gas piston and an operating rod which transmits the force of the gas, and the breechblock. The recoil is remarkably soft.

About eleven inches forward of the breech on the 58 is the barrel ring. This ring passes around the magazine tube and within the ring, which is brazed to the barrel, are two gas vents. These ports jet the powder gases back at an angle into the gas cylinder. This cylinder is located in the front end of the magazine tube; as a matter of fact the forward end of the tube instead of holding cartridges as it used to do, now serves as the gas chamber. Within the chamber is a gas piston and hitched to the piston is a double-bar operating rod. This rod is hinged to the breechblock. When the gun fires the propellant gases push the shotload and wadding up the barrel and passing the two gas vents in the lower surface of barrel an inconsequential quantity of the hot stuff pours into the ports. Here it immediately strikes the piston and sets it in motion. The piston moves rearward approximately .5-inch, taking the double-fork operating rod with it. This time interval of several miliseconds, permits the shotload to reach and pass the muzzle before the weapon unbreeches, thus pressures subside to safe limits before the gun opens.

The empty is ejected and a live round is chambered. An un-welcome angle in the operation is that a more-than-needed quan-tity of the hot stuff always gets into the gas cylinder. If something wasn't done with this over-pressure the gun would soon be dam-aged by slamming the bolt to the rear too hard. Remington solved this one by ventilating the magazine tube that holds the gun to-gether. It also acts as a gas escape for the gas cylinder; by simply drilling three vents in the thing excess gas is permitted to escape. Going beyond this, the engineers placed a rotating collar on the cap, and by a one-sixth turn the gun is instantly made ready for either light uplands or heavy duck loads.

The cap is engraved with a series of "H" and "L" markings. Twisted to "H" it readies the shotgun to digest 1¼-ounce loads (or heavier); turned to "L" trap, skeet and lightest uplands car-tridges can be fired. On "H" all three vents are opened; on "L" two of these are closed off. The tiresome business of fiddling with friction rings as on last year's auto-shotguns is a thing of the past with the new Remington.

The 58 is a 3-shot. Two cartridges are held in the magazine and the third is carried in the chamber. There isn't any possibility the capacity will be increased since the magazine tube is limited by the utilization of its forward end for the gas system. With bag limits as scanty as a Russian's sense of humor, there isn't any need for more than a 3-shell capacity. The new model is made in 12 gauge and 20 gauge. The 11-48 will continue to be carried, at least for the present.

The M58 looks just like its forerunner, the 11-48. You have got to stack the two side by each to distinguish one from the other.

Snipe shooting.

Shooting hand-thrown clay targets is a good pre-season practice.

The gas system has been so neatly stowed inside the forestock it cannot be spotted at all. The newcomer is advertised to weigh seven pounds, actually it runs 7 pounds six ounces, unloaded. The 11-48 is advertised at 7½ pounds but no one has ever gotten one that feathery yet. In view of the current swing to 10-gauge loads in the 12, *i.e.* this fad for 1½ ounces of lead, it is a good thing the 58 doesn't run any lighter!

The present crop of automatics are for the most part built for uplands and not duck loads. The Browning Double Auto scales 6¾ pounds; the Franchi, an Italian import, hits 7 pounds; the Breda, also from the land of spaghetti, runs 7½; and then we have a heavyweight in the shape of the J. C. Higgins at 8 pounds 5 ounces. Anyone who sets off a couple of dozen of these new standard magnum (1½ oz.) 12-gauge loads in an auto hefting seven and a half pounds or less will sure know he has been in a shootin' match. The punishment is something like going three rounds with the Abominable Snowman. Heavy loads are for heavy guns.

The Remington is available in three barrel lengths, 26, 28, and 30 inches. Likewise three chokes are yours for the selection; improved cylinder, modified, or full. With 28-inch barrel the gun has an overall length of 47⅞ inches. By comparison the Browning DA runs 46¹³⁄₁₆ inches; the Winchester 47⁹⁄₁₆ inches; the Higgins 48³⁄₁₆ inches. The stock has a length of pull of 14 inches, a drop of the comb of 1½ inches, at the heel of 2⅜ inches. These measurements are okay for length of pull, but the stock is so "straight," *i.e.* the drop of only 1½ inches at comb and 2⅜ inches at heel, that this chopper will throw its pattern 10-12 inches high at 40 yards. This is just too, too rosy for rising game like mallards bounced off a slough where the target is a towering one. Or just the McCoy for regulation trap shooting, or for trapped live-pigeon gunning as done on the Continent, and for any winged thing that affords a rising mark. But for many a gunner it will cause him to miss. Especially if he is one of these dead slow Joes who holds hard on and not beneath his game.

The forestock has all the objectionable depth of the average self-ejection model. From the center line of the bore to the place where your fingers wrap around the fore-end is 2⅛ inches. A good over/under shotgun similarly measured shows a bare 1 inch. It is axiomatic that the lower the forward hand is beneath the barrel the more sorry the scattergun points. The shiny new Remington is an average offender.

The new gun has a trigger pull breaking at 4 pounds 8 ounces, it is creepy, spongy and poor. A Winchester I had pulled 4 pounds 11 ounces; a Browning the same, although the pull was as clean as a pine smell; a Higgins similarly tested ran to 4 pounds 3 ounces; a Franchi would not go at 4 pounds 12 ounces, and a Breda, while a full pound lighter, was graced by a series of stops

Clay targets from this perch can be made extremely difficult, but are good practice.

in the trigger. The inability to get a really first-water pull on an
auto springs from the fear of the maker that if he puts a decent
release on the trigger, it will double. As a result pulls from 4 to
6 pounds are the rule.

I received a Model 58 with two barrels. The first of these was
an FC, 30 inches long. The bore ran .729-inch which is commonly
accepted as full cylinder in the 12 gauge. At the muzzle the
measurement pinched in to .695-inch. This is a few points shy of
what the manufacturers like us laymen to believe is full choke.
However, it has been my observation after miking a good many
tubes that few U.S. makers now choke a 12 the 40 points they
once did. Improved cartridges produce full choke percentages
with less constriction. Some $1\frac{2}{32}$-inch behind the muzzle the barrel
measured .702-inch; at .55-inch it ran .704-inch; and 2 inches back
of the snout the gauge showed .724-inch. It is likely the choke
is a swaged job.

The skeet barrel, shown in the propaganda releases as 26 inches,
actually runs $25\frac{5}{8}$-inch and sports a handsome raised ventilated
rib with two bead sights. The muzzle measured .724-inch, which
is routine for skeet (IC) choke. The bore from the forcing cone
to $17\frac{1}{4}$ inches forward held to a true cylinder diameter of .729-inch.
But at this point, some eight-and-a-fraction inches behind the
muzzle, was a tight spot. So constricted was the barrel at this
point that a .724-inch plug would not pass. At $10\frac{13}{16}$ inches down
the tube was another ring, this one was not so tight; it would
not let the .729-inch gauge pass but would accept the .724-inch
plug. Still a third peculiarity was discovered. While the very
muzzle held to a dimension of .724-inch and should, normally,
have been the most tightly constricted portion of the barrel, there
actually was a spot $1\frac{19}{32}$ inches back of the muzzle where the
.724-inch plug gauge was stopped.

In effect this barrel has a series of three wave chokes in it. A
most novel situation; and while I have heard of wave choke all
my life, this is the first time I have had the exceptional good
fortune to look one squarely in the business end. If Remingtons
are now reaming wave chokes, I think it is hiding their light under
a bushel not to make the enlightening fact known. Of course there
is some possibility that in their overweaning haste to get into production on this new shooting iron, an inspector or two along the
way just goofed.

I have not patterned the skeet barrel. However, it breaks clay
targets like Abdel Nasser busts the UN rules, so I guess those
three waves I got (in addition to the muzzle constriction) must
give me my money's worth. Four chokes for the price of one!

When I got the Remington, I was busy field-testing a number

of automatics. I took the newcomer along with the others and tossed it down on the desert and then covered it over. The piece was loaded. It fired once when I gathered it up, the round in the barrel. I cleaned the weapon and pumped 100 target loads through it in less than 10 minutes. It chiruped beautifully, malfunctions of somewhat minor nature were the only troubles to develop.

I then fired the gun 50 times upside down, 50 times with the ejection port upward, and 50 times with the port downward. Of these 150 shots in the out-of-the-ordinary positions, two jams turned up.

I shot 3-inch 12-gauge magnum loads. The gun does not kick unpleasantly and extraction and ejection when the big round is loaded singly was normal. With a big 3-inch in the chamber and another in the magazine, it functions most of the time. The magazine will not hold two of the 3-inch cartridges. The 58 is chambered for the 2¾ inch case. The longer shell should not be used. I test-fired the gun with this cartridge solely to see what would happen. The practice is not recommended.

Slug loads pattern well and function perfectly in the shotgun. The company suggests that the "L" setting be used on the gas cap when firing the single ball. I found it did not matter. I fired 25 of the new 1½-ounce standard 12 magnum loads, the 13th shot caught a jam. This load is about as pleasant to shoot in the 7-pound 6-ounce Remington as an afternoon of bareback Brahma bull riding. You really know you have been to the cleaners!

I poleaxed a couple of inches off the 28-inch tube and shot the musket. It rattled right along. Nothing daunted, I proceeded to whittle off another one-sixth foot. This produced no disaster. On the next amputation I went down to twenty inches. At this abbreviated dimension standard target loads would not function the action. However with 1¼-ounce duck loads and with Federal 1½-ounce magnum shells the shotgun put on a perfect show. I found that the gas vent had to be set to "L" and not to "H" to gain this desired performance.

My interest in the Model 58 with 20-inch barrel stems from the fact that for guard and riot purposes, for consideration by the military and for future sale to the police, all of which demand a 20-inch length, it is important to know how the gas job is going to behave.

Chapter 19

SHOTGUNS ARE GROWING PRETTIER

EVERY SHOTGUNNER who admits to fifteen cents worth of affection for his fowling piece dreams of the day when he will possess a deluxe model that will drip more gold than the Aga Khan's begum and be only slightly less ornate than a Chinese hearse. He has in his mind's eye such a bauble as to necessitate a cabinet all of its own—a cabinet, if you will, with a glass front —wherein will repose a shooting iron to be hauled forth for company to envy, as sleek and clean as a blue-grass filly, with his initials on the trigger guard in gold, and his measurements in the fiddleback of the mainstock.

I used to shoot with a Virginian who had laid a cool grand on the line for the One-Thousand-Dollar-grade Parker. He would part the brush before that kingly fusee like he was clearing a path for Grandma Moses. He couldn't have been more solicitous had the smoothbore been made of Wedgewood china. Some may think this was silly. I could understand.

The shooting man who doesn't pleasantly titillate at the sight of an extraordinarily fine gun misses one of the lusty thrills of the shooting sport. A fine and graceful firearm rouses all the pleasurable emotions in the gun lover's breast that stir the horseman at the sight of a Derby winner. It doesn't require a set of bifocals to appreciate the grace of line, the rich, warmly glowing walnut of the stock, the sleekness of the barrels with a depth of bluing that comes only when the tubes have first been burnished to new-dollar brightness. And lastly engraved by a master craftsman; finally a weapon as responsive in the hands as a thing of flesh and blood. What a deal of pleasure such a shotgun can bring a man!

Our mass-produced firearms are notable for utility, and are equally conspicuous for a beauty about on a par with single-trees and pick-mattocks.

But a swing toward the more aesthetic is noticeable. Before the war sight of a finely appointed firearm was as rare as complete accord in the United Nations. Since the Big Shooting the deluxe model has made its appearance. A number of factors, some at-

Handsome Marlin Model 90 over-under shotgun made for the old-time Western movie hero, Tom Mix.

tributable to the tourist-like journeyings—at governmental expense, between 1942 and '45—of several millions of our young citizenry to the Continent, where with the American pilgrim's unerring eye for the bargain they very thoughtfully took unto themselves many thousands of ornately turned shooting irons and fetched them home, has had no little to do with our awakening taste for fancy shooting hardware.

These liberated powder burners were for the most part stocked with a very good grade of French walnut, sported a deal of engraving, and possessed other appointments seldom viewed on this side of the Atlantic.

This was the beginning. Directly after the war a full score of importers, led by energetic peoples like Tradewinds, Galef, and Firearms International, as well as that famous sporting-goods emporium, Abercrombie and Fitch, commenced the regular importation of fine European arms. These guns invariably outshone our standard models in the matter of fine wood, decoration and engraving. True, they cost more, most frequently much more; but they possessed a customer appeal that quite often overrode the customer's Scottish instincts to save his money. Where before the war the sight of a finely turned Continental smoothbore was as rare as a Papago squaw in Times Square, since the fracas we are confronted with the photoed likeness of the handsome European model on the pages of all our sporting journals.

This steady indoctrination of the American shotgunner has not gone unnoticed by our alert manufacturers. First to react was Browning.

The handsome Browning over/under shotgun, as streamlined as a Nike missile and only slightly less appealing than Gina Lolabrigida, was settled on by the dynamic chief guru of the Browning outfit, Val Browning, for the full treatment. The result was not

Browning makes the splendid superposed model in six grades. This is the Grade V.

a single engraved gun but a whole bevy—a pride, if you will—of beauties. There are now Browning O/Us in grades II, III, IV, and the lordly VI! Ascending the scale the shotgun grows more handsome as the grade—and price—soars. The Grade VI at a little more than one thousand bucks, to my not at all humble notion, offers more shooting value, intrinsic goodness of design, materials and workmanship coupled with a beauty of wood, checkering and engraving than you will find anywhere else today for three times that money.

The deluxe Browning over/under series was an instant success. Reaction to this straw in the wind was not long in forthcoming. The company introduced the new two-shot auto-loader and when the gun was offered in standard model there was a most appealing dollop of scroll engraving on the receiver. The decoration adorns the sides of the somewhat flattened receiver and serves to set the gun off most pleasingly. The subsequent introduction of colored receivers for this latest Browning, available in black, green, russet and grey, have been nicely calculated to further show off the stylish engraving.

Winchester now offers all its more expensive scatterguns suitably engraved. The Model 21 is available in six styles and degrees of engraving; the Model 12 repeater and the new Model 50 auto-loader in a full eight different designs. This engraving is after the English scroll and in the fancier grades includes any amount of gold, sliver or platinum inlay. Stockwork and checkering keeps full pace with the richness of the metal engraving.

The most handsome Model 21 probably ever built, to my notion, is in the hands of T. K. "Tackhole" Lee of Birmingham. This is *the* "Tackhole" Lee, a remarkable *hombre* who a generation ago was a national champion with the shotgun, rifle and pistol. Today, he makes the Lee Center Dot, a telescopic sight reticule. The Model 21 in question was made for an Indian potentate. When delivery time finally rolled around, some 10 months having elapsed while the gun was being prettied up, the British, who were then very much in the saddle along the Ganges, refused to permit the nabob to accept the weapon. The price was a trifling ten thousand bucks. Mr. Lee bought the shotgun after Mr. Nehru's fellow citizen backed out on the deal.

All our arms people make very handsomely appointed shotguns. Ithaca frequently pictures a Model 37 repeater which carries a going price of one thousand dollars. It has only slightly less gold on it than we have buried at Fort Knox. Remington also features a series of deluxe models in the 870 repeater and the new gas-operated Model 58 automatic. Grades range through the 'Tournament' which has a going price of $484.55 for gun and engraving; and the "Premier" grade which sells in the Model 870 pump repeater for $1,665.25, with gold inlay, or $933.10 sans the inlay.

We are seeing a veritable rash of standard-model shotguns offered these days with some crude line drawings either acid-etched or chisel-gouged and alleged to be engraving. This is a sop to the newly acquired taste of the sportsman to possess an engraved shotgun. It is common work and I doubt very much if it fools the shooter, much less pleases him. If engraving at least on a par with the pleasing effect Browning achieves on the two-shot automatic cannot be offered, then it would be in better taste to leave the action as clean as a hound's tooth. Like the Model 21 in standard grade.

The Browning outfit is making shooting irons in various colors. Yep. That is right. You can now have a shotgun to match your socks and tie. Or your girl friend's green eyes. I consider it the most revolutionary offering the sporting firearms field has seen these past many decades.

Since time immemorial a sporting gun has been either blued or browned. It has remained for Browning, one of the most progressive, energetic and wide-awake outfits in the gun-making business, to knock cherished tradition into a cocked *sombrero*. Brownings in beige are now the rage. Or if you don't like your new "Double Automatic" in beige, you can have it in chartreuse. And should you just happen to purchase a sports jacket with an appealing plaid you can doggone near get a new Browning to match.

The new Browning auto-loading shotgun with the aluminum alloyed receiver can now be had in four colors, these are Dragon black, Forest green, Autumn brown and Velvet gray.

The new colored receivers are limited to those made of alumi-

The fine Beretta over-under shotgun is beautifully engraved.

The $1700-grade Ithaca double gun. No longer in manufacture.

num alloy. The color has been added by a process of anodizing the metal. Aluminum boats meant for use in salt water are treated much the same way. The color is a permanent thing, unlike old-fashioned bluing which wears off in surprisingly short time, this new finish will never disappear.

The standard Browning automatics made with steel receivers are not available in colors. They are not likely to be offered in anything save conventional blued finish for a long time to come.

Undoubtedly it is going to shock a lot of staid old shotgunners to contemplate a shotgun as green as a freshly peeled grape. But the boys who profess to be outraged that a gun shall have any color except blue are hidebound and archaic. Autos now look like a rainbow in full blossom, like Saturday afternoon on Peachtree Street in Atlanta, like a pansy bed in April. And to get even more personal, some of these hombres who turn out in the wild Aloha shirts will probably be the same gents who complain that a shotgun receiver with a little color on it is an atrocity. I don't agree.

Personally I am thoroughly sold on the color scheme for powder burners. I like it and I think the resulting effect is handsome and effective. However, I must confess that of the black, green, brown, and gray combinations that are offered, the Dragon black with its gold engraving appeals to me most. I believe this indicates I still cling at least to some extent to the old conventional blued finish. The color I least like is the Forest green. It is atrocious. The Autumn brown is tasteful and I wouldn't be surprised if it doesn't prove the most popular of all. The Velvet gray isn't new.

It came along when the new "Double Automatic" was first announced.

Colors in shotguns may strike some shooters as a new thing. Actually it isn't at all, although Browning has carried it a step beyond anyone else. The very highly engraved shooting iron is invariably left in the white, a variation of the "Velvet Gray" that Browning now offers. This is done to better show off the art work in the metal. Then there is the Parkerized finish which is a dull black and uglier than Tobacco Road sin; the old-fashioned browned (as opposed to blued) finish which left a gun with a high gloss that showed a very deep rust color well beneath the surface. And then there has been the chromed or nickel-plated surface, seldom seen on shotgun or rifle but common on sixguns.

The stock, much more than the barrel and receiver, has blossomed with all the colors under heaven. The conventional and most beautiful color is the time-tried walnut, but there are myriads of other shades. Maple and myrtle woods make up into stocks that are hideous in their brightness; cherry is only a jump ahead with its first-cousin affinity for crimson; mahogany and many other hardwoods are so dark as to possess little beauty. And then there are those laminated abortions.

The new Brownings were first shown at Vandalia at the Grand American. They were enthusiastically greeted by a shooting gentry about as conventional as a gaggle of Boston Back Bay bankers. Subsequently Brownings tried various dealers to sample the potential market and found a reception that was startling in its response.

We have colors in our houses, cars, hats, socks, and the little woman's hair; I cannot see why a little touch of mauve in the old shooting iron isn't strictly in keeping with the times.

Chapter 20

HOW GOOD IS THE RAISED RIB?

THERE ARE FEW ACCESSORIES about a shotgun that add points to the score or birds to pocket like a raised rib. An interesting fact about the rib is that many double guns have always had a rib of a sort. Not the very elevated job we see today but a low and rather ineffectual extension. I was looking at a Manton shotgun made more than a hundred years ago and one of the first things I noted about this English fowling piece was an unmistakable rib which extended from breech to muzzle. It was too low to be efficient, not rising as high as the barrels but a rib just the same.

Just what good is a raised rib on the shotgun?

The long ribbon of metal serves as both a front and rear sight. It does a neat job of catching the gunner's eye when he brings the powder burner to shoulder, and by smooth inducement persuades him to follow the strand of metal right out to its forward end. Off that very obvious front end is a flying target, it requires no effort at all to align the rib with it.

This in effect is its best purpose. In shooting a shotgun we aren't conscious of first seeing the tail end of the rib, then running the eye along its stippled surface and thence to the target; nevertheless this is what happens. It is done so quickly, so simply, the full mechanics aren't realized.

A gun without a rib, and let us consider the current crop of autos and repeaters of pump persuasion, provides no smooth continuity of sight picture. The gunner is conscious of a large bumpy receiver directly before his eye, and beyond that he sees the muzzle. Those portions of the barrel between receiver and muzzle, if seen at all, afford no help in the alignment of the gun. And why not? Simply because there is a shoulder between receiver and barrel which produces a gap, something like looking over the Grand Canyon. You can see both sides, but what emptiness between!

The shooter who depends on the muzzle as a front alignment device courts serious trouble due to the ease of cross-firing and the extreme difficulty of discovering the fault. If the face is slapped to the stock too tightly, or conversely, too lightly, look out! It may

The Simmons rib is adjusted to eliminate low shooting, a hazard when a raised rib is attached by any but an expert.

The Simmons raised ventilated rib on the Model 21 Winchester.

The Simmons on the Winchester Model 12 pump gun.

be argued that this cannot be blamed on the lack of a rib or the use of the muzzle as a front sight but on the negligence of the marksman. Quite true, but one thing compliments the other.

Much as I like the variable choke devices, I think everyone of them should be used with a raised rib. They are huge, and without the rib I am satisfied they induce cross firing in some measure. Take the same gun and put a rib on it and the problem is licked.

The raised rib has other advantages in addition to its obvious goodness as an accurate alignment device. It is a great eliminator of heat and mirage. Especially valuable during a long string of shots when the gun grows steadily hotter and radiation commences to blur and distort the sights and target. Not all raised ribs have the virtue of heat dissipation. If the rib is solidly attached to the barrel it may exaggerate the problem. The rib has got to be free floating like the Simmons and Winchester ribs to be entirely effective. Both these ribs are made in such a way as to produce a joint between the rib-supports and the rib proper. The transmission of heat from the barrel to the sighting plane is thus interrupted and little or no interference with the aim occurs.

The Browning auto here sports the Simmons raised rib and the Cutts Compensator.

The Simmons rib is free floating.

Once Remington actually machined the rib as an integral part of the barrel. This necessitated boring the barrel from its original forging off-center, a difficult and costly job, and retaining enough stock on top to machine the rib. Such a rib might be solid or it might be ventilated. When the gun was heated up, as when firing a 100-bird match, the tube tended to warp since it got much hotter than the rib. Radiation off the top was an added problem. Various models of the old Remington Model 11 automatic, the pump 31, and the over under Model 32 were made with such raised ribs.

Several years ago one of our big mail order houses commenced to make a pump repeater. On this gun they placed a raised rib. Some of the first of these guns would shoot a foot-and-a-half low at 25 yards. The reason lay in the rib and has long since been corrected. A rib has got to be adjusted either at front or rear, or both, to produce the desired elevation. If you take a good shooting gun and simply slap a rib on it the weapon will automatically shoot lower because the line of sight has been raised, thereby lowering the muzzle and so producing a low-shooting gun. Probably no one understands this problem better among the manufacturers of raised ribs than Simmons. These people can produce any kind of a ribbed gun desired.

The Simmons Gun Specialties are the acknowledged leaders in

the raised-rib manufacturing field. Ernie Simmons is a shooting man and an enthusiastic one; his daughter has been National skeet title holder among the younger gals a number of times. Ernie, when I visited him a short time ago, was turning out a little less than a thousand ribs per week.

The Simmons rib is the raised ventilated type, and it floats. The rib is anchored at one point only, directly over the chamber, this permits a ready expansion and contraction of the barrel without any distortion. The rib supports are small, are silver-soldered to the barrel, and the rib proper is dovetailed to ride upon these supports. The front support directly beneath the front sight is kept purposely small as a precaution against radiation. The Simmons rib is made for all gauges and all types of shooting irons. I have yet to see one that gave any trouble or find the shooting man who was not content with the device.

The shotgun rib must be knurled, stippled, or otherwise finished so that it does not reflect the sun's rays. One of the finest finishing jobs I've ever seen was done by hand and consisted of an extremely fine checkering which had sloped each of the tiny diamonds forward. It could not possibly cast any reflection toward the eye. The ordinary stippling job is quite satisfactory however.

Usually the rib is one-quarter inch in width. I have seen them on English Churchill doubles that were only half that width. This is altogether too narrow and defeats the purpose. Despite the fact that the quarter-inch rib is probably the ideal width—especially from the cross-fire angle—the most popular size today runs 5/16-inch. It is easier and faster to see, which undoubtedly accounts for its wide acceptance. This rib as made by Simmons weighs less than four ounces. His quarter-inch rib is about an ounce lighter.

Some gunners can use a long stock, others cannot. Some shoot heavy guns and still others must have them featherlight. There are those who want a muzzle choke and others who stick with the unadorned muzzle; some of us want that scatter-barrel bored as open as a drunken sailor's pocket-book, and others swear nothing will do but a full choke. Regardless of these and our many other notions, all of us will profit by the steady acceptance of a raised ventilated rib.

Chapter 21

ARE YOU NEGLECTING THE TRIGGER PULL?

IN CASTING ABOUT for a logical explanation of why we miss on occasion, we are prone to blame the ammunition, the boring, the fit of the stock, the presence or absence of a raised rib, the pitch down or up, the length and breadth of the pistol grip, and any of a dozen other things. But the little item that almost invariably escapes taking the rap is the trigger pull.

Rifle shooters are a sticky bunch when it comes to trigger let-off; and so are pistoleers. But does the shotgunner ever rear up on his hind legs and complain. No, indeed! He pours out his *dinero* for a custom-made stock, a raised ventilated rib, a variable-choke gadget—all good improvements, mind you—but does he do anything about a 7-pound soapy trigger? Right there lies the root of a whale of a lot of his trouble.

Shotgun triggers on all our repeaters, whether automatics or pump guns, stink. If the trigger is clean-breaking then it is heavy enough so you can hang the gun on a nail, safety off, muzzle down. But generally it isn't clean-breaking; quite the contrary, it creeps from hell to breakfast, and will weigh five pounds or better. Because a shotgun is triggered off in a microsecond the gunner fails to realize the harm done his work by a rasping, overly hard sear. He swings to cover the target; and if the gun then had a clean, sweetly-breaking trigger, nothing would interrupt what is a good lead. Instead, by the time he hauls up on seven pounds of slack and runs through the bumps and grinds on the ordinary pump gun sear, his perfect lead has gone awry.

The speed with which the whole art of wing gunning must be played hides the harm done by a creepy, stop-and-go trigger let-off. Recoil hides the crime compounded by a dragging, mushy sear. Just at that instant when the conscious should be recording the fact that the trigger will not yield, thereby spoiling a perfect lead, the fusee explodes and the comb whacks the gunner a sharp belt in the jaw. He isn't conscious that the kick amounts to anything but it is just sufficient to knock any recollection out of his mind of the harm that miserable crawling trigger did to his lead.

180

A trigger pull on a shotgun ought to be just as good as the pull on a Model 70 bull gun, or the Model 52 smallbore rifle, or one of the target handguns. It should weigh not more than 3½ or 4 pounds and should be as short, sharp and clean-breaking as glass. If, with the weapon empty, any perceptible movement can be detected when the trigger is pressed, then the pull is not what it should be. When the exact poundage, say four pounds, is exerted, the sear should "break" suddenly, without mushy forewarning, without any sponginess or double pulls. Recently I weighed the triggers on five of our current crop of auto-loaders, each gun from a different manufacturer and each a latest model. Gun No. 1, 3 lbs. 14 oz.; Gun No. 2, 4 lbs. 11 oz.; No. 3, 4 lbs. 12 oz.; No. 4, 4 lbs. 3 oz.; and Gun No. 5, 4 lbs. 12 oz. Of the five but two had cleanly breaking sears. This feature is of more importance than the weight of the pull. It is easier to successfully shoot a scattergun with a 6-pound let-off provided the release is clean than to shoot a weapon with a 3½-pound pull afflicted with the creeps.

Many triggers are badly positioned and ill shaped. Worst of the lot is the double gun with just as many triggers. It is customary to figure length of pull to the forward trigger. This means when the gunner shifts to the rear trigger his hand will be cramped because it is a full inch behind the front. Or if the rear trigger happens to be the more comfortable the forward trigger is then out of reach. A further liability is the common practice of design-

The pump and auto-loading shotguns are bad offenders on the score of poor trigger pulls.

ing all double gun triggers with very narrow bearing surfaces. The thin trigger adds to the beauty of the weapon but it contributes mighty little to good trigger execution. Actually a trigger should be broad and not too sharply curving. Rifle and pistol target shooters have found that an accessory shoe added to the trigger broadens the face and is a real aid. It, in effect, provides the finger a greater working surface and thereby seemingly lightens the pull. What is probably more important is that the tendency to push the gun sidewise during firing is considerably dampened. Because of the speed with which the shot is delivered a great deal more than the required four or five pounds of pressure is exerted against the trigger. The smallbore rifleman fires a 3-pound trigger. When he gets down in the prone position and laces into his sling, cradles the 12-pound rifle and proceeds to take a minute and a half to squeeze off the pipsqueak cartridge, he exerts only one ounce more than the 3 pounds needed to fire his piece. Not so the shotgunner. He has only fractions of a second to mount the weapon, catch his lead and pull the trigger. His pressure is apt to run 6 or 8 pounds because of the speed of his game. That extra force he applies to the trigger very often moves the gun sidewise or downward. The trigger had better be the best possible shape so that these faults are minimized as much as possible. The broad face is one answer.

Many shotgun triggers suffer from backlash. This is a false play apparent after the trigger is pulled and the hammer falls. The trigger instead of coming to a halt once the sear is released continues rearward. This unwanted and undesirable movement adversely effects the arm during those very critical microseconds when the hammer is in travel, later during the ignition of primer and propellant, and lastly while the shotload is trundling up the bore. It is at this time that the marksman is trying to maintain a lead which he believes is his best and he does not need a long-traveling, loosely hinged trigger to upset his calculations.

The trigger needs what is referred to as a "stop" in it. This is a shoulder which halts its rearward movement on the instant that the hammer is released. Our best target rifles all have trigger stops. The smoothbore needs such an improvement. Clever people like Alex Kerr, Frank Pachmayr, and Ernie Simmons could, if there was any demand, develop excellent stops for all our pump and auto-loading scatterguns. The demand does not exist because most shotgunners fail to realize what a lot of harm is done their work by faulty triggers.

Everyone has his own particular style for pulling the shotgun trigger. Mostly this takes the shape of pushing the finger through the trigger guard as far as it will go and then bending it into a sharp U about the trigger. It is questionable if this is so good. The

The recoil covers up the flinch, a common fault with a hard trigger.

most sensitive part of the trigger finger is the tip end. Here the nerves come to an end, here is the greatest sensitivity. For a more perfectly controlled and more uniformly balanced pull the finger between the very tip and the first joint should be laid against the iron. Another common fault is to ram the finger through the guard until the pressure is applied along the right side of the receiver, to the edge of the trigger guard, and to the side of the trigger. If you don't believe this has an adverse effect on scores then you are missing a bet! Pressure on a shotgun trigger wants to be straight rearward and not at any cockeyed angles.

Some shooters slap a trigger. This is okay if you are trying to trigger off 3-shot bursts from the 30-caliber BAR but it isn't so hot with the scattergun. The real trigger slapper does not touch the trigger at all when he mounts the weapon. He positions his finger a fraction of an inch ahead of the "go" button and when he decides his lead is just what the doctor ordered he hits the trigger, or slaps it, sharply. Oddly enough I have known any number of very successful trigger slappers. They say they cannot flinch when they perform these gymnastics. Seems a fine point there; as if the whole business isn't a fine exhibition of flinching!

A shotgun trigger should be pressed fast and decisively, but the force should not be applied roughly. The finger wants to find and rest on the trigger an instant before the pull commences and once the decision is made to fire, the pressure should be smoothly continuous. It most distinctly should not be a yank. A properly adjusted trigger pull should be 4 to 4¼ pounds. Because of the speed with which we mount, aim and fire, it is difficult to apply only the 4 pounds needed to trip the sear. However that is the goal we seek. A 4-pound pull should have not more than 4½ pounds of pressure put against it. A shotgun weighs 7¼ pounds, if when you pull the trigger you slam 6-8 pounds of pressure against the trigger you are going to move that gun in some unwanted direction. The recoil coming so soon after your rough pressure will cover up the error and you'll be wondering why you called that target dead and yet it went sailing on.

Chapter 22

THE WOODSHED REBLUE JOB

VISIT ANY OF THE BIG ARMS COMPANIES and you will see stacks of guns returned by the users awaiting repair. These busted-up fusees hit the repair division at one time of the year—two weeks before the hunting season gets into full swing.

There is no other peak period. The gunner who had trouble with an ejector when the bird-taking time pinched to a close last year doesn't send his old cornsheller to the manufacturer during January. Nope, he waits until mid-September. And what's more he decides to shoot the works; he asks that not only the ejector be made like new but also put in a new bolt, a new carrier, tighten up the barrel joint, remove all the rust pits from the choke, install a de luxe grade stock and reblue while it's there.

This put the fix-em-up department in the plant in a tizzy. There are just so many mechanics in the place—it is never a profitable division—and since things are pretty slow for the other eleven months of the year, the company cannot afford to double the force just to see that during the 12th month Hiram Hayfork gets his shooting iron returned on a 48-hour turn-around.

Col. Shelly Smith, the big tycoon at Ithaca, tells me that they have shotguns in their repair for years. And why? Because people have shipped them without placing their names on the guns; with incomplete return addresses; without tagging the weapon to indicate what the owner wants done (the factory attempts no maintenance unless the gun is tagged to show the repair desired). And then, says Shelly, letters to those owners who have failed to provide the needed instructions go unanswered. As for those Ithacas that have been shipped sans owner's name, or lacking a full return address, these ofttimes are never claimed. Hence my statement that Ithaca actually has shotguns in their repair division for years, weapons that lie on the repair shelf gathering dust and taking up needed space.

If your old Bacon-Gitter has reached that state of decrepitude where a trip to drydock is advisable, get it into the mails right now! Otherwise you cannot reasonably expect it for those first juicy days of bird season. Lace a strong tag through the trigger

185

It is not difficult to reblue your own gu
and the cost is trivial. Your druggist c
mix a blueing solution that has been su
cessfully used for forty years. Besides th
blueing mixture you will need files, eme
cloth, crocus, and steel wool for removir
dents and scratches and for all eliminatic
of the original blueing. Too, you will nee
a half-dozen dowel pins, plenty of clea
cotton flannel cloth, a small can of lye, cc
ton gloves, gun grease, and a small sectic
of sheepskin. The kitchen gas range wi
provide the necessary heat; and a bluein
tank, size approximately 36" x 4" x 4", whie
may be built at the local tin shop or pu
chased from any hardware store, and yc
are ready to go!

This mixture has been in constant use fc
the past forty years and is completely tim
tried and satisfactory. Ask your pharmaci:
to mix the following:

3	drams	tincture of iron
3	"	spirits of niter
1	"	sulphur
2	"	vitriol
1	"	corrosive sublimate
½	"	nitric acid
1	"	copperas
12	ounces	distilled water

Druggist will blend in colored glas
bottle. Set away for two weeks to age. Stor
in dark place. Do not use at once; solutio
must have time to work.

A firearm cannot be reblued unless it i
completely disassembled. All springs mus
be removed, the heat will do them seriou
harm. Such other accessories as ivory and
plastic sights, etc., cannot be left in plac
during the operation. Tear the weapon dow
completely; it is likely if it is in need o
a refinishing that the stock and forestock
will also need a redoing.

One of the great secrets of a successful reblue job is getting the metal properly prepared. The preliminary step is to remove all evidence of former hard use; nicks, dents, and scratches must be filed out and later the file marks eradicated by the successive application of finer and finer emery cloth.

After the file use emery cloth and gradually reduce the coarse sheets until crocus is applied. The surface has got to glisten like a mirror and be just that smooth!

Grease the bore with some good grade of rust preventive. Gunsmiths are divided on this one. Some contend that the bore should be left dry, as there is some danger that the grease will seep about the dowel pins and thus contaminate the work. In my experience this rarely happens, and the grease is necessary to keep the bore from accumulating condensed moisture caused by immersing it in boiling water and then permitting it to cool without removing the dowels which so tightly cork breech and muzzle.

Secure dowels of the proper size and boil them for 30 minutes in lye-water. Then dry thoroughly in the sun or over, artificial heat. Drive these pins into breech and muzzzle with a hammer. Leave at least 6 or 8 inches of the dowel protruding; the ends provide handles for the steps that follow.

Burner element is a 3-place gasoline Cole man stove. It is necessary to have a serie of burners beneath the blueing vat, or tank so that a uniformity of temperature can b maintained. Tank should be sufficiently lon as to take barrel and action, as shown i photo. Any tin shop can fabricate the tan in 30 minutes and cost is nominal. Afte fabrication, boil out tank with a lye-wate solution for 2 hours. Tank should be galvanized iron, and this contains greas that must be gotten off all surfaces. Ly (½ can) should be mixed with distille water for boiling out, and for actual re blueing operation always use distilled wate. Tap water will contaminate the bluein solution because of presence of chemical

To a full tank of clean, distilled wate add ½ can of common lye. Bring to violent, rolling boil. Immerse barrel an action of the gun. Be sure dowel pins ar in place at breech and muzzle. Suspend th weapon on hooks made of common # wire. Boil for 25 minutes. Withdraw an rinse immediately in clean, distilled wate boiling violently. This is to remove lye Do not touch metal surface! Wear clea cotton gloves at all times.

While weapon is still hot, dump tank c lye water and replace with clean, distille water. Bring to rolling boil. Place bluein mixture in Pyrex jar in one end of tank permit solution to come to boil, or nearl so. Hang gun on the #9 wire hooks (i must not rest on bottom of tank, it will ge too hot there) and boil for 10 minute Then lift weapon by one of dowels, an dipping a canton flannel swab, wound abou a clean, sap-free stick, into the blueing mix ture, paint the weapon in long, sweepin strokes from end to end. Operator here i spooning up blueing solution to cover a obstinate spot on receiver. Be liberal an generous with mixture!

No! No! No! A thousand times no! This reblue job is destined to failure before the amateur goes any further. The metal is cooling rapidly, jerked from the tank as it has been; and the blueing solution cannot be kept at a sufficinetly high temperature to achieve the desired finish. Keep the mixture in one end of the blueing tank where it will boil all the time, and see that the barrel and action are immersed in the violently boiling water at all times except when lifted to paint on the blueing solution.

After the gun has been thoroughly swabbed with the blueing solution, remove it from the bath and stow it away in the dampest place you can find. If you are near sea (salt) air, so much the better. After 24 hours examine. All metal surfaces will be found covered with a fine and even coating of rust. Wipe off the loose rust with a previously boiled and completely clean canton flannel cloth. Then immerse the gun in the reblue tank, the vat again filled with violently boiling distilled water, and swab it all over with a second dosing of the reblue solution. Set away for another 24 hours. This should be repeated at daily intervals for five or six days.

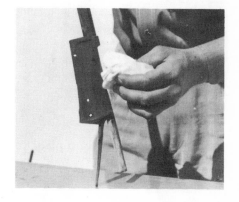

Should there be some patchiness, this is an indication that you have not sufficiently cleaned away the old finish. Go over these spots with steel wool and then immerse the weapon in the vat and reswab the places with many applications of the blueing solution.

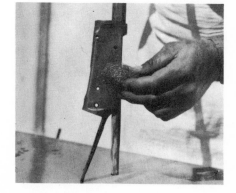

After the sixth day (and sixth application), boil the weapon for 15 minutes in plain, distilled water, remove it from the tank, and while the metal is still hot, swab the piece with pure linseed oil. Take long sweeping strokes and this time use a section of sheep skin. Permit the linseed oil to dry on the weapon. On successive days add more applications of the oil. This brings out the finish and adds lustre and beauty to the metal. Actually the process is more of a "browning" than a true blueing—a finish highly prized by the old English gun makers. It has a depth and quality to it not found in the usual factory blued finish.

The reblueing job is relatively simple and certainly not costly. The old favorite takes on added value all dressed up with a new finish, and the satisfaction felt by the owner is huge indeed!

guard and on this card place your name and address, and a listing of precisely what you want done. Address the package like this:

Attention: Repair Division
Winchester Repeating Arms Co.
New Haven, Conn.

In due time, and don't hold your breath until the boys in the fix-it shop get around to writing, you'll get a letter telling you how much the damages will total. Not until you reply to this billy-do giving your okay will repair commence. Be prompt, Gretchen, be prompt!

Of course there's them as say to hell with the factory, I'll do my own fixin'. The manufacturer, let it be noted right here, is heartily in accord. He will provide the parts by return mail with his blessing. He also does a big business with the *hombre* down on the corner who sharpens lawnmowers, makes keys, and fixes shooting irons on the side. You ain't gonna make the Remington, Ithaca, Browning, Winchester, or whatever company a bit mad if you do your own maintenance. Generally what you do is plenty amateurish and looks like hell, but it's your gun and it is at least quicker.

Probably nothing appeals to the owner quite as much as the possibility of renewing the finish on his favorite field piece. Factory blueing is a pretty thin coating. After a single season, whether at skeet, or at the more strenuous business of field shooting, the blue is marred. If the gun happens to be a new one the marks of battle are saddening to behold. No one, absolutely no one, can do a bettter job of reblueing and making the gun like new than the people who built it. They are in the business and their facilities are unexcelled. If, however, you want to do your own, that is also possible.

Not only can the sportsman reblue his shotguns, rifles and sixshooters but he can do it cheaply. More cheaply, let me point out—and infinitely more satisfactorily—if he has a number, say a half-dozen to refinish. Initial cost runs into a few dollars, but what is more significant is that the more·reblueing he does the more expert he becomes.

To be reblued a firearm must be completely torn down. Every nut, bolt, screw and spring has got to be shaken out. If the weapon has ivory or plastic sights, these must be removed. Tear it down and lay the parts out so that they will remain undisturbed until you are ready to reassemble the weapon.

The old finish has got to be removed. This is the major secret of a successful reblue job. You must first start with a file and remove all dents, nicks and scratches. If the barrel is dented, a mandrel of bore diameter must be entered in the tube and the dent tapped out. After filing has removed scratches and other marks of hard usage, then change to emery cloth of fine texture and smooth away the file markings. Follow the emery with crocus cloth until the surface shines like a mirror. *Every last evidence of the original blueing has got to be eradicated!* The external surfaces must be mirror-like.

Have your local tin shop make a tank of light sheet stock, size 36″ x 8″ x 6″. This tank must be heated on a gas burner that will maintain an even temperature from end to end. A three-burner gasoline camp stove is just the huckleberry. Place this tank, once finished, on the stove, and fill it with distilled water. Boil it out for two hours. This is to eliminate all greases and oils that may adhere to the sheet iron. Dump the boiled water and again fill with distilled water to which has been added a half-can of common lye. Bring to a boil.

Drive dowel pins into either end of the gun barrel, permit the dowels to extend a few inches beyond the breech and beyond the muzzle so that handles are provided. The bore should be greased before the pins are driven into place. Make hooks of No. 9 wire for all the minor parts, drape the parts on the hooks and hang in the tank of boiling water. Drop the barrel, action, and other major parts into the boiling water on these hooks. Never permit any part of the weapon to rest on the bottom of the tank, else it will come into too direct contact with the flame and have the temper drawn.

Boil for one hour. This is to cook off all the greases and oils and is an extremely important part of the process.

Before commencing the actual operation, as a matter of fact at least a week or ten days before, have your local druggist mix the following:

3 drams tincture of iron	1 dram corrosive sublimate
3 drams spirits of niter	½ dram nitric acid
1 dram sulphur	1 dram copperas
2 drams vitriol	12 oz. distilled water

The druggist will blend these chemicals and pour them into a colored glass bottle. Store the bottle in a dark place and permit the solution to age. Actually the longer it ages the better and never in any event less than a week.

Slip on a pair of clean cotton gloves. From now until the completion of the operation do not touch the parts to be blued with the bare hands.

After the disassembled gun has been boiled in the lye-water bath for 60 minutes, dump the water and refill with perfectly clean distilled water. Bring to a boil and immerse the parts once more. Place the blueing solution in a Pyrex glass jar in one corner of the blueing tank and let it come to boiling temperature or very nearly so. With water boiling violently and barrel (or other part) up to similar temperature, lift the tube by one of the dowel pins and holding it vertically swab on the blueing mixture. Use a swab made of previously boiled canton flannel wrapped about a clean dowel pin that has been boiled in the lye-water. Apply the blueing with a long sweeping stroke. Be generous with the amount you slop on. If the formula is not boiling then stir it occasionally.

After the barrel, action, and other parts have been thoroughly covered, remove from the tank and store for 24 hours in a fairly damp place.

Inspect. You will find the weapon is covered with a fine, even coating of deep red rust. Rub off the loose rust with a clean cotton cloth. Again immerse the weapon in the boiling water and after it has been brought to temperature, swab on the blueing solution just as you did the first time. The process should be repeated daily for a full week—and twice that long if necessary.

After seven daily treatments wash the barrel and all other parts in boiling water to check the further action of the solution and then go over the weapon with a clean soft cotton cloth, drying with great gentleness. While the metal is still hot apply liberal quantities of pure linseed oil. Abandon the cotton rag this time and apply the linseed oil with a woolen cloth. The linseed oil is quite necessary for it serves to set the color permanently. If the color is not as deep as desired, simply add additional coats on successive days until it approaches the shade you are seeking. This process is as old as the tall stories told by all Texans. It is time-tried and well nigh infallible if the doer will just follow instructions. The final finish is actually more of a browning than a true blueing but it is a joy to behold!

Chapter 23

WHO LOADS THE FASTEST SHOT SHELL?

IT IS A NEVER-FAILING source of conversation around the club to champion one load over the other because it has a little more zing. Maybe a hundred or a couple of hundred feet more per second and so you can cut down on your lead. What maybe is more surprising are the number of people who will believe you.

And then there is the hogwash about how one load kicks more than another; patterns better, mutilates the shot less, burns cleaner, and a dozen other claims.

Maybe there is one load that is better than the others. I shoot all the time and I haven't found which one is this super-duper. I'd like to know.

There is a tight little circle in which all the shotshell manufacturers travel, and just to keep it chummy they call themselves the Arms and Ammunitions Manufacturers Institute. It is just like the Baptist Ladies Sewing Circle. Once a month a big-wheel representative from every one of the manufacturers meets in New York; and while the members thus getting their heads together probably don't personally care for each other much, that doesn't in the least effect their hashing over current problems.

Everyone lays his cards on the table and if there are any secrets they are small ones. Once we had 1400 shotshell loads; between the Arms and Ammunition Manufacturers Institute and the Simplified Practices Committee these have been reduced to a few dozens. Once each shotshell loader could develop any velocities he liked, use any shell case he chose, load all the powder and lead he wanted. The result was anything but satisfactory. The wing gunner accustomed himself to a certain lead then changed loads and had to rediscover all his leads.

Now, thanks to the intelligence of the shotshell people, all velocities are the same, powder charges and shotloads are uniform, and a shooter may switch from load to load with the assurance that performance will be such as to not play hob with his leads.

There are three manufacturers of shotgun powders in the United States. These are DuPont, Hercules and Olin Mathieson. The latter firm, Olin Mathieson, are exclusive manufacturers of ball powder and have limited distribution of this new propellant to their

Quail in the briars along the North Carolina coast.

subsidiaries, Western and Winchester. Ball powder is a war-time development and was first successfully used in small-arms ammunitions, *i.e.* pistol, carbine and rifle. It has been modified to permit firing in the shotgun and is characterized by fine uniformity, cool burning, and stability.

The DuPont Co. makes a powder known as MX. Hercules produces the famous "Red Dot." There are other powders manufactured; DuPont, for instance, makes a fine bulk smokeless, but our discussion here will be concerned only with these better known and more largely used types.

Modern smokeless powder is made in lots, that is in batches. A lot may run anywhere from a few hundred pounds to as much as five tons. No two lots are ever exactly the same. This is due to the involved chemistry which is an inescapable part of the process. Man, despite his cleverness, has not yet reached that point where he may mix nitric and sulphuric acids together with a few scraps of cotton linters and a bucket of water and do it each time so exactly the same as to have the resulting propellant just like former mixes.

As soon as a lot of powder is finished it is immediately tested for speed of burning, pressures, and other characteristics. Both manufacturers, *i. e.* Hercules and DuPont, follow a system of attaching a number to the powder lot. Thus; Red Dot 1, or Red Dot 2; MX-1, MX-2, etc. The lower numbers indicate the faster

Scene of the Annual Great Eastern Skeet Championships, Lordsburg, Conn. The Remington Arms Co. sponsor these great matches.

burning propellants. Numbers may run as high as 10. After the propellant has been tested to establish its inherent characteristics, the powder people then test the lot in the cartridges of each of the shotshell companies. This is done because each shotshell manufacturer makes a slightly different kind of primer, uses different cases and has his own ideas about wadding, strength of crimps, etc. After these tests the powder is shipped in various quantities to storage near the cartridge-loading company.

In passing it might be well to comment on the extremely fine red dots that are found in all Hercules Red Dot powder. These tiny discs are an inert material placed in the propellant to identify it. An excess or almost total absence of these tiny objects has nothing to do with the performance of the powder. They do not contribute one iota to the performance of the propellant.

The Arms and Ammunition Manufacturers Institute establish velocities for all skeet, trap, and game loads. However, these velocities permit the manufacturers a leeway of 20 feet per second plus or minus. Let us look for a moment at the standard trap load, 3 drams equivalent of powder and 1⅛ ounces No. 7½ shot. This load is aimed at developing 870 fps. When the manufacturer sets up to run a lot of this particular loading, he adjusts all his machines to throw a charge of powder which will give him 870 feet per second.

The wheels commence to turn and immediately the ballistics department carts away samplings of the run, and these are rapidly fired and chronographed. If it is noted as this testing goes on, and it is continuous, that velocities are dropping down around 855 fps, the powder charge is increased a grain or two grains and tests quickly run. Should velocities on the other hand commence to climb, say up around 885 feet per second, the charge is just as promptly reduced. In this manner, by a never-ending inspection and testing system, the velocities of the skeet, trap, and game loads we use are kept within uniform and extremely close limits.

This brings us to another interesting practice of the *hombres* who make our cartridges. That is the hocum about "drams equivalent" stamped on the boxes and the overshot wad. When we loaded with bulk black powder, 'way back around the turn of the century, a dram was a dram and meant something. Today it doesn't mean

All the gear necessary for a crow-shooting afternoon. Best loads for crows are those most effective on duck.

a thing. It is a term held over from black-powder days and should be junked.

Actually the manufacturer is striving for a certain well established velocity in his shotshell and he measures his powder in grains (7000 to the 16-oz. pound) and he doesn't pay any attention to drams measure at all. In a lot of skeet loads there may be a variation of several grains weight between shells, nevertheless every top wad will carry the same figure "3 drams equivalent." It just ain't so. Every cartridge will attain its desired instrumental velocity, that is, 870 fps, plus or minus 20 feet, but it does not mean every last shell is charged with precisely the same quantity of propellant.

Not too many years ago we had quite a dazzling array of shot; it was called "chilled," "drop," "lubaloy," etc. Chilled shot was hardened either by alloying the lead with antimony or treating it with arsenic. Drop shot was pure lead. "Lubaloy," an interesting development of Western, had a coating of electrolytic copper added. This resisted deformation in the bore quite markedly. The only drawback was the cost, which was rather high. Anyway drop shot, the pure leaden article, fell into disrepute. It was looked upon as a poor performer and to be avoided. This saddened the ammunition tycoons because it was expensive to alloy the shot and thus produce the "chilled" variety. The Arms and Ammunition Manufacturers Institute considered the problem and came up with a neat solution. It was decided that hereafter all shot would be referred to as "Standard." And so it has been. Drop shot is still made but the shooter isn't worried anymore. He uses it in all his light to medium game loads and if you ask him he will tell you his favorite quail or dove load performs very well. Chilled is used in all skeet and trap loads and in all the so-called super and express cartridges for ducks and geese.

Another interesting development of modern shotshell manufacture is this matter of breech pressures. Any number of old Damascus and twist steel barrels are in use. The owners believe if they buy the lightest 12-gauge loads to be had there is no danger in firing the fifty-year-old model. Let us look at the facts. Our very heaviest 12-gauge load, fired in a 3-inch case, employs 4½ drams of powder and 1⅞ ounces of shot. Breech pressures vary between 11,000 and 12,500 psi. The lightest 12-gauge load, 2¾ dram and 1⅛ ounces, in 2¾-inch case, develops a minimum of 11,000 pounds per square inch.

How can this be, you will ask? The answer lies in the choice of powder. The super magnum 12 employs a very slow and progressive-burning propellant, thus giving a moderate thrust to the great weight of shot. Starting in with relative gentleness and building up the pressure after the inertia of the shotload has been overcome. The 2¾-dram load on the other hand is propelled by a fast powder which reaches peak pressure with great rapidity. Therein lies the answer. And what is more important, there lies the danger and the fallacy to continued use of the antiquated shotguns.

Chapter 24

OPERATION SLUG-LOAD

THE 12-GAUGE SLUG-LOAD packs enough oomph to upend the Abominable Snowman. At 40 yards it splinters more than a dozen well-seasoned ¾-inch pine slabs and whistles on. But at thrice 40 steps you'd have to cross a whitetail buck with one of Nehru's holy cows to foal a target big enough to catch the erratic lead.

The load is put together for shotguns from 410 to 12, and an ever increasing fraternity are compelled by state law to quest for the annual venison with the squaw gun charged with the conical ball. The absence of bitching on the part of the slug-shooting clan indicates the single ball gives small cause for complaint.

But just how efficient is it?

The average shotgunner knows about as much of the performance of the slug as he does about the interior ballistics of the 280 atomic cannon.

I determined to develop some sound facts on the single-ball missiles. I decided to fire the 20, 12 gauges, test all chokes, and learn which seemed to digest the leaden pills best; what barrel lengths were to be selected; what were optimum ranges; maximum distances; group sizes; were rear sights desirable; are modern scatterguns properly stocked to effectively handle the slug; and other related facts.

With this as the project, I commenced by firing the various gauges, and shot each in improved cylinder, modified, and full chokes. Barrel lengths ranged from 26 to 30 inches. I experimented with side-by-side doubles, over/unders, slide-action repeaters and autoloaders. All the firing, practically, was from a bench rest. I commenced shooting at 25 yards and eventually worked back to 300. Most of the target punching, however, was limited to 25, 40, 50, 75 and 100 yards.

Before we get up to our hocks in the actual powder-burning, suppose we take a quick look-see at the slug. The 12 is the best, we'll examine it first. Trot out the kitchen knife and let us dissect the victim.

To begin with the bullet is commonest lead. It isn't alloyed with anything, as a matter of fact it is so soft an *hombre* with a real big mad on can chew on one of these one-ounce slugs like it was so much Wrigley's Juicy Fruit. The ball is made not by casting the molten metal into a mould but by swaging in the cold state under pressure. I like the system, it produces a finished bullet that is full size, diameter, and weight.

Variations between 25 bullets that I weighed showed an extreme of only 7 grains. This small difference in no wise effects the accuracy. Diameters, likewise, ran surprisingly similar. Of 25 samples which I miked the smallest ran .676-inch and the fattest, .681-inch, the average was a neat .678. The bore of the 12, another strictly relative thing, has an average dimension of .729-

Optimum accuracy is gained with the slug load when the shotgun is equipped with scopes.

Slugload testing is best done with a rest if accurate findings are to be gained.

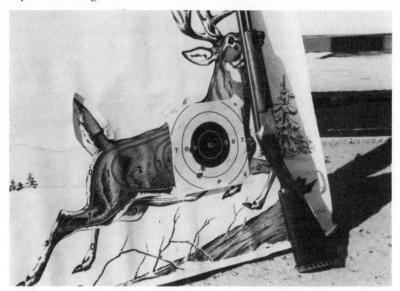

The over-under shotgun is not a good performer with slugs.

inch, when full-choked at the muzzle this dimension shrinks to .690-inch. It may be readily appreciated from the above that the 12-gauge ball is a rattling good fit.

Scarcely any two of the bullets possess the same overall length. The average head-to-tail reading is .722-inch. Between the shortest and the longest slugs of two dozen measured there was a difference of .044-inch.

The nose is flat like the business end of an English pit bull and behind this exceedingly blunt point is an ogive as ballistically well contoured as an old-fashioned bathtub. Elsie Maxwell, if you could launch the old sister, would have about the same flight characteristics as this shotgun slug. Be that as it may, the hunk of lead gets down the range.

Behind the ogive, which constitutes approximately one-third the length of the missile, is the body proper. This main portion is serrated with 14 lands and just as many grooves. These ornamentations have an abrupt right-hand twist, a depth which on a guess I'd say was .066 to .068, and lands and grooves are of similar width. About the base of the slug is a leaden belt which in no wise increases the diameter but does do a most effective job of closing the groove channels at the tail of the missile. No one has said so but it is obvious that the flutes are supposed to impart a spinning motion to the slug through the passage of air along the grooves. The aforementioned lead belting about the hip-pocket extremity denies this.

Actually the shotgun slug develops about the same rotational speed as that of a fat gal caught in a revolving door. The lands and grooves hacked out of the soft flanks are strictly eyewash, put there to bamboozle a gullible gunning public. The spinning motion is precisely nil—but there are more ways than one to skin the feline, as we shall shortly see.

The base of the conical missile is hollow. This cavity is sizable; it extends for three-quarters the length of the ball. This arrangement of the mass produces a thin side wall at the base; but as the cavity ranges noseward, it pinches inward with an attendant preponderance of weight in the very bows. The center of mass is nudged 'way up forward and any tendency to tumble is delayed

Studying slug-fired targets.

Slugs were fired in every type of shotgun.

The slug load deals out plenty of punishment in the way of recoil; is most pleasant to shoot offhand.

The Williams shotgun sight is a great help on the slug-throwing scattergun.

to very considerable distances (somewhere beyond 300 yards by actual test!) since ballistically the light stern end simply cannot forge ahead of the much heavier nose section. The slide-rule wizard who whipped up this one was a plenty astute *hombre!*

As a result of the design the slug does not need to spin on its axis, and as for that matter it has not been subjected to any influences likely to induce rotational spin. The grooves are whittled into the slug solely for decorative purposes. Some brainy ammo manufacturer, probably a former sales manager risen to the lofty seat of head guru, knew the shooters would be happier if they were led to believe the shotgun load spun like a rifle bullet. So he added 'em. The flutes do no harm to performance, but so far as serving any useful purpose are strictly in a class with mammary glands on the human male.

Most 12-gauge slugs are not round at the base. Variation of .05-inch is an average. The misshapen butt ends are a result of rough handling during and after the bullet has been swaged. The slugs are dumped, tossed, and poured like so much popcorn. Tar-

The Williams shotgun sight on the new Browning Double Automatic.

get performance would be improved if additional precautions were taken during the various handling operations.

I attached a relatively cheap scope, 4X, to an Ithaca 12, the Model 37 pump gun, and fired five groups of five shots each at 40 yards. The gun is bored modified choke and sports at 28-inch tube. The average of these five groups ran 4⁹⁄₁₆ inches. The stunt was repeated at 50 yards and the group size for the 25 shots (again five groups of five shots each) averaged 5¹¹⁄₁₆ inches; at 75 yards the groups had grown to an average of 10¾ inches; finally at 100 yards the average spread between widest shots was 13½ inches. For acceptable lethality on a target the size of a Virginia whitetail the slugs must fall into a pattern that has not more than 12 inches dispersion vertically and not over 14 inches laterally.

Holding to the notion that the slug, because of its non-spinning proclivity, would soon tumble, I shot it at 150 yards, then 200 yards, and finding it was still ambling along nose foremost, I dropped back to 250 and finally wound up at 300 yards. The bullet went through the paper nose foremost giving evidence of remaining stable flight characteristics. How much farther it would travel before it tumbles I do not know, but I'd wager it will go to maximum ranges without keyholing. The hollow base simply cannot get ahead of that weighty nose until velocities have dropped to galloping speeds. At 300 yards, from a bench rest and utilizing the same scope, the slugs cannot be kept on a target six feet high by four feet wide. Definitely the 12 gauge with the conical ball isn't for woodchucking!

The next shooting was with the new Browning 2-shot autoloader, known as the "Double Automatic." This weapon is a 12,

bored improved cylinder, 28-inch barrel and not graced by any
manner of rear sight. At 40 yards the usual 5-shot groups indicated an average of 4¹⁵⁄₁₆ inches; 50 yards 5⅝ inches; 75 yards
12⅞ inches; and at 100 yards 13¼₆ inches. At 100 yards it was
significant that the groups printed an average of 11¾ inches above
the point of aim and 3¼ inches to the right. With telescope or
receiver sight this deviation could have been corrected.

A Browning Superposed (over/under) followed its stablemate,
the Double Auto, into the lists. This barrel-above-barrel model is
a duck gun, a 12, with 30-inch tubes, and is bored full choke in
both pipes. The only sight is the tiny front bead perched atop
the solid raised rib. At 25 yards, I noted the under barrel planted
'em 4 inches above the point of aim and the over barrel did the
same although it grouped an inch to the right as well as shooting
a mite toward the moon. At 40 yards the under barrel ranged 5½
inches high, the over tube 7½ inches above point of aim. Group
spreads tallied an average of 6⁷⁄₁₆ under and 7¹³⁄₁₆ over barrels.

At 75 yards (I did not fire at 50 yards with this number) the
lower barrel printed 16 inches high and 4½ inches to starboard.
Groups ran 15⁹⁄₁₆ inches. The upper tube threw the slugs 11
inches above the point of aim and like its twin required a small
horse blanket to catch all the lead. Group average was a full
20¹¹⁄₁₆ inches. At 40 yards the upper barrel shot higher than
the lower; at 75 yards this was reversed. The over/under shotgun has the tubes regulated to place both patterns to a common
center at 40 yards. When you work out to twice that distance,
the axis of each bore has crossed, causing the lower barrel to shoot
higher than the upper.

At 100 yards the gun shot 24½ inches high and made a series of
groups that measured 21¾ inches, average. This from the under

One of the best shooting of the several guns tested with slug loads was this
Ithaca Model 37 equipped with low-power scope sight.

barrel; the upper grouped better, 16¼ inches, and 21 inches above the aiming center.

The over/under as indicated by this firing would not remain within our acceptable dispersion zone at 75 yards and definitely was 'way over at 100. I did not shoot the weapon at 50 yards, I am sorry now I did not, but obviously its capabilities as a deer-slayer are limited to distances within the 50-75-yard bracket.

Group fired at 50 yards on man-sized silhouette.

Subsequent firing with a 16-gauge over/under and a 20 of the same type indicated that these guns are not as satisfactory for slug use as the single-tube pump repeater and/or autoloader. Both are limited to 60 yards or thereabouts. Accuracy is good at 50 yards but the 16 shot 16 inches high although the group was tight enough. The 20 did not shoot too high but beyond 50 yards groups ran over our permissible 12"x14" dispersion factor.

Likewise I exhaustively tested a 12 Ithaca side-by-side, bored improved cylinder in both 28-inch barrels. This old piece, it is more than 40 years of age, grouped the slugs from the right barrel precisely 19 inches from the group formed by the slugs pooped off out of the port tube—and the distance was only 50 yards. A 16, another Ithaca of the same era and vintage as its brother, developed the same peculiarities. At 50 yards the elevation was well nigh perfect but the left barrel shot left and the right went over by the smokehouse, distance betwixt was 17 inches. You cannot be sure of killing winter meat with performance like that. In summation, leave the over/unders and side-by-sides at home when you decide to hunt buckskin with the conical round.

And while we are making with the do's and don'ts the firing I did with a Model 12 pump gun, 20 gauge, equipped with a variable muzzle choke device was very revealing. At 50 yards the group—that is those portions that I could catch—printed 15 inches high. With regularity there would be a flier. I have not the least doubt that the slug made the jump from the end of the true barrel, moved through the ventilated portion of the muzzle device, and hit the choke tube off center. This caused the fliers.

I placed a target behind a dense clump of mesquite and shot at it. The 12-gauge ball will mow down brush like the grim reaper wielding his scythe. It doesn't make a hoot whether the branches are directly in front of the game target or placed midway of the range, the soft lead whittles it down and keeps on. Not until I set up a forest of sticks, each selected for a half-inch diameter, did the slugs have trouble. By the time the ball bores through a half dozen of these it is apt to miss the mark. Any jackass ought to know he can't shoot through a couple of California Redwoods to bag his game, even so the one ounce of lead turns in a highly satisfactory exhibition.

Buckshot was used long before the slug came into the picture.

An average group fired with Winchester pump 20 at 40 yards.

There is more information floating around about what buckshot will or won't do than there are tales about the sex life of Calamity Jane. Sagas about dumping a fleeing mossy-horn at a full hundred steps are as common throughout the South as grits and hawg jowl. Just how does buckshot stack up when compared to the conical ball?

Buck runs in several useable sizes; me, I prefer double or single 0. The 00 in 12 gauge runs nine to the load; the single 0 contains

The slug load is essentially for use on white-tail deer.

A 12-gauge load of single O buckshot at 60 yards. Not so hot!

an even dozen of the pellets. There are other and smaller sizes, but for serious meat-taking I have little confidence in other than the two sizes enumerated.

Many times deer have been killed with a single buckshot, but these lucky shots cannot be depended upon. After all the marksman managed to place the one pellet in head, neck, or heart quite by good fortune and not by any particular display of skill. What we must depend upon is placing not less than three of the spherical leads into the game. A moment's consideration will indicate why three buckshot are the allowable minimum. The 00 buck has a per pellet weight of 58 grains, three together total but 174 grains. This is none-too-much metal especially when we realize that the buckshot starts at a moderate velocity, sheds this speed and as a consequence energy at a rapid rate, and finally possesses about the saddest imaginable shape for deep penetration.

I tried a 12-bored improved cylinder at all ranges from 50 to 100 yards with 0 buck. It was a rather hasty firing and results are not as conclusive as I'd like, nonetheless I give them here as an indication. The target was the outline of a deer, dimensions as close to the real article as the artist could make 'em. At 50 yards, 1st shot, 3 pellets; 2d shot, 8 hits; 60 yards, 1st shot, 3 pellets; 2d shot, 3; 70 yards, hits 3 and 1. At 80 and 100 yards there were no pellets nicked the unprotesting deer.

With a modified barrel I tried the same thing. At 50 yards I scored 3 hits with the first and 2 with the second shots; 3 hits and 5 at 60 yards; 1 hit and then 2 at 70; a clean sheet at 80 yards with both rounds. At 100 yards out of the 24 pellets hurled down range (each load contains 12 buckshot, remember) a single ball struck the target.

Sticking with the same single 0 buckshot load, I then switched to a full choke 12. Results were like this; 6 hits, and then 4 at 50 yards; 4 hits and 3 at 60 yards; 1 hit and 0 for the two shots at 70 yards; and at 100 yards I hit the deer target with 3 pellets out of the two blasts unloosened.

This shooting was immediately followed by a stint with the larger buckshot, the 00, which as I have said runs 9 to the cartridge.

I again ran through the improved cylinder, modified and full choke borings and of course whanged away at all ranges from 50 to 100 yards. Results were very similar to my findings with the smaller pellets. At 70 and 80 yards the margin was ever so slightly better for the double-0 buck. However, the difference was small.

In summation what we find is that to place our required 3 buckshot in the deer we cannot fire beyond 60 yards, and it doesn't matter a hoot whether the shotgun is as open-muzzled as a B-flat

clarinet or as tight as a Boston banker's heart; likewise the choice
of buckshot size seems to influence the equation precious little.

On the other hand the conical slug-load in any run-of-the-mill
scattergun, in pump repeater or self-loading models, extends this
range to a full 75 yards. And if equipped with radar I doubt that
the rattling hunk of lead could be corraled in the carcass of a
beastie as small as a white-tail at much beyond the 100 paces.

BALLISTICS OF THE SLUG LOAD

'Gauge	Range Yds.	Velocity	Energy	Mid-Range Trajectory
*410 ga.	0	1470 fps	460 ft. lb.	————
	50	1180	295	.5-inch
	100	1030	225	3. inches
	200	855	155	16. inches
20 ga.	0	1410	1245	
	50	1213	923	.5-inch
	100	1071	718	3. inches
	200	910	520	15. inches
16 ga.	0	1436	1600	
	50	1243	1205	.5-inch
	100	1100	940	2.5 inches
	200	940	690	14.5 inches
12 ga.	0	1470	1995	
	50	1269	1485	.5-inch
	100	1120	1165	2.5 inches
	200	640	830	14. inches

————

* Worthless for deer.

Chapter 25

LIVE-BIRD SHOOTING ON THE CONTINENT

THE MADRID PIGEON CLUB annually sees a kill of 50,000 live birds. The shooting goes on nine or ten months of the year and is limited to the afternoons of Saturday, Sunday, Tuesday and Thursday. Three or four matches are banged off each afternoon and are limited to 3-bird, 4-bird and 7-bird tourneys. The entry is not too steep, cost per event ranges from two-fifty to seven-fifty, plus approximately forty cents per bird. The winner gets back a healthy percentage of the entry, ordinarily second and third monies are distributed as well. Once monthly there are matches in which handsome sterling cups are awarded in addition to the money.

The Madrid club, known as the *Tiro de Pichon de Madrid,* is north of town on the highroad to the palacio of Dictator Franco, is a tiled-roofed and picture-windowed little cottage only a dozen years of age and costing something around a half-million bucks in the building. It squats atop a hill known as the Somontes, and saw some rousing gun-work when Franco and his bully boys decided to take Madrid from the north a couple decades back. Spain had a rootin', tootin' civil war back in the 30s that most folks have forgotten.

The pigeon club has several hundred members. Membership is not steep, it runs a little more than a hundred bucks annually, and at least theoretically any Joe can join. Significantly the board of governors scrutinizes the applications with all the thoroughness of caste-conscious Europeans.

The "let's-don't-hurry-boys" attitude of the Spanish gunner gives the American gunner the willies. You'd think with a shooting club, the finest in Spain, and one of the most ritzy on the Continent that there'd be no less than a dozen pigeon grounds and all of 'em would be going full tilt. Not so. The Tiro de Pichon has a sum total of one live-bird field. Yep, one shooter can perform and all the others must wait with whatever degree of patience heritage and training has given them.

Ordinarily on a shooting day the marksman will go to the club at 2 p. m. and have lunch in the splendid limed-oak dining room

211

Billy Perdue of Mobile who walked off with the European live-bird championship fired at Madrid during June of 1952.

which looks through huge picture windows onto the shooting field. Here he orders up a dinner and as he eats a steward drops around and takes his entry. He need not pay then, but later on during the week the club will send a second steward to his office in Madrid and then he will straighten his accounts. The entry made, he sits back to enjoy his Solomillo and bottle of excellent Marques del Riscal wine together with volumes of conversation with mutual *amigos*.

The first event, a warm-up, gets under way. Finally the loud speaker calls his name. He gets up leisurely, passes some quip with his voluble fellows, wends his way in no hurry at all into the main lounge, passes the gun rack where the stewards have thoughtfully stacked his AYA double, thence onto the terrace, and at long last to the firing point. Meanwhile the fifty other entrants are all settled back in the comfortable confines of the club house, either finishing their *comida* or, having gotten the business of the food out of the way, are relaxed with cognac and cigars. If it takes a single contestant a full five minutes to move from his food to his shooting stand no one complains.

Every member has a published handicap. Distances vary from 16 to 26 meters, and of course the handicap is based wholly on the shooting success of the individual. The gunner, once he reaches the shooting box, takes up his position. The gun, invariably a 12 double, either side-by-side or over/under, is loaded with two rounds. The shooter places the gun to shoulder and as the butt cradles he says to the operator, *"Listo"* (ready). The button-pusher answers *"Listo."* The marksman then points his twin muzzles directly over the center box and calls, *"Pajaro"* (bird), whereupon the button is pushed and the game takes wing.

There are before him five pigeon traps with a bird in each. These traps are steel boxes with collapsible sides. The opening of the box is controlled by an intricate mechanism not unlike a slot machine. Electrically operated, when the button is pressed a series of cams are set in motion, and neither the operator nor any other human may influence the mechanism. The trap containing the pigeon opens with a resounding clatter and so frightens the bird he instantly takes wing. Unless the game is killed before it crosses a low 3-foot enclosure approximately 20 yards from the traps, it is lost. Very frequently the bird is killed stone dead in the air, but so great is his forward momentum, plus the impact of the shot charge, that he will be carried outside the boundary fence.

The pigeon used for live-bird shooting has been bred for hundreds of generations for the game. He is turbo-prop powered with JATO-booster, a lightning-charged bundle of feathers that bounces 10 feet into the air in a hundredth part of a second and then takes off for the fence, climbing, angling, and corkscrewing. And just to make it all the more sporting, his tail feathers are plucked so he doesn't know himself what he is going to do!

The gunner has two shots and generally he uses both. The load is 1¼ ounces of No. 7 shot. Because of a lack of dollars, few American cartridges get into Madrid live-bird shooting circles, but they are highly prized. Current favorites are Italian loaded; and now the Germans are back into business again, the kraut 12s will undoubtedly be fired plenteously. Spanish cartridges are held in small esteem by the local gentry.

But to get back to our gunner:

Having fired, he falls back and the next shooter approaches. After everyone has fired the marksmen who have bagged all their birds are placed in a shoot-off. It is then miss and out. It seldom takes long to settle a match once the eliminations begin. A wingman who can bag 10 straight Spanish pigeons is shooting exceptionally well; if he can run 20 straight, he is in the championship class. Any resemblance between the Spanish bird and the barnyard variety, seen in every corner of this country, is purely coincidental. The former is ten times tougher to connect with. Long runs in this country are not duplicated on the Continent, and any number of our ranking shotgunners who have thought to clean up at Monte

Carlo, Estoril, and Madrid, basing their belief in themselves on
their showings on our stodgy pigeon, have found that the European cousin is a *paloma* of a different feather!

Guns are for the most part conventional doubles. There is a
sprinkling of O/Us but they are decidedly in the minority. No one
would think of firing anything save the 12. The load used sticks
pretty close to what we consider the standard 12; that is, 3¼
drams of powder and 1¼ ounces of shot. The No. 7½ shot is unknown on the Continent, instead there is the No. 7. This shot
size differs between countries, and in Spain the No. 7 is our
normal 6. Barrel borings differ as much as do shooters. By and
large a modified choke is most common, although there are many
who use improved cylinder, quarter choke, and full.

The gun stock on the pigeon gun is painfully straight. A drop
at comb of 1½ inches is most used, but many elect to shoot stocks
that are as straight as 1⅜ and 1¼ inches. Billy Perdue, who won
the European live-bird Championship in '52, shot a Purdey that
had no down pitch at all. The all-important first shot is loosened
at a wildly rising target, and for that reason the weapon that
tosses its charge quite high is to be favored.

Barrel lengths run 28 to 30 inches. Sometimes you see a 32-inch,
and as well, many fire the 68.5-cm. tube which is 27 inches long.
Beavertail forestocks are virtually unknown, and strangely the
Monte Carlo stock, the checkpiece, and other innovations which
we have accepted from the Continental gunner are seldom seen
at live-bird tourneys. Another oddity is the absence of single triggers. Despite the fact that his follower shot must be whipped in
with blinding speed, the pigeon shot seldom has any save a two-
trigger gun. One reason for this is the lack of really dependable
single-trigger mechanisms.

Live-bird shooting falls into the doldrums in Madrid when the
partridge season opens the last week in October; it does not
revive until the gunning draws to a regretful pause the first of
February. From then on the *palomas* really catch hell! There is
a circuit which commences in the south of Spain at Seville, Cadiz,
Malaga, and other cities of Andalucia, and gradually works north-
ward as the spring freshens. Next to Madrid the most important
shootfests are held in the summer capitol at San Sebastian and
in Barcelona. The gunner who has the *dinero* and the time may
tread this glittering powder trail from midwinter until the Chukar
beckons again in the fall. And if the Spanish *pinchon* pales on him,
he can take a quick flyer to Lisbon where he will find the Portu-
guese offer just as sturdy competition as the Castillian; or he
may warm up his guns on the French Riviera; or take a swing
through live-bird circles in Italy. Wherever he goes he will find

shotgunners who are tough and quick. Any quaint ideas we may have that we are the best shooters on the face of the earth are pretty rapidly dissipated in the live-bird trials of the Continent. During four years of steady shooting with the Spanish, both at the pigeon sport and in the field, proved to me that I need go only a couple of pistol shots from my own dunghill to meet my match.

Besides being a whale of a sweet shotgunner, the average Spaniard is a practicing sportsman. If you enter his club a stranger and do a thorough job of wiping his eye he'll put aside his Old World dignity that dictates that he must not get familiar unless you are an old friend, and will come up and tell you what a fine piece of shotgunning you have done. And he means it too! I have never shot with more thorough-going gentlemen.

The Madrid Club has a skeet field; the San Sebastian pigeon fathers have another. I believe there are a number of other fields throughout the country. The Spanish championship was fired over the San Sebastian grounds during '52, and at Madrid in 1953. Believe it or not, the championship was decided on 25 birds! There were shoot-offs of course. An interesting innovation at Madrid in '53 was the ruling of the officials that all the entries would fire station No. 1 before moving on to No. 2! The Spaniard simply is not interested in any shooting game in which nothing dies. His shotgunning is not unlike his taste in bull fighting. He wants to see blood flow. For this reason, clay target shooting is not popular.

Chapter 26

A TEXAS "DUKE" HUNTS IN SPAIN

THE SHOOTING BOXES stretched like a line of skirmishers from the higher reaches of the valley to its confluence a full three-quarters mile below. The posts were arranged just under the crest of the ridge, situated to deny the partridge view of them until the game came booming over the rise. Then it would be too late.

On my right, some sixty yards above, stood the Duke de Luna; downhill waited the Duke de Peñaranda, nephew of the former king, Alfonso XIII. Luna is one of the first guns in Spain. This morning, certainly, I was bracketed where I'd have to turn in top performance!

The crowd was so distinguished the very air seemed slightly befogged with a royal bluish haze. There were besides Luna and Peñaranda, still a third duke, Algeciras, equerry to the Pretender, Don Juan, and if this were not enough there was a whole bevy of marquises. Besides Fausto Saavedra, Marquis de Viana, our host, I counted the Marquises de Haro, Acapulco, Sales and Valdesevilla. And there were quite as many counts: Taboada, who is also a Spanish grandee, and Pozo-Rubio, Grijalba, and Montealegre.

And finally there was old Askins.

Now bird shooting in Spain isn't quite as simply done as on the Kansas prairies. To begin with, the game isn't hunted, it is beaten. This requires some three-score-and-ten peasants to do the driving. And if this wasn't a considerable requirement on the personnel side, every shooter must have a *secretario*. This worthy is gun bearer and handy man and tags along to tote your spare fowling piece, as well as several hundred cartridges, coat, sweater, whisky, shooting stool, and whatever else fancy dictates.

If this seems a bit on the plush side, let me assure you it is.

The *secretario*, besides making life more comfortable for you, will, if he is worth his salt, sally forth when the drive is finished (there are six drives during the day) and gather up not only all your downed birds but a number of those belonging to your neighbors as well. He is a very valuable and important accessory, this institution known as the *secretario*.

He can be sporting too. When the game commences to wing

216

over, at first by the dozens, later by the score and finally phalanx
on phalanx, it is his job to keep your spare double charged and pass
it up to you from his crouched position. Often, being an untrained
campesino, unaccustomed to handling firearms, he will manage
to load the gun, and in passing it along to you during the ex-
citement of the flight, will inadvertently get his finger in the
trigger; and if the hurtling one-and-one-quarter ounces of No. 7s
do not neatly part your hair you can count yourself fortunate.

This is not supposed to ruffle or disconcert you. The etiquette
of the occasion demands that you turn casually and inform him
in a gentlemanly roar clearly audible from one end of the firing
line to the other that he is a stupid ass and does he want to kill
you?

Directly after the second drive of the morning my *secretario*,
an intelligent and willing country Spaniard who had fought with
Franco during the first Communist attempt to engulf a country,
turned to me and in Spanish said, "Senor, are you a *conde*
(count)?"

It appeared an innocent question and while most Spanish sportsmen do not deign to chat with their gun bearer, I always did, as
much to practice the language as for any other reason. I looked
at my man searchingly, replied: "Certainly not!" I put on my
haughtiest air, lisped in my best Sunday Castillian, "I am the
Duke of Ysleta."

The rest of that day and all the next he addressed me very
respectfully as *"mi Duque."*

It should be explained in passing that Ysleta, for which I had
just created a dukedom, is a tiny little Mexican pueblo about a
dozen miles down the Rio Grande from my native El Paso, Texas.

My poor *secretario* after a careful analysis of the situation had
come to the conclusion that he was saddled with some *corriente*
(common) Americano who had no title and, what was probably
worse, little standing socially. When these facts became known
he would most surely be held up to derision by his more fortunate
companions, each of whom had a member of the nobility to serve.

His relief upon learning that he was buttling for no less than
a Texas duke eased his perturbation and to show his satisfaction
he scuttled out after the very next *ojeo* (drive) and not only re-
trieved all my birds but got four clearly the property of the Duke
de Peñaranda and seven dropped by Luna.

Fausto Saavedra, Marquis de Viana, owns estates throughout
Spain and this one, "Las Romanones" was one of the top spots.
Handily, it was a bare 20 kilometers from Madrid and could be
reached in thirty or forty minutes from my quarters. The Marquis
is a sailor, a full captain in the Spanish Navy; and during the

Netting migratory pigeons high in the Pyrenees of Spain. Birds here just struck the net, the trigger has been sprung, and net is falling.

Spanish war, a blood-letting now past some 20 years, he had elected to support Franco.

The Nationalists, as Franco's forces were called, were a bit shy on naval craft, so Viana cranked up one day and hied him over to pay Mussolini a visit (this was back in '36, remember) and after a brief conversation with Il Duce bought a destroyer from his own pocket and presented it to General Franco. "She was a sorry craft," he laughed.

Be that as it may, he organized annually one of the finest shoots in Spain. During the gunning extravaganza of which I write we bagged, the first day, a total of 542 partridges; on the second, 782. High gun was the Duke de Algeciras with upwards of 200 Chukar fallen to his brace of deadly Purdeys.

The game is the red-legged partridge. I dubbed him Chukar— actually he is not. But so close is the relationship only an expert can differentiate between them. He is called *"perdiz"* by the Spanish, a word meaning partridge; and since it is the only one of its kind on the Iberian Peninsula, the sobriquet serves very well.

Dr. Gardiner Bump, one of the long-hairs of the U.S. Fish and Wildlife crew, set me right on that score. Doc stopped off for a few days in Madrid en route to Turkey where he has been busy every year trapping the Turkish version of the Chukar for transplanting in selected areas of the United States. The Chukar, very properly speaking, comes from much farther east than the Spanish bird, Bump explained. The Spaniard is the red-legged partridge and is peculiar to the Mediterranean, being found on the African side as well as on the Continent. I recollected I had shot him in Tunisia during the slugfest of 1939-45.

Doc Bump had never shot driven game so I invited him to Quintanilla, a lodge owned by that prince of Spaniards, Don Publio Vazquez. Don Publio, a handsome bachelor and sportsman, had built a comfortable many-roomed chalet on his vast acres solely for the enjoyment of his shooting guests. At Quintanilla, I found, there was always a cook in attendance, a handy man to look after your needs, and the *finca*, a farm of more than twenty thousand acres, could provide a hundred beaters any time.

The first day the shooting was especially heart-tingling. I recollect we killed upwards of 300 birds and my worthy game-man got his baptism of fire on beaten partridge. He had a venerable old Parker shotgun, a 12, non-ejector. During one drive I glanced over to see him wrenching at the miserable empties attempting to claw them out of the chambers before the flight was done. Everyone uses two double shotguns—not one—and ejectors are a must. While you are dragging down a brace of targets with the first gun the *secretario* is busily charging the second weapon; swapping empty gun for loaded is a sort of legerdemain which shooter and loader achieve in the space of a heartbeat. Bump suffered along with his venerable firelock.

At the end of the first day's gunning the Maestro of the Hunt took tally. Bump had accounted for precisely eight birds.

The day following our luck held handsomely, although the total bag was not quite so high. As I remember that weekend we came

Returning to the hunting lodge, Province of Cordoba, southern Spain.

The Marquis of Valdesevilla, who this past season killed more than 1,000 partridges.

away with about 500 partridge. High gun had accounted for almost a hundred—there were a dozen of us shooting—but interestingly *amigo* Bump had again scored exactly eight perdiz. I smiled to myself, Doc, not a bad wingshot, must have seen to it that he deliberately missed many. Our good fish and wildlife minion did not intend to let it ever be said that either at home or abroad he exceeded a reasonable bag.

And that brings me to a comment on the business of Spanish game bags:

The perdiz belongs to the landowner and not to the State. If the *haciendado* wants to kill all his game in a single shoot he is perfectly at liberty to do so. He has nurtured the partridge through a twelfthmonth, has waged no-quarter war against vermin and predators by payment of bounties, has hired full-time armed guards to patrol his acres and ward off poachers; and after all this, the State looks upon his partridge as little different than his chickens, pigs and goats. He can shoot them as he sees fit and if he wants to invite a dozen good *amigos* to aid and abet, that is perfectly ducky.

Partridge are sold in all the markets in Spain.

Bags as high as 2500 from a two-day *caceria* are not at all uncommon.

Don Rufino Yanci, ardent Basque sportsman, invited me to shoot pigeon at his club in the Pyrenees. This club, I found, was as common as an old shoe. It had a membership of precisely six members and so rigid were the rules no others might even petition to join. Outsiders shot at Echalar only by invitation of one of the half-dozen club members.

The shooting grounds were some 35 miles northeast of San

Sebastian, in the very tops of the towering Pyrenees; and our game, as I was to find, sometimes was killed in Spain but fell in France—we were astride the border. Gunning of the *paloma*, Spanish style, is an entrancing business, as I was to learn; not at all the staid business of lying in wait around a waterhole on the desert, as I'd long been accustomed.

In the very tops of the mountains are series of natural passes. Here the Basques hack out long alleyways in the timber, first making sure that below the pass are extending ridges. At the near end of the passage nets are stretched, these look for all the world like the nets used by the fisherman on the coast far below. Each snare is approximately 60 feet in length by 40 feet in height. Beside each is a cleverly concealed blind, within this blind an operator crouches, his hand on a triggering device. When a flight of pigeon hit the net, he trips the mechanism and the mesh falls like a plummet entrapping the hapless migrants. It sounds simple, actually it is quite complex, there are many intangibles not readily apparent to the uninitiated.

There are three varieties of pigeon that make the fall migration, a flight that invariably takes place during the latter three weeks of October, and provide the Basque sport. The lesser of the birds is the *tortula*, a dove bearing a striking resemblance to our own; then there is an intermediate flyer, the *choloma*, twice the size of the dove and truely a pigeon; and finally there is the *piéce de resistance* of the Pyrenees gunner, the lordly *torcaz*.

This is a great blue pigeon, with a wing spread of 14 inches and all the speed of a gerfalcon.

The gun is the Browning Grade V over-under bored full choke in both barrels, excellent medicine for the hard-to-down Chukar partridge.

The Master of the Hunt tallies the kill. Quintanilla, Central Spain.

He flies, as do the others, only when the wind is under his sternsheets, which means it must come out of the northwest. Nothing else will bring him down. This makes the shooting a bit sporting, for the sportsmen must motor out from San Sebastian, an involved journey which necessitates a daily dispensation from the *Guardia Fronteriza* (Border Guard) to travel thus closely to the border, and may find on arrival that not a single band will pass that day, the wind having switched to the northeast.

But when the wind is right thousands of pigeon will wing over on their march to the southermost provinces of Spain and to not-so-distant Africa. It is then that the shooting attains the heights!

Considerable strategy is involved in the netting of the wily migrants. A full mile below the nets, on either wall of the canyon, wooden towers are constructed. These towers are fully one hundred feet in height and perched there are keen-eyed young Basques especially trained for their jobs. The tower observer scans the skies over France, always watching toward the northwest; and when he spots an oncoming *banda* of pigeon, he tootles shrilly on his horn. Immediately everyone at the nets takes cover.

Watching the flight, which may include as many as two hundred birds, the uninitiated will see, to his dismay, that the flight is going to wing above the pass by fully a thousand feet. No use to be concerned about this band—but wait, what gives?

As the pigeons draw near the two towers, the men stationed on the platforms suddenly commence to hurl a series of wooden discs, each painted a vivid white, into the canyon below. These saucer-like objects, brilliant against the background of pines, arch out widely and fall for hundreds of feet into the defile below.

The flight leaders upon seeing this immediately conclude that another band has been attacked by hawks and evasive action is in order. All in an instant the flock hits the deck. Swooping from an altitude which would have enabled them to clear the nets by a thousand feet, the *torcaz* seemingly fold their wings and like as many arrows hurtle groundward—just in time to crash into the nets!

If it were not for the strategy of the flashing discs, curving and arching into the abyss, scarce a pigeon would be snared, much less shot.

The guns are stationed not at the nets but behind and below them. Long custom (pigeon have been trapped at Echalar for

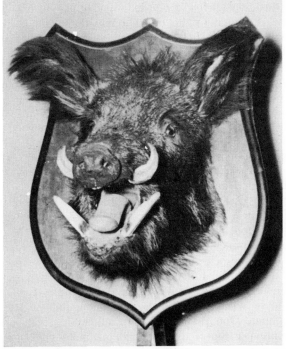

The wild boar of Europe is found in numbers in the cork forests of Andalusia, the southernmost region of Spain.

more than six hundred recorded years) dictates very stringent shooting rules. You must not fire before the band strikes the net or spills above it; however, if a flight becomes wary and flies above the mesh you can fire; singles escaping from the strands are fair game; but never, never must you toss a charge of shot into the net itself!

Don Rufino and I arrived at Echalar just as the sun was dissipating the night's shadows. We hustled into the blinds. Gunfire drummed in from the right. "The President of France is shooting over there today," a Basque, busy with the crates that would later hold the netted birds, nodded casually in the direction of France.

I settled back. Whether I killed a single pigeon or not, this was an exhilarating experience. Here I was perched among the highest peaks of the Pyrenees, a glorious view revealed below me, at my elbow an agreeable companion; while the hustle of those who were preparing the nets lent a tense expectancy to the scene.

Minutes passed and time dragged into a half-hour; finally forty-five minutes had came and gone. Suddenly the silence was sharply broken by the trilling of the bugle. Instantly there was a frantic scurrying in every direction. "*La bocina,*" Don Rufino was all smiles, "*Estas preparado?*" I nodded eagerly.

My view extended to the tip of the net, on the flanks to the sky-scraping conifers; if I was to shoot I must take my game during that exceedingly brief interval from the nets to my post. I was going to have to be fast.

The bugle was mute; we waited tensely for a full three minutes and not a single flying critter put in an appearance. Finally it spoke again with a long continuous note. "*Carramba!* The birds have turned aside. We may relax," my companion was obviously disappointed.

But we had not long to ponder our lack of targets. The bugle made its music as before, and again there was a great activity as we got under cover.

With a swooshing, metallic-sounding roar fully 200 *torcaz* crashed into our net, it fell as though made of steel. There was a wild flapping of wings, showers of feathers almost hid the net, and there was a yammer of shots from guns to either side.

All in the space of a heartbeat great blue targets were hurtling over and around the fallen mesh, targets that sped outward as though pursued by the hounds of hell. I snapped two shots at a booming mark with no visible return. "How far are we shooting at the *palomas*, Don Rufino?" I inquired.

"From the very top of the net to this blind is forty-two meters, for I have measured it with a line," answered my friend, "and from the tops of the trees is at least 55 meters."

Wow! This beat pass shooting on mallards. The next *banda* to swerve above the nets saw me ready. I am sure I was leading the forward pigeon by not less than a dozen feet. The load was heavy American—Spanish shotshells are a bit erratic—and when that great *torcaz* came windmilling down as dead as Steve Brodie I knew I had the zero!

It was a memorable day. We stayed until the chill of the high dusk made the game no longer worth the candle. Passing the blinds where the Basque netters had been so busily engaged through the long hours of the day, I inquired, "What was the take today, *amigo?*"

"We have counted a hundred and twelve dozens birds, Senor," and then with a sly grin, he added, "but small thanks to the guns; the most of those have fallen to our snares."

Chapter 27

SHOTGUNNING IN INDO-CHINA

THE SHOTGUNNERS' mainstay in Indo-China is the lordly dove. In those 27 states of the USA where the dove is looked upon not as a song bird but in fact as a game target, some nineteen millions were bagged last year. More, interestingly enough, than any other feathered target. The harbinger of Peace is just as plentiful in this corner of Asia, but by no means were any 19,000,000 shot; neither in '57 nor for that matter any year since Confucius.

An intriguing peculiarity of the Asiatic dove—there are three variations—is that he is apparently non-migratory. You see doves all the way from the 17th Parallel—that demarcation line between ourselves and the Ho Chi Minh Commies of the North—to the very southern tip of the peninsula. You hear his plaintive co-o-o throughout the season of the monsoons and stretching into the months of heat and dust; from Tet until the rice is laid by. A hunting grounds likely to hold an afternoon of lusty gunning in July will be just as hospitable in the fall.

The Vietnamese do not eat the "Con Coo," neither do they know anything about shooting him. Even if they did admit to lethal intention there are precious few scatterguns and even fewer shotshells. Blessed by an almost complete absence of human enemies, you'd assume the messenger the doughty Noah dispatched would be so tame you'd have to chunk rocks to set him a-wing. Perish the thought. The Indo-Chinese version of the Rio Grande flyer is wilder than a Mex prostitute on a marijuana jag.

Doves aren't gunned in old Annam after the time-honored manner of the Texas Southwest where you wait them out around the sundown waterhole. Nor do you seek out an inviting Kaffir corn patch and walk him up as in Oklahoma. Nor has the coolie farmer been introduced to the obvious advantages of a dozen acres of Georgia black-eyed peas, locale par excellence for strafing the *paloma*.

There is water here in such plenty as to provide a sup every furlong, and as for food these tropics abound in such quantities of grain and insects it is a wonder the birds move about at all. Interestingly, we hunt the birds not over the watering places, for

these are beyond number, nor yet on the feeding grounds which
are everywhere, but in those few spots where the game goes in
search of the fine gravel so necessary to the digestive well-being
of many fowl. Here is best gunning of all. Here the speedsters
flock by the tens of thousands.

The birds after an early morning breakfast rise and by two and
threes and forties flock in for the dessert—the gravel-and-small-
pebble pie. And where do you suppose this places them? Why on
the half-dozen hard-surfaced roads of Viet Nam. These few high-
ways are built with a rock and asphalt base over which tar and
finest gravel are strewn. The top layer of pebbles is more savoried
by a Chinese pigeon than a double snort of Lydia E. Pinkham's
Vegetable Compound by a Bible-belt dowager.

Shooting can be done on the traveled roads. Sometimes a car
will not pass in a pair of days. There is no law forbidding this
shooting. I make it a practice, however, to find those abandoned
stretches of hard-top where the Viet Minh during the eight years
of war destroyed the bridges, thus compelling detours. Here there
is no traffic and here "Con Coo" flocks in numbers.

I was gunning for doves one rainy morning near M'Drak, some
hundreds of miles north of Saigon. The game had proven especially
cooperative and I was beginning to feel some faint twinges of
conscience over the mouting heaviness of the bag and worrying
not a little over my dwindling shell supply.

I had dropped a pair of the russet birds—a dove stranger to
me with a spectacular saddle-brown upper feathering but otherwise resembling our American—and walking over to retrieve the
brace, I ran a tie with a critter I had never seen before, nay,
failed to realize was closer than Australia.

I beat the co grass seeking my game and had gathered up the
first bird and was moving ahead where I had marked down the
second when I came face to face with a dog. Not a fox, nor a
jackal, nor a wolf. A dog. He looked surprisingly like the dingo.
His ears were as round as those of a hyena and quite as upstand-
ing. He had neatly pocketed my pigeon, the feathers hanging out
of either corner of his mouth. Backing a full step he whirled and
ran. The tail carried like a coyote was bushy and the body only
a little more hefty than that of a Springer. His hair was short
and exceedingly coarse. I watched the audacious little poacher
dash from the secure cover of the dense co and angle directly
across the road, a move tactically as stupid as a Nasser. But he
was safe from my charge of 7s-and-a-half, for I am too fond of
canines to shoot even a specimen as interesting as a true wild dog.

Later along the same stretch of abandoned hard-top, I marked
a bird down and was certain from the way it folded up that it

was dead in midair. I beat the dripping grass and was just in time to see a python, a runty little fellow maybe 10 feet from stubby snout to blunted tail, slithering off my game all but disappeared in the great splayed mouth. It was evident to me that my gunning had an audience that was not always composed entirely of the hapless pigeon.

While the dove may possibly be non-migratory, we have a snipe, a Wilson's if I've ever seen one, and he most certainly is a traveling man. With the coming of mid-October snipe appear in practically every marshland.

We were shooting them one day, Ngo Van Chi and I, and with us we had a Moi hillman, Ken, who acted as our retriever. We had threshed out a low ground and were traversing a bracken of jungle intent on gaining a second marshland. We had gotten into a dense stand of Dao and vine and were making heavy going of it. I had been halted by the octopus-like tentacles of the "wait-a-bit" vine and was slowly backing up, the only effective method for breaking the grip of this jungle nuisance, when I caught the lightest of movement out of the tail of my eye. Hardly had I swung about when a great bird, with all the shrill complaint of a Dakota ringneck, took to the air, threshing a veritable storm of leaves from the branches as he bored through. In a thrice he had placed a tree between us while I gaped in astonishment. And admiration. That bird had fully a 5-foot tail and it streamed out behind him, presenting such a picture of winged beauty as I shall not soon forget.

It was a peacock. A great old rooster. Regal in full plumage. He had raised within a dozen feet and I could have shot him twice over had I not been so stunned. I was glad afterward that I had

Indo-Chinese jungle fowl and doves.

The greatest hunter, in the opinion of the author, this side of the Chinese Wall, Ngo Van Chi of Dalat, Viet Nam.

been shocked to inaction. Peacock I shot after that, many of them, but the memory of that first great, gaudy cock will ever remain the most vivid.

Snipe, I learned quickly, were found where little mounds of earthen balls the size of marbles dotted the marshland. These infinitesimal hillocks were cast up by a great worm, a member, truely, of the angleworm tribe but running magnificently to thyroid. The probing beak of Jack the Snipe bored deeply into these mounds and he feasted greedily on these succulent tidbits.

"Ten-lo 'clock gu'd times shoots s-s-nipes," Chi offered. "S-s-nipes hungly then. But mus' hunts with sun at black. S-s-nipes have veely blig eye, when sun shines in eye no can see hunter veely gu'd." So we hung old Sol over our left shoulders and waded into such myriads of the uplands game as I'd never seen before. At times we had Ken, our G-string retriever, seeking as many as five of the grassed long-bills at one and the same moment.

Coursing the marsh, the water of such a depth as to barely trickle over shoe tops, we skirted a herd of forty buffalo. The great beasts lifted their heads and regarded us with a menacing curiosity. The wind, fortunately, was in our favor; had the reverse been true, we'd have been foolhardy to have trod out so blithely. In a land which harbors such fauna as tiger, elephant and gaur, the buf is regarded by all veteran hunters as the more dangerous of the four.

We continued our sweep, working to the solid wall of jungle

The live feathers from the royal peacock. The shotgun is the new Browning Double Auto.

a full kilometer toward the west. Then we angled back, crowding the tangle of vine and fern, and this time approached our game from a different quarter, careful, as before, to work out of the sun like the old Luftwaffe of World War II. In 50 minutes we collected forty of the zig-zagging aerialists.

Returning to the jeep, I swept the hunting grounds with a warm and appreciative eye. Surely, I told myself, this cannot be central Indo-China. The scene might well have been laid in the Tidelands of Virginia, or the marsh country of Louisiana, or perhaps plucked from that appealing savanna above Savannah. Might have been except for the reality of the great backswept horns of the buf, who now getting our wind and not liking the malodorous smell of me, the gringo, were edging in to give us a closer look; might have been except a glance at my Asiatic comrade-at-arms persuaded that here was no Virginia planter nor yet a Cajun muskrat trapper.

Pulling back to the jeep we inspected the pug marks of a great cat directly atop our tire marks and all made within the hour. "Leopa'd," Chi barely glanced at the spoor, "Him clum' fin' clipples."

I had packed my favorite Winchester Model 12 when I hied me off to Viet Nam. This Winchester sports a three-hundred-buck engraving job by Aranzabal of the AYA Company, and has an exceptionally handsome Arrizabalaga stocking job, this together with a ventilated Poly and a Simmons rib. The fact that in this case I have pretty much gilded the lily is evident when the truth comes out that I bought the pumpgun in '45 as Government surplus for twenty-six bucks.

Contemplating a year of hard usage in the rains of the tropics, I removed the lovely Spanish stock and replaced it with the original and much-battered wood. Other than that (the engraving on the receiver has been chromed, the barrel chromed by Marker), I did nothing. I proposed to shoot the gun and if it must suffer so be it.

Once arrived in Saigon, along came a honey of a second smooth-bore, the brand new Browning "Twentyweight," the 12 with the weight of a 20, a shade over six pounds. I have since divided my gunning between this pair. For the little duck shooting I have done I have clung to my sturdy old M12 for that adjustable Poly instantly readies me for the vagaries of the webfeet. For snipe and jungle fowl where the improved cylinder boring and the feathery feel of the Twentyweight are a combination ideal to a degree, I have used it.

From Saigon south to the waters of the Bay of Siam, and from the South China Sea on the one quarter to the unfriendly borders of Cambodia on the other, South Viet Nam is one great rice paddy. During the monsoon it is inundated and the roads fail, and all movement, practically, is by water. Here one would presume there would come a migration of tens of millions of waterfowl. Here is to be found everything an old drake could possibly ask; food, that succulent rice-grain, water as far as the eye spans, cover, protection, and an almost total absence of natural enemies. Here you would believe would be the duck-shooter's Happy Hunting Ground.

In preparation for what I knew was going to be a tremendous concentration of waterfowl, I frantically gathered shotshells and sat back and waited. And waited. And waited. After a solid year I am still waiting—but no longer hopeful.

With everything to offer a wandering goose we have no geese. With a made-to-order mallard paradise there are no canard. True, there are a few thousand ducks 60 minutes below Saigon as I write. But the silly things are non-migratory. They don't *sabe* about this business of winging up to Red China for a few months to take care of this nest-building dodge; and then wing back again when the paddies are flowing with rice and food is for the gobbling. Nope, they just stick around year-long. It has been one of the greatest disappointments in a land which has dished up few frustrations gunning-wise.

We have that gaudy progenitor of all barnyard fowl, the jungle cock. He is of a size to be twin to his domestic bantam counterpart. As for color, he outrivals Cinemascope and he flies with a wing-

Ducks in Vietnamese rice paddy.

beat that puts to shame the rangiest Dakota pheasant. And he is as forever alert as a Nike search-radar. His mate is a drab, shy little chick in no wise as handsome as her lord but first-water gunning target for all that.

Like the dove, the jungle chickens are much given to searching for gravel along the surfaced roads and it is everyday humdrum to count fifty during a jeep jaunt of 25 kilometers.

Sitting over a tiger bait the other morning, my *mirador* (blind) on the ground and some 20 steps removed from the malodorous remains of two maggot-riddled elephants, I was entertained by a lusty pipsqueak of a rooster whose plumage catching and turning the first rays of the probing sun put to shame the most pristine hues of the rainbow. He marshalled a little harem of five or six skittish biddies.

The harem, I noted, like that of Ibn Saud, was composed of some old dowagers who like old hens the world over clacked disapprovingly as they went about the business of getting breakfast; and then there were a few young chicks. These latter were much given to flitting their tails saucily under the Old Boy's beak, and seemingly were obsessed with the notion that the largest and most succulent leeches were to be found in the blackest shadows hard on the flanks of the tiny clearing. Papa with many scoldings and cluckings explained that a leopard might even then be lurking in these murky patches.

Three times he shooed one doll back and it was obvious he was fast draining dry of patience. Minutes later she strayed again.

Dropping his wings, ruffling his feathers and extending his neck, the Head of the House overhauled this mincing bit of fluff before she had gotten well under way. He caught her by the topknot with a dexterity born of long practice and then as they say in the Victorian novel "he had his way with her."

This union seemingly had a most salubrious effect. The little biddy shook herself, settled her feathers, and clucking a happy little refrain trotted over and joined the old hens. Soon she was scratching as contentedly as any unfrustrated chick you'd ever want to see.

I was shooting jungle cock on the Plei Ku Plateau. This table-land, some dozen kilometers north of the village by that name, is a country that had me pinching myself to be sure I was indeed in Indo-China and not in fact back again near Raymondville and gunning over those vast acres that are a part of the mighty Kleburg enclave, the King Ranch. The plateau where I tramped might well have been lifted from the very center of that famous Texas cow pasture. Here was a dense but not too dense stand of brush, a bush most surely first cousin to the Texas chaparrel. Here was a flatness and broadness that blotted out all comforting land-marks and unless the hunter was equipped with some manner of built-in radar soon had him floundering, neither recognizing North nor that other direction 180 degrees opposed.

Here was the same short but luxuriant stand of what appeared to be Grama grass. And on occasion you rounded a clump of brush and found yourself looking right down the throat of the huge and only partly domesticated Asian buffalo. On the King it is the same. There you come face to face with the Santa Gertrudis, a breed originated by the Kelburg dynasty. Partly Brahma, the high-humped Ganges bovine notable for a temper, and an admixture of Black Angus with maybe just a dash of Texas longhorn, he looks only slightly less poisonous than the great black buf of Plei Ku.

Snipe shooting near Djiring, Viet Nam. The natives are Polynesian eth-nically, are called Moi.

The chickens were there in quantity and I gunned them through a blissful afternoon and until late evening when with much scurrying they executed one last concerted assault on the weed grain and the big-as-your-thumb hairy caterpillars.

Now it was late. In minutes my game would be gone, flown to roost after the habit of the jungle cock to rise and fly for hundreds of meters before settling for the night in some likely tree.

I had moved perhaps a short kilometer since dropping a single old cock, and my gun stilled, and walking soundless in the Bird-shooters, I edged around a clump intent on poking into a little clearing that I could see through the limbs. This would be my last whack at the fowl, for the shadows were long and the sun had sometime since dropped below the tallest of the chaparrel.

I Injuned around the last bit of foliage, and gun at the ready, swept the clearing. There wasn't a jungle cock in sight—and for good reason. There precisely in the middle of the two-by-four opening was the biggest damned tiger I have ever seen!

He stood four feet at the shoulders and to the top of his head was at least another 16 inches. He was as long as a Lincoln Continental and his stripes shone and glistened as though he'd just had the works down at the corner barber shop.

We were maybe five paces apart. So close I could look him in the eye and I noted I did not have to glance down to do that. He never once blinked those glittering yellow orbs and they were locked on me like a fix-radar. He just stood and surveyed me and I stood and wondered if a load out of the Browning would get there in time to blind him. Five paces is awfully close. The gun was stuffed with No. 7s-and-a-half backed by a peewee charge of 2¾ drams of propellant, a loading Harold Russell pushes quite strongly for trapshooting but has never advocated for tiger killing. While quite keen at the moment as to what Old Stripes' intentions might be, it ran through my head that if I survived this jolly encounter I'd just dash off a hasty memo to Val Browning suggesting he might give some thought to adding another round to his two-shot auto-loader.

It seemed like a long time that the old Bengal and I looked at each other. In retrospect, I have decided that it probably wasn't more than a half-dozen seconds. It seemed at the time considerably longer than that. Finally the great cat turned his head, a bit disdainfully I thought, and without a backward glance and as much as to say, "Just another one of those puny humans. No danger there," he stalked into the bush.

Chapter 28
ANALYSIS OF THE HUNTING ACCIDENT

FIGURES SHOW THAT the most lethal man in the field today is a boy under 29, of some 600 accidents caused last year, half were attributable to young shooters. This fall it is reliably predicted that we will field an additional three-quarter-million of new sportsmen. From what ranks will the most of them come? Why from those youngsters redhot to be shooting men.

Statistics go on to indicate that the older a gent becomes the more cautiously he handles that shooting iron. He has learned with what healthy respect he must accord that ounce and one quarter of No. 6s. Of the 600 casualties, those oldsters 40 and beyond accounted for but 144 of the accidents; of these 33 were chalked up to men 60 and beyond. The longer you handle a gun the more safety-conscious you become, obviously.

If some jerk loads up his bus on Saturday night with four other gentry of like caliber and they all proceed to get highly incandescent down at Duffy's Tavern and then along in the shank of the eve they pour the auto into a 35-mile-per-hour turn while doing an easy 85 and all wind up as fit subjects for the last sad rites, it earns one quick piece in the morning *Times*. But just let two of these same class go for woodcock in the fall and one dose the other with a 12-gauge treatment of some 444 little 7½ pellets, and it is good for not only the local news sheets but the AP, the UP and every TV show in town. The same class of citizen who foisted Prohibition on the country is just as busy trying to toss all our shooting irons down the drain. Every hunting-casualty report is seized on as eagerly as finding a four-leaf clover. Arthur Brisbane, a leading Hearst columnist of two decades ago, was a howling advocate for the eliminating of all sporting firearms. He also recommended that all dogs have their teeth pulled so they would not bite people.

A careful analysis reveals a lot of most interesting data about those Joes who shoot other people, and themselves. We jump to the hasty conclusion that probably hunting deer in Michigan, Pennsylvania, or New York is fraught with more peril than tampering with the other man's frau, but this ain't so. The most dangerous

game in the hunting fields today is the lowly cottontail. More
gunners get their hip pockets filled with searing sixes while
pursuing the ubiquitous rabbit than any other of our fauna. Next
in line, believe it or not, is the pheasant. Old John Chinaman, as
big as a B36 and just about as fast moving, pursued by only a
relatively small percentage of our shotgunning gentry, accounts

Of 600 accidents involving firearms last year, oldsters 60 and beyond accounted for but 33. The oldtimer is a cautious man with a gun.

for a lot of folks peppering each other. The deer ranks third, with
151 casualties, as against 227 for the rabbit and 167 for the ring-
neck.

Of a little more than eleven hundred accidents which were
studied all resulting in some one getting ventilated, 775 occurred
when the visibility was good. During murky weather when
visibility was poor, but 16 accidents were recorded. In this same
connection of 796 hunters who were killed or wounded, a whop-
ping five hundred were pinked in the open fields or brush. Wildfowlers got an almost clean bill of health in this study, but 38
turning up.

Of those people who were shot by someone else, generally a
shooting partner, it is suspected, the victim more often than not
was unseen by the gunner. This does not intend to say that the
poor soul was mistaken for a Virginia whitetail, but means that
the covey broke and swung 'round the bush and our Hero followed them and poured his two cartridges where he thought

they had disappeared—which happened to be right where his buddy was standing.

Let it not go unexplained, however, that people, despite red coats, red hats, and red eyeballs, still stop their share of 30-'06 bullets; of 591 eligible for the hunting field Purple Heart, 103 were mistaken for game. Fatalities from this 591 ran 122. The high-

Statistics indicate the most dangerous game to hunt today is the lowly cottontail rabbit. More people pink themselves and one another while hunting rabbits than any other game. This safety photo posed by Dot Lind.

powered rifle with an expanding sporting-type bullet is a messy thing; considering all accidents caused by rifled arms, a round 25% resulted in death. The scattergun was not quite so lethal. Despite the awesome proportions of a charge of birdshot at distances below 10 yards, but 14% got into the obituary column.

The crew who compiled the hunting accident data thoughtfully came up with the distances from muzzle to wound. By far the most with the rifle were from zero yardage out to only 10; the shotgun showed a major percentage shot at the same point-blank range. Of a grand total of 309 casualties attributable to the rifle, only 36 fell between 50 and 100 yards; 41 at 100 yards and beyond. By the fact that most accidents are right at the muzzle I am inclined to believe that a lot of sportsmen shoot themselves.

Oddly a total of 14 woundings occurring with the shotgun (out of 627) were at distances beyond 100 yards. Now No. 2s and 4s will reach beyond a hundred steps and do some damage, but can it be these 14 accidents are accountable to buckshot and pumpkin ball?

We have always made much of the hunter who cripples himself while negotiating the farmer's fence. Reams have been written about how to climb a fence, detailed studies showing with diagram and photographs where each foot is placed, and how the piece of clothes line is tied about the stock of the gun and it is dragged beneath the lowest strands of the barbed wire. Figures indicate that only slightly over 6/10th of 1 percent of game field accidents happen when crossing fences.

The hombre who says he has never had an accident with a firearm is either an advocate of the longbow, a complete stranger to the powder burner, or one of the greatest liars unhung. Anyone who has even a nodding acquaintance with guns will have accidents with them. Fortunately more than ninety-nine times out of a hundred these accidental discharges do nothing more harmful than shake the aplomb of the gunner. Cold analysis almost invariably indicates that he had gotten careless. A ceaseless vigilance is the price we must pay if we are going to improve our safety record. You find too a species of jerk who gains superficial knowledge of his newly acquired prize and finally comes to look upon it as something of a toy. Like a new set of golf clubs, a Lincoln Continental, or a blonde in ermine. A gun is no toy, neither is it a friend; it is like nothing so much as a coiled and deadly rattler ready to strike the instant you get careless and let your guard down. Shooting irons are an abiding passion with me but I never get footsy with them. It's too dangerous.

Here of late we have been attracting almost a million new marksmen yearly to the ranks of our sportsman clan. The end is not yet in sight. This upsurge in hunting interest commenced directly after World War II, the impetus the military training provided accounting for the new blood. Countless numbers of these young sportsmen are not properly schooled in gun handling. Nor will they ever be. The shortened hunting season, the press of modern existence, countless other sports, and many more things preclude the new hunter's ever really learning his weapon. Our National shooting orders, the NSSA, the NRA, and others catch a minor percentage of these newcomers, but regretfully, far too many are only casually interested. Their interest only extends to the purchase of a hunting license (thereby being counted) plus one or two forays afield during the year. This vast majority are the unfortunates who wind up in the casualty column more often than not.

They are the gents who do old-line sportsmen inestimable harm as well. For every wounding during the duck-buck-and-pheasant season is ammunition for a certain breed of reformer who would emasculate us all; would leave us with our pants just as broadly at halfmast as were the English after Dunkirk. Sometimes I wonder if the campaign to register all our firearms, decry every hunting accident, make ammunition of every robbery and killing involving firearms isn't a part of the Communist master plan to reduce us to the impotency which they so earnestly seek.

Chapter 29

IF YOU CAN'T SEE IT YOU CAN'T HIT IT

SKEET SINCE ITS BEGINNING has been a game notable for youthfulness of its devotees. But that doesn't mean that everyone who toes the line has yet to cast his first vote. A whale of a lot of gunners were around when Henry Ford said the buying public could have any color of his auto they wanted as long as it was black. This opus is directed toward that vintage of shooting man, and most particularly it is concerned with his ability to see. Can you tell a house from a horse? Had your bloodshot old peepers in the shop lately? Or are you one of the clan that just get an arm-stretching instead of bifocals? And what do you know about getting a proper fit in shooting glasses, anyway?

There are three species of eye doctors; the opticians, optometrists, and oculists, or as they sometimes prefer, ophthalmologists. Each of these buckos has a legitimate place in the scheme of things, but each is a specialist and it pays to know something of the medical background of all three. The optometrist examines eyes, he has a degree in optometry. He specializes in refraction examinations and is licensed by the State just like a medical doctor; he can fit you with spectacles quite satisfactorily and is highly skilled.

The optician grinds lenses and assembles glasses, he is a technician in the sense that he can accept a lense prescription from an optometrist or an oculist and come up with a pair of specs that are perfectly okay. An optician is not qualified to do refraction examinations but many fit glasses by a sort of trial and error method wherein he utilizes a large tray of sample lenses, running through the supply until the patient informs him he can see the chart clearly.

Probably the best qualified of the eye doctors is the oculist. He is a doctor of medicine who has specialized on the eye. He can, of course, perform eye surgery and he is especially well qualified on diseases of the eye. Shooters with especially difficult problems in getting a satisfactory sight-and-target picture should not despair until they have given the oculist an opportunity. He is the eye specialist par excellence.

While it doesn't too much effect distant vision, the eye trouble

240

common to a great many shooters is presbyopia, or "old sight." This is a condition that hits practically everyone after 40 and is simply a condition whereby the eye lense loses its elasticity and its ability to promptly focus on near objects. The oldster cannot read the menu at a normal range anymore and he holds it at arm's length, giving rise to the remark, "I could still read the newspaper all right until my arm got too short." Presbyopia isn't too serious with wing shots since the end of the gun barrel is generally sharp enough and the target equally so. Riflemen and handgunners are not so fortunate for they must see a rear sight that is usually pretty fuzzy.

Nearsightedness is far more serious and calls for a careful fitting of shooting glasses that will call for the painstaking efforts of a qualified specialist. There is no particular difficulty in refracting for a nearsighted person. Concave lenses of proper strength will accomplish wonders in clearing up the target. Astigmatism, regardless of how minor, must be corrected. As little as one-quarter diopter of astigmatic error must be compensated. It is not easy to detect errors this small but it is essential that they be found.

The shotgunner has a peculiar problem, unlike either the rifle or pistol marksman, in that his target is constantly moving. Sometimes it starts very close and rapidly moved away from him; at other times quite the opposite is true. The target first appears at a distance and approaches him at great speed. The marksman who fires rifle or handgun encounters few of these headaches; his target, more times than not, is stationary and he has plenty of time to focus his eyes on it. Good though our eye specialists may be they are compelled to make compromises, and we must accept them. The spectacle hasn't yet been developed that can focus near and far objects with equal sharpness. In any choice between the two the shotgunner should elect to gain greatest sharpness at a distance. If the sighting rib is a bit on the hazy side, the front sight very slightly blurred, but the target bright and clear, he'll get along.

How about colored lenses? Most skeet shooters wear some kind of shooting glasses and a great many use those with color added. So-called sun glasses are popular and not all of them are worn by the movie stars whipping down to Malibu Beach. These glasses have color added, and besides being widely accepted by many people who must be out in the sun are frequently utilized by our gunners. A startling number of these specs aren't made of optical glass at all, are not properly ground, and introduce some serious refractory errors.

Before we get into a discussion of tinted lenses, suppose we take a hasty look at this business of color physics. Light is made up of radiant waves of energy of varying length. The wave length pretty

The yellow lens shooting spectacles improve definition under poor conditions of light.

accurately pegs down the position of light of different colors in the spectrum. Ultraviolet is an ultrashort wave length in the spectrum, and wave lengths range through violet, blue, green, yellow, orange and red. The eye sees best yellow and green which range through the central portions of the spectrum; conversely the eye has the most difficulty with the violet and red which are on the flanks.

The eye, unfortunately, constitutes a single-lens optical system. It is not achromatic. The violet and blue waves come to a shorter focus in the retina in front of the green and yellow which in turn are in front of the orange and red. The green and yellow come to the sharpest focus on the retina. The ultraviolet rays focus in front of the green and yellow and cause 75% of the chromatic aberration of the eye and hence are responsible for blurred vision and halo effect. By eliminating these rays with a suitable lens visual acuity can be increased markedly.

The visual sensitivity curve of the eye is an attempt by nature to correct the chromatic aberration by selecting for vision those rays that cause the least aberration, namely the yellow and green portions of the visible spectrum.

Tinted lenses when they are properly chosen are a most worthwhile aid to improving visual acuity, protecting the eyes, and adding to the comfort of the wearer generally. Colored lenses for general outdoors wear are usually worn to protect the eyes from ultraviolet and infrared rays. Excessive ultraviolet radiation is definitely harmful; infrared are heat rays and are equally harmful; in any case both are of no aid to vision. A proper tinted lens will exclude these radiations.

For general outdoors wear undoubtedly the most popular color is the blue-green. These lenses are made by all our leading makers of sportsman glasses; Mitchell, B&L, American Optical, and others. These lenses very definitely reduce visible light for comfort and all of the better ones from such companies as those enumerated above are characterized by an almost total opacity in the ultraviolet and infrared. Shade densities are standardized by the use of the letters A, B, C, and D, or by the numbers 1, 2, 3, and 4. Either system indicates transmittances of about 75, 50, 25 and 10%.

During the heat of summer when hot, irritating, uncomfortable and even painful scenes beat upon the unprotected eye, the new blue-green lense will transform the view to one of cool and bearable pleasantness. The ultraviolet and infrared are barred, glare is reduced by limiting the amount of light that is permitted to

Major Charles Askins with a bag of desert quail.

reach the eye, and visual acuity actually increased. If the shooter needs a corrective lens this should be incorporated in the tinted lense.

When shooting outdoors in good light, and by "good light" we mean in bright sunlight with no cloudy overcast, the new blue-green lenses are best. About a shade D (or 3) seems to be correct for most individuals, weaker shades do not seem to reduce the glare enough.

For hunting in deep woods, for use during the very early morning hours, or just before dusk in the evening, for any manner of overcast or cloudy condition, the yellow lens is best. This very remarkable lens will change a dark, dull day—or a dark and obscure target—to a brilliant, beautifully sharp and clear one. Almost regardless of the kind of hunting or shooting, the yellow lens is a help. A yellow lens transmits 90% of light as compared to 75% for the best of the blue-green shades.

There is only one word of caution about the yellow lens; because of its light transmitting qualities it definitely is not for wear as a sun glass. It will not protect, it passes and even seems to intensify the rays of Old Sol!

I wear the Mitchell Yellow Lens shooting glasses. I have used them for the past year in Indo-China where the rain forest and other jungle conditions of murky half-light have proven the value of this color tint.

Yellow lenses for shooting specs are made, as I have just commented, by the Mitchell Shooting Glasses Co.; by Bausch and Lomb; the American Optical Co.; and probably others.

A set of shooting specs made up with the yellow lenses and containing the gunner's prescription carefully arrived at by a qualified oculist will not only account for more crushed targets but will give him a deal of satisfaction in the game fields.

We are all fond of saying that we abuse our eyes, most of us actually think we do over-use the old orbs. Careful checks have been run that indicate that after a full eight hours of steady use-age at close work the eyesight suffers only about 2 to 3% loss of visual acuity. There may be some additional nervous and muscular tension; but as for the eyes failing, they seem to stand up very well.

When the TV hit the American scene there were many doleful complaints that over-indulgence, especially among the younger fry, would have us all in specs at a tender age. Subsequent wide acceptance of television doesn't seem to have harmed the American point of view. On the contrary, many oldsters have discovered as a result of watching TV that instead of the screen doing harm to their eyesight it actually pointed up the need for corrective glasses.

Some shooters believe they should abstain from all TV shows and movies, and some actually refuse to read the morning paper before and during shooting tourneys. This is pretty much hocum. Undoubtedly over-indulgence in television, the movies, or reading during a shootfest would be apt to be harmful, but a normal routine is far the more sane course. What is more important is to be sure that your working conditions are visually adequate, that the light you read by each evening is ample, and that your home is properly and sufficiently lighted.

For prolonged reading such as newsprint, bookkeeping, fine type, etc. a minimum of 50 to 100 ft. candles is needed. For ordinary prolonged reading of ordinary type, such as this, 20 to 50 ft. candles is required. Do not read in a darkened room with only one light source over your chair or bed; by the same token don't work over a bench with the same arrangement. People with uncorrected refractive errors sometimes attempt to compensate for these errors by using a stronger light. If you find that you demand a stronger light than fellows around you, then immediately be suspicious of your eyes. A refractive error or even one-half diopter requires twice the amount of light to overcome this deficiency in vision.

Chapter 30

TAKING A PEEK AT THE CRYSTAL BALL

IT IS INTERESTING to speculate where our shotguns are headed. Since 1948 all our leading manufacturers, with the exception of Savage, have produced new automatic shotguns. Remington got the jump on the pack with the 11-48 model. This self-shuffle job shed a sizeable amount of undesirable weight and provided us with a receiver that had all the handsome lines of the pump gun. The 11-48—the numbers are a combination of the year 1948 and the model number of the original Remington—has been a popular addition.

After the Remington we had a tolerable sit before anything new in the self-operating category showed over the horizon. However, 1955 produced a pair.

These were the Browning Double Automatic and the Winchester Model 50. Both were startlingly new.

The Browning for the first time utilized short recoil operation. The Winchester is also built around short recoil. A most novel system functions the Model 50.

It has remained for the High Standard Manufacturing Co., a sort of shirt-tail relative of the Sears, Roebuck Co., to birth the most revolutionary of the new crop of automatics. This is a gas-operated shotgun. Now Remingtons have a second, the Model 58.

It may be appreciated that the past eight years have seen more developmental work on the automatic than at any time during the twentieth century.

New developments in the pump-gun field, on the other hand, have been about as lively as the last convention of the Grand Army of the Republic. Winchester continues with the Model 12, a shotgun engineered 46 years ago and virtually unchanged since. Remington have their comparatively new Model 870 pump, first of the rapidly expanding Remington "family of firearms"—an after-World-War-II number—a sweet piece and packing an appealing price tag. Sears, under the J. C. Higgins by-line, sell a sturdy if too heavy repeater, the Model 20. Ithaca peddles a pump gun, the Model 37, and so popular is the weapon that they make nothing else.

Police guns. The muzzle wrappings are for use at night and improve the aim.

There is a pump repeater from Savage-Stevens, the first known as the Model 77. The line is completed by the inclusion of the Nobel Model 40.

In any consideration of future improvements among shotguns, we cannot rule out a trombone. Certainly nothing new has been forthcoming for many a long year. However, the manufacturers sell more pump guns than any other model. There will be nothing new as long as sales maintain a satisfactory level, and certainly the slide action gives little cause for complaint. It isn't that the antiquated old pump action couldn't stand a good face lifting. There hasn't been anything really new in trombone models since Teddy Roosevelt charged San Juan Hill.

The pump repeater has a receiver that is too long. Should either of the leading arms manufacturers today want to design a really modern shotgun of this type they could provide us with an action

considerably shorter and of less depth. Magazines are far too long
and by the same token too heavy. Federal law and most state laws
limit the magazine to a capacity of only two cartridges. There is
no good sense of a tube to hold four rounds when you cannot stuff
that many in it. The throw or travel of the slide is a holdover
from the kerosene-lamp-and-button-shoe era; there's no good reason
it cannot be engineered to move only half its present distance.

Watch the pumpgun, it may well be next for a modernization
treatment.

A shotgun that appeals to the discriminating is the conventional
side-by-side double. This smoothbore has almost disappeared.
Winchester offers the superb Model 21 for a trifling three hundred
and fifty bucks, which puts it out of the reach of everyone save a
Texas oil tycoon's playboy son. Beyond that the offering is scant
indeed. And there's the Fox Model B-ST which recently has been
improved by the inclusion of a non-selective single trigger, but
still has no ejectors.

A bright spot is the Sears Model 100, which not only provides a
single trigger but is graced by selective ejectors as well. This
number sells for $130.

The makers cry that they cannot build a double-barreled shotgun with single trigger and ejectors, and do it cheaply. The single
trigger doesn't seem to kite the price as much as the selective
ejector system. I refuse to accept the contention that ejectors cannot be designed that would be entirely reliable and yet not boost
the price. The trouble lies in the lack of research and developmental

Test-firing one of the new crop of auto-loading shotguns.

Better balanced and faster handling than the repeating shotgun, the double-barrel models—here shown is the $1,000 Ithaca, now discontinued—do not compare in popularity to the magazine-type smoothbores.

effort. We are still using ejectors that were around when Sitting Bull lifted Custer's blond locks. Our systems were developed by the English before the turn of the century and remain basically unaltered to this day.

The conventional double gun would be once again a popular model should the manufacturers decide to center attention on its improvement. People like Savage-Fox and Marlin have shown us that a satisfactory single trigger can be designed and not boost the price. But one remaining improvement need be realized, the automatic ejector, with an attendant moderate sales tag.

If our crystal-ball gazing is going to give any weight to the almost utter lack of attention to the side-by-side these many past decades, then very possibly our next new shotgun can be a modernized version of the best of 'em all.

Directly after World War II one of our biggest manufacturers of shotgun shells decided he'd get five more yards out of his 20-gauge gun, so he just tacked another quarter of an inch on the case. This gave him quite a bit more space into which he had his people cram some more powder and an additional $\frac{3}{16}$ ounce of shot. The resulting load measured up to the skeet 12 cartridge. This super magnum 20 was kept under wraps for years; it had been made for a man who was a remarkable wingshot, and at first it was used exclusively by him. But it was too good to keep and now the magnum 3-inch 20 is common property.

The Roman Candle 20 set off a spiral, a trend which hasn't yet seen an ending!

A little more than a year ago all the ammunition boys came along with super magnum loads. The 20 was stepped up to hurl as much lead as the 12; the 16 equalled the express 12; and the 12 was so increased in oomph it set the old 10 completely in the shade. All this was done without increasing the length of any case. Case lengths in every instance remained at the standard 2¾ inches.

The fine engineering served to set a number of loads in an obsolescent state if not completely retire 'em. The 20-gauge 3-inch number, forerunner of the super magnums, found its performance

equalled by the 20 in standard case; the 12-gauge 3-inch, for years
available in loading of 1⅜ and 1⅝ ounces of lead, was outdistanced
by the standard magnum, which now holds a full one-and-one-half
ounces of shot.

Likewise, the introduction of the super magnum 10 shotguns by
concerns like Clark, Continental Arms, and Silver & Co., weapons
that handled the 10-gauge 3½-inch shell, a delicate little number
crammed with 5 drams equivalent of powder and 2 full ounces
of shot, killed the old standard 10 gauge deader than Cock Robin.

Now the 3½-inch magnum 10 is mightily threatened. Now ap-
pearing is a 12-gauge cartridge that will belch out a walloping
load of 1⅝ ounces of No. 4s!

Where is this rash of A-bomb loads to end?

That's the 64-thousand-buck question. Like the proposition of
crowding more HP under every new auto hood. One manufacturer
gets the jump on the others and manages to tamp an eighth of
an ounce more pellets into a given cartridge, and there's nothing
for it but the others must follow suit. Right now the door is
wide open, and as for myself I like it! There are more new loads
in the hopper, of that you may be sure.

Whether it is realized or not there isn't anything new about
shotguns. The squawgun is about as new as the politician's promise.
Until Val Browning came along with his short-recoil automatic,
closely followed by the Winchester with its separate chamber, we
hadn't seen anything really revolutionary in scatterguns since Fred
Kimble stumbled onto the choke bore three-quarters of a century
back. So to see some new shotgun cartridges—and with the promise
of more to come—is glamor news indeed!

What are the implications of these new hulls? To begin with,
all are wild-fowling loads, the medicine for the webfeet. Secondly,
but not nearly so importantly, all are great medicine for wildly
rising ringnecks; for jackrabbit shooting in the West; for turkey
and fox. But primarily these busters are going to be loosened at
duck and goose.

Are ducks plentiful enough to persuade that instead of using
a standard (old standard, that is) 12-gauge 1¼-ounce load of shot,
a fellow should invest in some of the super magnum 1½-ounce
atomic paralyzers? The average bag over the country is four ducks
and two geese, pretty conclusive indication that the ultra heavy
load isn't needed. A duck hit with one-and-one-half ounces of load
is over-killed.

But the proposition has another side which has a whale of a
lot of merit. It is true that bag limits are low and that a good
wingshot may drag his entire daily bag out of the first flight that
passes, but generally he does not. As a matter of fact the average

shotgunner today is a mighty ordinary marksman. He does relatively little hunting, he is far too busy in this highly competitive world making a living to shoot much. A Spanish marksman casually mentioned to me one day between Chukar drives that he never got into good shooting form until he had fired five or six thousand shots in a season. The run-of-the-mill American sportsman won't burn up a case of shotshells in the game field per season. As a result he is a spotty, sometimes terrific, more often decidedly mediocre hitter. The new family of super loads provides an edge which compensates in some part for his lack of skill.

The new magnum doesn't increase the range of the shot pattern any but it certainly does sweeten it up! A count on some twenty-five thousand ducks and many thousands of geese by the Fish and Wildlife Service indicated that one duck in every five and half of all geese placed under a fluoroscope were carrying shot pellets. Very evidently a thicker pattern, consisting of pellets driven at higher velocity, would have brought many of these fliers to bag. The new loads will, in my opinion, very materially reduce losses of cripples. More birds will be killed cleanly in the air and as a result more will be found.

Despite the fact that the super magnum fodder spews out more lead, and velocities are very slightly increased, the increased range isn't anything to beat the drums about. This isn't too well understood as yet. It is a pity because there has always been an idiot fringe with us who want to kill ducks at 70-80 yards. These boys are experimenting with the Big Bertha hulls in the belief that they are going to bring 'em to bag 'way out to hell an' gone. These are the goons who do their little-boy best to fill one duck in every five and half the geese checked by the F & WL Service with out-of-range lead. The super magnum cartridge is a more lethal killer but it kills at reasonable ranges through delivering more weight of lead at the target.

Chapter 31

PLAYING THE GAME

PATIENT WAITING has finally brought us into the best time of the year, the hunting season. A shooting time peculiar for bag limits that are samplings, seasons that are abbreviated and a rising army of game questers. The circumstance of these factors coupled with the press of modern business usually sees the average sportsman get into the field no more than a half-dozen times during the season. When he finally does win free he has the feeling that the hunt has simply got to be productive; a good killing round is going to see him return at end of day satisfied he can still hit, and besides it is going to impress his shooting mates.

In line with these sentiments Lansing A. Parker of the Fish and Wildlife Service wrote a simple little piece almost 10 years ago entitled, "What is Par for a Day's Hunting?" that so neatly sums up proper hunting psychology that I think it should be published in every shooting magazine in the country. This story first appeared in the Minnesota Game Department monthly bulletin and was later picked up and saw light in the *Pacific Northwest Sportsman*. Lansing has put together the fundamental causes for our shrinking game; and while indicating the reasons our wild things are on the decline, he holds forth a cure:

"How was duck shooting today, Jim?"

"Not so hot. I got only half a limit and was out until noon. How did you do on the ringnecks?"

"Great! We brought home the limit after only a couple of hours hunting."

Have you heard reasonable facsimiles of these conversations? Of course you have, and chances are good that you have made similar statement yourself as a hunter.

What is the significance of the reference to limits? Why is it that so often the success of a hunting trip is measured by the number of daily bag limits taken? What makes it so necessary to assume a par score like a golfer does in order to evaluate a day's hunting? Why is there so much personal satisfaction about the limit of game?

252

Marauding coyote killed by the author with duck loads. Near Obregon, Sonora.

I believe the answer to the above questions lies in the cornerstone of American democratic free enterprise, which has developed a keen desire for competition amongst all of us. No people in the world are gifted with as much competitive spirit as the Americans. If a man cannot compete against his friends and acquaintances he will compete against himself. Witnesses to that fact are the popularity of golf and bowling.

Jungle fowl shot in the coffee near Ban Me Thuot, Viet Nam, Indo-China.

What is the effect of this trait as applied to hunting? At one time in this country man was obliged to hunt wild game to supply meat for his table. The pioneer who always had a quarter of venison or several brace of partridge hanging in the smokehouse no doubt was regarded as a good hunter. He was a man of standing in the settlement, for his larder was always well stocked. It implied he was able to outsmart the game, stalk it more cunningly, and then make his shot more effective.

Pulling in a high-flying squadron of crows.

In later years it has no longer been necessary to hunt wild game to provide for the table. Game became scarce due to the advance of civilization upon wildlife habitat and man's myriad ways of directly or indirectly reducing the numbers of wildlife. As a result bag limits were adopted as a conservation measure to help, in part, perpetuate the sport of hunting. Instead of permitting a party to kill a wagonload of prairie chickens or a boatload of ducks, conservationists recognized that the annual increase must be spread out for every one of the rapidly increasing number of hunters.

When a hunter was limited to a maximum kill per day, by what means could he gauge his skill and prowess? Quite naturally the bag limit became par at which he was shooting.

The net result of unconsciously recognizing that the killing of a bag limit was the mark of a good hunter has caused sportsmen to overlook the pleasures of a hunting trip simply because the maximum bag take was not attained. The hunter often fails to recognize that hunting today is not a meat-getting expedition or a killing orgy but rather a form of recreation and relaxation. Even should there be a meat shortage with attendant high prices, the average hunter will find that wild meat is extremely expensive when all the attendant costs are totaled against the pounds of edible meat brought home from a hunting trip.

Unfortunately the competitive spirit that prompts hunters to kill the limit often leads to practices which are illegal and unethical.

Roadside hunting for pheasant, doves, quail and rabbits, done by riding the fenders and utilizing pick-up trucks, is a good illustration of violations sometimes employed to fill the limit bag.

Fortunately for the game not all hunters are able to make a limit kill every time they go out. If they did the game population would be wiped out in a very few seasons.

Another angle to the problem of shooting the bag limits is the utilization of the game. Some hunters feel that they are happily satisfied when they have killed the game, but beyond that point cleaning and preparing it for the table is an unwanted job. Generally friends and neighbors enjoy a meal of wild game; and if the sportsman or his family are unwilling to dress and cook it, the people next door will be glad to do so. Every true sportsman recognizes the cardinal law of preventing wanton waste. Yet many hunters shoot the limit without any thought of how they will use the meat. The first rule that all hunters should follow is to limit their kill to what can be conveniently utilized.

What does all this discussion add up to? Simply this:

There is more to a hunting trip than the amount of game a shooter has in his bag at the close of the hunt. The whole trip should be based on relaxation, recreation, exercise, and the opportunity to be out of doors. If you are hunting with a friend, the satisfaction of comradeship and demonstration of fair play is ample reward. If you use a dog, there is untold satisfaction to be derived from watching and directing its performance.

The work of a good dog in itself is worth the time and effort spent on an afternoon's hunt. Then too there's that satisfying tired feeling that comes over you after an all-day hike in the weeds and brush. It's hard to describe but certainly it is different from the tired feeling you get mowing the lawn at the wife's command.

Taken separately or in total these are the things we must learn to enjoy about a hunting trip. The bag regardless of how large is the premium, the extra something thrown in for good measure if we're lucky.

Chapter 32
WING SHOOTING

WE HAVE THOUSANDS of expert shotgun shooters in America, and very little instruction in the art of wing-shooting. Two men are capable of giving instruction, the man who has just learned what he is to teach, and the man who is teaching as a calling. The student who has recently graduated from college makes a good instructor in the branches he has just acquired. Not only is everything still fresh in his mind, but he knows and can analyze every step by which he acquired his knowledge. If he continues to give instruction, as would a college professor, his treatment of the subjects may be staled a bit but will yet be effective. Memory is short, but the mind always remains young, and is forever acquiring new things at the expense of the old. A foundation is laid and on it a building is erected, growing steadily during all the succeeding years. By and by the building is to be seen, but the foundation under it is forgotten even by the man who laid it. Now the building could never have appeared without the foundation under it, and a student of architecture must study the foundation first. The man who has just built that foundation can tell him all about it, to the last stone and how and why it was put in place. Not so the man who hasn't thought of foundations for twenty years. In the same way the expert can show you how he shoots, but he cannot tell you of all the successive steps by which he acquired skill; these having been forgotten long ago.

All this, you understand, is a sort of apology for the shortcomings of this essay on wing-shooting. I have forgotten much that I once knew, and in fact may have forgotten more than I now know. However, if no one else, both willing and able to write, is undertaking the task, then it seems to fall to me. An Englishman wrote a book on wing-shooting. The substance of his advice was: Don't close an eye, don't potter, don't swing, keep the eyes fixed on the mark, throw up the gun and pull trigger as the butt touches the shoulder, and down goes the bird. Just so! But suppose that bird doesn't go down? What is to be done then? I have been game shooting a long time, and the only thing I never could learn was to pull trigger as the butt struck my shoulder and kill the bird.

Neither could the Englishman, but he could remember that he pulled trigger when the butt hit his shoulder, and that is all he could remember connected with the shooting—all contributing factors being forgotten. For example, what happened before the butt hit his shoulder?

I was as good a shot and maybe a better shot twenty years ago than I am now. I wrote my first book on wing-shooting seventeen or eighteen years ago. I could write a good deal more positively on the subject then than I can now. If I have learned anything in this last twenty years, it is to be very tolerant of the views of others who may differ from me. Twenty or thirty years ago, like the skilled duck shots of that day, I'd have said that the shooter couldn't hit ducks unless he swung on them from behind, swung along and passed them, pulling trigger and "carrying through." If any man wrote or told of killing passing birds by tossing his gun up ahead of the mark and pulling trigger without swing, I set him down at once as not a duck shot. In my opinion he'd never learned how to properly take ducks, and did well to kill one bird in three that was well within range. I was a swinging shot, you see, and not tolerant of any other style.

By and by I became curious to know just what could be done by intercepting ducks, not swinging with the passing fowl. For an entire year, when I had a good many opportunities, I did not swing on a bird nor with him, but steadily intercepted, not with a gun that was raised vertically, but one that intercepted at an angle to the flight. At the end of the year I found that I could shoot ducks just about as well one way as the other. The only thing necessary was to stick to one style of aim or the other and not mix up swing with interception, because the lead was a bit different. Then I knew that the man who told of throwing up his

Spanish peasants act as beaters during the partridge season. Here walking in for the midday "break."

gun, raising the piece in front of the mark and firing could do just what he said he could—hit the bird. In fact, though this is not the place to dwell upon it, lead with an intercepting gun is more accurate than lead with a swinging gun, but correct elevations give more trouble.

All of which, with other things eventually led to the conclusion that a man could learn to hit game with any old style he cared

A shotgun is not thoroughly known until it is patterned extensively.

to adopt, if he stuck to it and mastered it. Except the first two or three years, when a boy, I have always shot with both eyes open. I considered this style the only way to do wing-shooting, and any other manner of aiming a rank error. In the course of events, however, some one sent me a shotgun with a Lyman peep sight mounted on the tang. When aiming through the peep I blinked my left eye more or less. I found the peep sight a bit slow but very accurate, and birds could be killed well. This Lyman peep led me to mount a home-made peep on the thumb-piece of the top lever, where it could be raised or dropped down at will. This sight was used on a quail gun, and whenever I found myself making inexplicable misses, I'd raise the peep and aim through it. Misses

The leading Spanish arms-building city—Eibar. There are 62 arms makers.

might still be made, but I always knew exactly why they occurred. During the past season as an experiment, I mounted a telescope sight on a shotgun, and discovered that good wing-shooting could be done through that sight, though it was slower than the peep at times, field being limited.

The gist of all this is that while the tyro had better follow accepted styles of aiming, yet if he doesn't there is no good reason why he shouldn't succeed anyhow. Any of us can learn to shoot with a straight stocked gun or with a gun having a tremendous drop; we can learn to shoot without any sight fore or aft, or we can learn to use two sights; we can learn to pull a ten-pound trigger or a three-pound trigger; we can snap, half-snap, intercept, or swing and still hit the bird—I have no sort of doubt but if a man swung his gun from left to right, while the fowl winged from right to left, he would still learn to hit it in course of time. I have never been able to hit anything shooting from the hip, but some men say that they can, and I do not doubt it, though I have never seen a good hip shooter.

It is common to assert that a marksman must have very keen eyes in order to acquire any sort of skill with shotgun, rifle or pistol. I do not agree with that entirely. All the vision a man needs is to be able to see precisely where the mark is. If he can do that, he can hit the mark even if his vision is not sharp enough to show feather markings. The man with poor vision, though, sure does need to keep both eyes open. Many years ago I shot with a fine old sportsman, Joseph Mest, who lived in St. Louis. He was about fifty-five years old, and his eyes began to fail. He said that he could see the bird well until he got his gun up, closed one eye for the aim, and then he couldn't find the bird. Probably his right eye was a little weaker than the left, but shutting one eye usually has the effect of clouding the other. I tried to teach Uncle Joe to shoot with both eyes open, but couldn't do anything with him as his shooting habits were too strong.

Quail hunters pause to count the bag and compare notes.

There is something peculiar about aiming a shotgun, or else the experience of one man must not be taken as applying to others. Twenty to thirty years ago, when game was more plentiful than it is now, I acquired the knack of shooting without putting cheek to stock or seeing any part of the gun. This was a sort of hip-shooting, except from the shoulder. I did all my quail shooting in this way and probably shot better than I ever have in any other style. The aim was merely a movement or the culmination of a movement, and was not directly governed by the eye. I looked at something, with head fairly erect, raised the gun and shot at it— hit it. Just to see how accurately I was holding, I put blinders over both front and rear sights of a rifle, so that neither sights nor barrel could be seen, finding that I could then stay in a six-inch circle at twenty yards, with ten shots. Most of the shots stayed in a four-inch circle, and squirrels and rabbits could be killed, but fine rifle work could not be done. I concluded at that time, however, and still believe, that if a man had time enough to practice with a rifle, he could kill deer and other game without a sight on the piece and without seeing the barrel when he fired. This is very much the "natural method" of shooting a bow and arrow,

Desert quail.

the necessary movements becoming habitual rather than eye governed, but the rifle without sights could be shot far more accurately than an arrow can be driven.

Now while on the subject of vision and gun aiming, let me say that if I should suddenly lose the vision of my right eye, I shouldn't change to the left shoulder nor procure a cutaway stock which would permit the rib to come in line with the left eye. I'd shoot from the right shoulder just as before, seeing the mark with the left eye, and then depending on the alignment of the hands and fixed gun movements to cover that mark. Would I hit it? I think so. Just recently, while shooting the telescopic sight on a shotgun, as mentioned, I concluded to put the leather caps on the glass and see what could be done then. Of course that big sight stood up directly in front of my right eye and I couldn't see anything over it or under it or around it. But when I fired at a flying bird he was killed just the same.

Understand, I am not advocating shooting without putting cheek to comb or seeing the barrel as the only method of aiming or even the best method. I discovered that when changing guns frequently this style didn't work so well. By changing guns the position of the hands changed, and correct elevation might be lost. The man who desires to shoot without placing cheek to comb or any other conscious alignment of the tubes will do well to stick to one gun.

My present style of wing-shooting on upland birds is not precisely firing as the butt strikes the shoulder, but is related to it. I pull trigger just as the comb touches my cheek. From long practice with that gun I know precisely the position my face must occupy in order for the cheek to barely touch the comb. As the bird wings off the eye follows it, and the face is lowered to exactly the place it will be in when the aim is completed. All that then remains to do is to bring the gun into this alignment with cheek and eye. No doubt when the piece is brought to the shoulder there is a momentary pause in the movement of the barrels, because one action is completed and another just beginning. It is the intent to bring up the weapon close under the bird, never too close and never too far beneath, never ahead and not too far back. No effort is made to see where the arm is pointed when it comes to the shoulder, since the man who cannot tell where his tubes are pointing without looking at them or sighting over them is not really a wing-shot. Keeping the eye on the bird, knowing where the gun is pointing, it is easy enough to close the gap between the two and pull trigger on time.

Previous to adapting this style of shooting upland birds, I tried the whole thing out systematically. Putting up a target at twenty yards, I took a .22-caliber rifle without sights on it, and fired on the target. Getting my elevation for that gun, I commenced making allowances as though for lead, now shooting a foot to one side, now to the other, now above and now below—always without seeing the gun. Then I'd begin taking a further lead on that stationary target, swinging on from under and to the right, swinging on from under and to the left, endeavoring to place a horizontal line of bullets six inches apart, for a distance of three or four feet, to either side of the bull. Lead was also taken above, and above at a 45-degree angle to right and left. This amount of skill can

Skeet above the Arctic Circle.

readily be acquired, and it is a good foundation for work that will be done later with the shotgun.

It is well known that the movement of a shotgun after the piece comes to the shoulder is either a horizontal movement or one at some angle upward, never down. If the gun came up too high, inadvertently, it would first be dropped, and then the closing-in, final aim commenced. The reason for this is that in the nature of things the piece must never be allowed to interfere with the vision and in fact, it is only in rare instances that the mark is fully covered when the piece is fired. In taking lead and elevation on a stationary mark, as described, I discovered certain things which might apply to me and to very few others. When the gun was raised to cover the mark, either coming up vertically or at an angle, I learned that the faster the piece was moved the more danger of under shooting or of shooting back of the point aimed at. Naturally when doing this kind of aiming practice, I tried out the thing with a gun having the horizontal swing customary in duck shooting. With the piece moving rapidly the trigger had to be timed to that movement, and there was where trouble started. The faster the gun moved the quicker the trigger was pulled with me, only the trigger acceleration more than kept pace with the speed of the gun, and I'd let off behind the mark and well behind where I was sure the bullet should have gone. That very thing happens when shooting at flying birds, a common fault firing behind and under. Logically, the thing to do if a man finds himself shooting behind on a horizontal swing, or under with rising tubes, would be to quicken the gun action, but the effort to move the barrels faster seems to be deflected to the trigger finger.

By way of making amends for this automatic inclination to shoot low, or low and behind, I deliberately select a stock measurement that will cause the gun to shoot fifteen inches high at forty yards, and if the weapon doesn't do this I'll undershoot. However, part of this is optical, as will appear sooner or later. We will take that factor up under head of binocular shooting or one-eye aiming.

The main thing that I am trying to impress in this chapter is that some system of aiming and some system of movements should be selected, and then train to that system until it is mastered. If the marksman believes that the correct system is to look fixedly at the flying mark, and then throw the piece directly on that mark so that the tubes are perfectly aligned with it as the butt strikes the shoulder, that contact with the shoulder being the signal to pull trigger, all well and good—follow that style until you learn that it either will work or it will not. Remember that such a style implies that the piece is neither moved up nor down nor to the right or the left, after the gun is up. That is snap shooting pure and simple and while I have never been able to master such a style myself, somebody else might. Anyhow, practice one set system of gun movements until they become automatic; for until this happens, fast and accurate work will be impossible.

Chapter 33

PSYCHOLOGY OF WING SHOOTING

PSYCHOLOGY, as it refers to the wing-shot, means taking the machine apart to see what makes it go. Occasionally we will find not only what makes the machine go but what keeps it from going.

Self-confidence is a great asset. Nobody ever got anywhere much without it. It is one of the things that the boss can read-in us, and if he is a capable boss he can tell the counterfeit from the real. We all know this and hence our effort to "play the part" of a highly self-confident man.

Confidence based on knowledge of ourselves, relative to the job to be performed, on maintained and sustained success in performing that very job is what we want, and not the "cocky" feeling that we can do anything that anybody else can do. It is best to stand square with the world and to be honest, if we can. You can fool some of the people all the time, but you can't fool yourself permanently or effectively. My grandfather used to say when asked if he could do a thing, "Well, I have seen it done." That might carry some weight, but it wouldn't enable a man to do wing-shooting. We hit a bird because we hit the one before that, and the one before that, back for a thousand birds, until the time comes that we know beyond accident that we are going to hit him this next time too.

When a bird gets up, you have to know that you can hit him; there isn't a thing to be done but what you know exactly how to do. The problem that has been solved a thousand times is no longer a problem. There is nothing to be gained in solving it except ease, facility, and rapidity. No mental debate, no thought process, no conscious effort is involved, but fixed habit is allowed to take control, and the shot is pulled off with the same certainty that a carpenter hits a nail on the head.

However, if a would-be carpenter got to wondering whether he would hit the nail or hit his thumb, you take it from me that he'd hit his thumb. In the same way if a duck is passing a good ways out, and you decide that maybe a six-foot lead would catch him, take it from me that the duck won't be hurt—you have to know, not guess. The shot that looks uncertain to us is worse than that,

Chukar partridge.

it is certain, a certain miss. The man who doesn't know that he can take snipe, from having taken them again and again, can't kill snipe. He might say that he could, and he might half believe he could, from having conveniently forgotten all the misses, but he knows that he can't, or he will know as soon as he gets a "fire under the tile."

The process of acquiring self-confidence is one simple enough, given opportunity and a certain decision of character. A man needs inborn stability. When he is performing a thing rightly, and he knows he is right, nobody is going to change him and neither is he going to change himself. Indecision and loose mental habits are hard things to contend with. Confidence can be lost by shooting as well as gained by shooting. The man who is never satisfied with his methods but keeps changing them and searching for better, will be an erratic shot as long as he lives. Make up your mind that the style that is effective for you is the correct style, and let the chap who thinks differently go hang himself.

Knowing how to do a thing, even if not in the accepted style, is far better than to experiment in a pinch. If you know how to take a bird, sure of hitting him, with one eye closed, and you don't know whether you can hit him with both eyes open or not, better close that eye if you want the duck. I noticed, one time, that a friend of mine was jerking his gun a trifle as he fired. He was hitting his birds well, but watching him I could always see that slight jerk. I told him about it and tried to induce him to remedy the bad habit. He did try to break himself of it, and he missed nearly all the birds from then on until he told me to go to pot, that he was shooting those birds and he intended to keep on shooting them in his own way.

This doesn't mean that an absolute bar should be put up against progress or a correction of bad habits, but when an individual has shot enough to acquire automatic or subconscious control of his piece, after his own fashion, then any radical change will simply break him up, and he will have to learn to shoot over again. If everybody says the right arm is the correct one to throw with, more accurate, less strain on the heart, best according with a brain development that has been in process of evolution for a thousand years, but you can throw left handed and you can't right, then hang it all, throw left-handed.

We have all heard of the man who is a fool and knows it; we can teach him a lot. We have all heard, too, of the man who is a fool and doesn't know it, and we can't teach him anything. Once on a time in my athletic days I was looking for a man who could take the measure of a lad who had bested me, in a broad jump. I wanted a youngster who could do 22 feet, and a youth promptly acknowledged that he could do it. There wasn't much room for doubt, not with a back yard right behind the house where I could try him. The Lord knows why he thought he could do 22 feet— must have jumped down a steep hill sometime, for the best he could do was 19 feet. We all know that kind of a bird, so don't imitate him; above all don't fool yourself. If you think you can do 22 feet, think it because you did jump 22 feet day before yesterday, and then I'll bet my old hat on you.

Can you concentrate on anything? Yes. Sure. What is the degree? The man who can eat without talking or quit eating and just talk, can concentrate, after some fashion. I have seen women who could talk without thinking, however, and that doesn't require much concentration. Deep concentration, sustained through a long period, marks the great trap shot.

In my rifle-shooting days I couldn't talk while a match was on, and if anybody spoke to me, that was an annoyance. Men differ and yet concentrate. I stood back of Laurence Nuesslein when he was shooting in the International Free Rifle match at Camp Perry. Nuesslein talked all the time between shots; he would fire a shot and then take up the conversation right where he had left off. I was interested in "Larry" and thought he had the make-up of a great rifleman, but was not being properly coached. Taking that up with the coach, I was told that Mr. Nuesslein couldn't shoot unless you allowed him to talk. Wishing to see if he really knew what he was doing all the time, I'd ask him where a shot went and he would call it within an inch or two, and also tell me how it happened to be pulled there. He was concentrating with one part of his brain and talking with another. I doubt if many men could do that. Anyhow, he made the best off-hand score of the match.

Spectators are required to keep silent while a golfer is making his stroke, and there is a reason. People are not required to keep still while a rifleman is aiming, and another rifle may go off within a few feet of his head without his knowing it. If he did know it, away went his good score. He is taught a deeper concentration than the golfer knows. The live-bird match shooter and the clay-bird shot are in that boat too—they must be able to ignore what is going on. Once on a time George Kleinman was shooting a match with John Winston. Winston never said a word to his opponent,

Increasing numbers of the fair sex are becoming shotgunners. Beth Coleman of Seattle.

but he cut up queer didoes. He'd mark off a cross on the ground, step over it and then step back, bless himself with his fingers, and do other odd things before going to his mark. His maneuvers got on George's nerves and irritated him, which was precisely what they were intended to do. Though much the better shot, Kleinman lost the match on a low score.

The expert duck shooter I have mentioned shot the barrel off his friend's gun without seeing it—never seeing a thing except the duck. I had a companion miss my head by a few inches because the quail he was shooting at jumped to pass over me and the gun jumped with the bird. I was in plain sight but had stepped into the path after the quail took wing. I have to look around carefully, under some conditions, to see that no dog or human being can get in the way, because I'll never see anything else after the bird gets up.

This kind of concentration is necessary in all wing-shooting. Kill that bird if the sun goes under an eclipse and the heavens fall. That is what makes quail shooting both attractive and difficult. When a bevy roars up it is absolutely essential that one bird be picked and the others no longer seen. If this is not done, if the eye and the mind is not fixed on one bird to the exclusion of the others, nothing will happen to any of them. It sometimes happens that we pick on the very hardest bird of the lot, this one doubling and twisting and swerving while all the others went off in easy fashion, but that can't be helped. The man who would start to aim at a bird and then change and take another would be hopeless. They used to tell me that the way to shoot a rifle off-hand was to go to sleep on the cheekpiece, to wake up with a 10, and the way to kill a bird is to go to sleep on that bird and not wake until you see him falling.

Much of the ability to concentrate is born in us, a part of our mental make-up, and the mind trains the body until it too, concentrates. Still, much ought to be done by training. Doubtless the professor who ran up against a stone wall and tried to gently push it out of his way so that it would not interrupt his train of thought, wouldn't have done that when he was a boy. Concentration had grown on him and concentration will grow on any of us. I have myself tried to push a tree out of the way when it came in contact with my gun, and waked up cussing the tree.

Nevertheless and for all of that, I doubt if such tremendous concentration is really necessary to shooting as a means of recreation. Except we are a noted trap shooter we don't have to be so grimly in earnest. What is a miss more or less anyhow among friends? The rifleman has to have it, but I have seen him come out of a match, in which he did not appear to be under any strain whatever, completely exhausted, not fit company for man or beast. For some such reason I like the company of the man who just shoots and if the bird gets away says, "Go it, you little devil." The man who enjoyed most of all the hunters I have known was no great shot, but missed with a laugh, and, win, lose, or draw, came home at night in high good humor.

Over-anxiety comes from too much ambition, from vanity, from nervousness, from lack of confidence, from selfishness, and from a number of other causes.

The overly anxious man is keen to show at his best and very

fearful that he might not. The man that is afraid cannot do anything well, except possibly run—they say a scared man can run faster than anybody, but I doubt it. I know that once a dog gets a jack rabbit scared he is sure to catch that jack, but scaring him is some job.

The anxious man shoots too quick, then he shoots too slow, then aims properly but pulls trigger too soon or too late. After which he goes about thinking of his misses rather than of the work ahead

Prized game of the shotgun hunter is the wild turkey.

of him. If his companion is outshooting him, that is a perpetual source of worry. I have a friend who tells me that he never shoots so poorly as he does when shooting with me. He may start the day by telling me how many birds he killed straight the other day, and of course he means to show me that he really did it and that he can do it again. Before long, as such things will happen, come a couple of easily accountable misses—misses that are bound to occur now and then. These start him well on the way to becoming "rattled" and ere long he is going from bad to worse. If I want to finish him, then, all I have to do is to say, "Jack, you are not shooting very well today, come up and take the shots for a while." If he does, more than likely he will miss the easiest kind of shots, and for him the day is ruined. I know how to help him and sometimes do. All I need do is to rattle off a half dozen misses while he makes a kill or two, and the mocking bird is singing again. Of course I have to cuss myself and appear worse rattled than he was, whereupon he grins and his nerves are restored.

Nervous anxiety affects nearly every athlete. Very often the prize fighter gets a licking before his nervousness is walloped out of him and his temper aroused. The batter who comes up when one hit would win a ball game, when he knows the eyes of his mates are on him, half hopeful, half despairing, is under a tremendous strain and he is a good man or lucky if the hit comes through.

The usual effect of over-anxiety is to slow one up, to make him more careful, which results in a direct loss of time, and away goes the bird. The more carefully he shoots the worse he misses, which is highly exasperating.

I suppose that everybody is set to guess at times as to just what is wrong with him anyhow. Occasionally I dope it out, as far as I am concerned, as staleness due to too much shooting. I am not being put under any strain at all, not enough, and all gun movements become too slow. The gun is not working to the eye, but falling behind, while the bird is just as fast as ever he was. Deciding that this is the trouble, I drop a seven-pound gun and take up a six-pound one, and the trouble is always automatically cured right then and there.

Staleness generally comes from shooting alone, since a mate will whip you up if he has no other effect. If then, a bad shooting streak comes it is caused by over-caution and over-care. Forget it, become utterly reckless, don't care a whoop whether you miss or hit, shoot without any aim—whatever you do don't aim, double-quicken the time, and presently you will just be knocking time out of 'em.

Once on a time, finding myself in a bad slump which refused to wear off in the course of a week, I concluded that I wouldn't kill any more birds but just see how close I could shoot to them without hitting them. Presently I got to shooting too close and did hit them. The hold would be a little off but I'd hit the bird anyhow. Presently I discovered that I wasn't missing any birds at all, nothing to it. I didn't have to hold right on them either, but the sole requirement was an indifference as to whether I hit or missed. Naturally, one man's medicine is another's "pizen," and I do not know whether or not this scheme would work out with everybody.

A youngster shoots with me whose theory is that birds are missed because you "don't put it on 'em." "I know what the trouble is," he'd say, "I didn't have it on him." The next shot would be delivered very carefully, followed by an exclamation. "He got away from me! I had it on him but he got away from me before I could shoot! Watch me put it on the next bird!" He did put it on them finally, but it was usually on some succeeding shooting day. Again the advice, when rattled and over-cautious, quit thinking, shoot recklessly, and see if you can't shoot a bird's wing off, right now, without hitting his body.

Chapter 34
CORRECT POSITION

MUCH OF GOOD WING-SHOOTING lies in taking the correct position. Watch a trap-shoot in progress and note the variations in position. Some of them are easy, while others are absurdly strained. Some of the strained positions can be explained psychologically. Some marksmen have learned that they can best concentrate the mind and become highly alert by first putting the body under a strain. No strain on the body and the mind takes it easy as well, according to this theory. For all that, I think the mind had better be whipped up in some other way.

We all know that trap shooters have a simple problem before them as compared with the marksman who has to take flying game that breaks cover unexpectedly and takes a trying course. Half the misses of the veteran shot who knows how to hold and where to lead are due to faulty position of the feet. He gets his legs tangled up. No matter how much foresight is employed that very thing must happen. A lot of training lies in placing the feet, so that the body will swing easily, without cramping, without any strain, perfectly balanced from the time the bird rises until the shot is fired.

For the reason that he is less spry than he used to be, the old man will often shoot better at the traps than he will on game, and he may shoot better on ducks than he does on quail or other birds that he has to walk up. However, he has the advantage of knowing when his position is right, if he has time to take it, and the novice may not know. I have seen a quail rise in the open and wing off straight-away; it looked impossible to miss, and the miss was inexplicable until I noticed the marksman hadn't taken time to get his feet under him, and was swaying, partly out of balance when he fired.

Of course, if a man is walking up birds, the wrong foot is just as liable to be in advance when the game appears as the right foot. Those feet have to be changed in a twinkling, with the speed of a ten-second-flat sprinter. The left foot has to be carried forward or the right foot back, one or the other of these movements becoming habitual. Usually in walked-up game, the left leg bears

273

the greater weight, and acts as a pivot on which the body turns. The right leg applies the force which turns the body. In a quick shot the left leg will probably be slightly bent, and the right may be resting on the toe only. I can usually tell whether a man will be a quick shot or not by the position he gets into.

Remember that a quail or a grouse breaks fast and reaches top speed of maybe 75 feet a second within the first fifty feet. If it takes ten feet of that bird's flight for the mind to realize that the bird is off, one fourth of a second to get the legs into position, and the bird breaks cover at 25 feet, then we have a total distance of 55 feet before our marksman is even ready to aim. The shooter is certain to note how fast the bird is getting away, and all his subsequent movement will be hurried and unsteady where they should be careful and steady.

Of course all these preliminary movements will be trained into us until they become automatic. Very few men can remember anything whatever concerning what was done with the feet, after the bird sprung. Now and then the thing will be brought home, as when he steps into a hole in trying to get into position or his foot hits a root, or something else happens. Then he may find that his gun hasn't come up quite right, or he has inadvertently swayed enough to miss. All these things are what makes shooting over level ground far easier than taking the shot from a hillside or when walking up- or down-hill. All this is a part of the game, and misses are to be expected from one cause or another; but don't make any more of them due to a poor position than you have to.

The duck shooter is situated differently, unless he is jumping the birds by walking. When he puts out his decoys and builds his blind he must do so with some thought as to the position from which he must shoot, or probably will have to shoot. As a matter of common knowledge, the right-handed shooter can take birds passing to the left with greater ease than he can fowl winging from left to right. His left hand is in advance of his right shoulder back. Now he can bring that right shoulder forward and swing to the left without any trouble, but if he has to swing that right shoulder farther back, farther than it is willing to go easily, it will put a twisted strain on him, which may cause him to jerk the piece. Try that out when no ducks are flying and try it from a boat.

The duck shooter has to practice other than the standing positions, though some apparently do not. Haven't we all heard of the shooter who sprang to his feet and took 'em? That is a fool of a thing to do if he wants easy shots. No man can spring up so quickly that the birds cannot see him, and they will be tying themselves into knots trying to jump and dodge and get away, just when he is attempting to aim. The proper position in a blind is kneeling, and do not get up to shoot. The pump gunner must have his arms free to work the action, but from a pit I have usually shot an automatic and a double gun while half reclining, with my back against the walls. In any event, about half of one's duck shooting will not be done while standing on the feet, and other positions should be practiced in order to make them comfortable and accurate. I have shot a great many jumped ducks from a boat, a small duck boat which would not permit any foolishness. Ducks can then always be taken coming in and passing to the left, but those passing to the right will be found next to impossible unless the gunner deliberately places himself partly facing to the right, whereupon he can take them either to the right or to the left.

This thing of how to carry the gun afield when expecting a shot has changed a great deal, by a sort of evolutionary process. I remember the first quail shooting on the wing that I ever saw done. The shooters were carrying their guns, held in one hand, up over the right shoulder, hammers down, barrels pointed up and back at an angle of about sixty degrees. Our quail shooters appeared to be going about for hours, carrying the gun just so. When a bird appeared the piece was jerked down, throwing the fore-end into the left hand, and then aimed. Unless the gun were carried just so, the man's aim was disturbed, or he didn't apparently know how to aim, except when the piece was so elevated to start with.

Thereafter appeared a period of gun carrying which lasted a long time, and which I acquired myself. The piece was held in both hands, barrels across the body, muzzle up at an angle of about 45 degrees. Everybody carried a gun like that, and just walked about with the gun held so, any time it was down from the shoulder. This position has appeared in a thousand pictures, and everybody knows it. No English shooting book ever appeared without showing the gun so carried. I discovered after a time, and so did everybody else, I suppose, that when carried in this position, the subsequent gun movements in covering the mark were too complicated and too slow. The barrels made a wide swing as they came on and then the muzzle invariably dropped too far beneath the mark. It was all a bit of foolishness which people acquired from imitating one another.

The gun should be carried in the position from which it can the most easily and surely be brought to bear on the mark.

All the body movements or arm movements in trap shooting are from the waist up, and he has learned that the most accurate aim can be taken when the body alone moves, swayed from the hips, no change in the arms. But that kind of thing will not always work in the field or on the marsh, and the arms must come into

action sometimes. The less arm action, however, the better, and
if the feet are placed right, a swaying, bending and raising of
the body will cover the bird. The secret, then, is to place the feet,
not exactly facing the bird as it comes in, but to permit easy action
in the direction the shot will have to be taken. For example, it
is to be seen that the shot will be passing at quite a distance,
the shot should be taken when the bird is nearest the gun, that

A fine example of how not to stand. This is the rifleman's stance. Feet are
too widespread.

is at right angles to a position looking forward; if the marksman
now takes the position adapted to a forward shot, and to that kind
only, be will be cramped in turning either to the right or the
left. I am repeating this for the sake of emphasis. Hence if the
bird is coming in, say from the north, and will pass to the west,
place the feet to begin with, in preparation for a shot to the west,
followed by one to the southwest. Possibly the shooter is using
a repeating shotgun, and only one shot will be fired overhead, and
the gun will then turn to take the birds from the rear, place the
feet to take birds in the rear, that is, reverse the feet and place
the right one slightly ahead of the left, or quite ahead.

Quail are the worst little scamps to tie a man into a knot, for
there are times when the Lord only knows what they will do when
they get up. Neither does anybody know how he will be situated.
I recall four different times last season when the birds broke

while I was astride of a wire fence. Birds were pointed along the fence but wouldn't get up. Then I'd say to myself, if I try to cross this fence they'll catch me foul, but after while I'd put a leg over that fence and away they'd go. On several occasions, too, I caught my gun against the brush in trying to raise it.

The trouble with getting out of position is not altogether strain or cramping, but with the twisting about, the cheek may be carried over the comb or away from it, leading to cross firing. Again, as the cheek slides forward and back the elevation will change, shots going over or under. In all this the trap shooter has a great advantage of the rest of us, but throw a bird back over his head unexpectedly and see what happens.

In readiness.

Chapter 35

SWINGING AND SNAPPING

IF WE READ ANYTHING about wing-shooting or instructions in wing-shooting, we are bound to read of swing, follow through, intercept, and snap. I have made an effort to separate and analyze the different movements, calling one a snap or a rough snap, another a half snap, a rapid swing, deliberate swing, and so on. These are gun movements, by way of covering the mark or by way of gaining the lead. However in actual practice one of these movements will merge into another, or the shooter may use one movement for a certain shot and a second movement for a different shot. For example if our marksman is wedded to a deliberate style of swinging and he finds his gun well behind the mark, he is going to swing faster in order to catch up and gain his lead, hence will be doing a rapid swing when he shoots. In the same way the man who snaps with his first barrel and misses, must in the nature of things swing on after the bird with his second barrel.

Therefore it is hardly necessary to use more than three terms in describing the gun movements, after the gun is up or the bird is up. The first is the snap, the second the intercepted bird, the third the swing or the swinging aim.

The first is the snap. Some men like to describe their work as snap shooting or the work of some one else as snap shooting. I am uncertain as to just how much of real snap shooting takes place. Nevertheless, this is the manner of doing it. When the bird is a-wing, the shooter concentrates his mind and vision on it. Not much, if any, thought is given to the gun, but it comes up and shoots right where our snap shot is looking, result a dead bird— all done in a jiffy. Only upland birds are snapped as a rule, generally in brush shooting. It appears logical that the marksman can shoot right where he looks and he is looking right at the bird, which is so close that no great lead is required where the piece is open bored. Hence it is argued that snapping is the correct manner of taking all birds that break cover close to the gun, yet affording but a very brief space of time in which the shot must be taken. Any man can fix his eyes on a stationary mark, throw up his gun, and shoot very close to where he is looking. A 24-inch

Dove shooting over the desert waterhole.

pattern at 20 yards ought then to make amends for whatever in-accuracy there may be in the hold and the bird should be killed. Very often it is and there are men who can snap-shoot very well.

Here is the weakness of snap shooting. There is but one gun movement, that of placing butt to shoulder and cheek to comb. This movement is or should be of lightning quickness, so that the bird is far outpaced and compared with the gun is practically staying right there in the air. The weakness of snap shooting is right there too, for once the piece is up the aim has been taken, and the shot is fired. The endeavor is to point the gun precisely where the eye is looking, but no man ever has been able to do that yet, whatever his sights, and whatever time he may take, so long as the piece is free to move. The snap is a complicated aiming movement, and hence the most inaccurate. The butt must strike the shoulder just so, the cheek must take the comb just so; the endeavor is to stop the gun just as it covers the mark; if the piece rises too high, the aim is inaccurate; if the trigger is pressed too soon, the aim is inaccurate; if the gun comes up to the right or the left the aim is inaccurate. Inaccuracies are never corrected nor detected, except by missing.

Birds should be snapped in the brush when it is to be seen that no time will be afforded for any other style of shot. A fast bird like a quail or a grouse can be snapped within twenty feet of where he rises, or within less than twenty feet of where he was when the aiming movement started. During this twenty feet of flight or perhaps it is no more than ten feet, the aim must be precalculated, that is, it must be known or judged where the bird will be when the movement culminates in a fired gun. The bird has twenty feet of flight in which to do the unexpected. If the flight period during the snapped aim could be cut down to ten that would be a great gain. At that the snapped aim demands a far longer period of time than any other style of aim. This requires some explanation.

The snapped aim requires the entire time and the entire movement from the position in which the gun is carried to that it occupies when discharged. The gun muzzle rises, falls, whips with the jar of shoulder contact, and steadies—all these movements being included in the aim. The swinging shot covers his bird first, and then makes a final very brief shift before firing. If he had to know where the bird would be before he started to raise his gun, and before he started his swing, you can imagine what would happen. In the same way the intercepting shot gets his gun up as quickly as he knows how, and just as close to the bird as he knows how, but he doesn't discharge it, not until he can see how close he is to the mark, after which he makes the brief shift needed to cover it.

I have tried snap shooting at rabbits, usually in the weeds where the little beasts could be seen for but one or two jumps. Generally I hit right where I had aimed, which was precisely where the rabbit had been but wasn't any more. Certain mental and nerve processes have to be studied to account for that missed rabbit. The eye sees something and the brain gives orders to shoot at it. Orders are carried out by nerves and muscles, the whole process demanding a very brief time, as measured in fractions of a second, but the actions do not follow the thought instantly. During the interval of transferring thought into action, the rabbit straightens his hindlegs and is no longer there. Even a man's perceptions are slower than he suspects. A rising quail will be ten feet on the way before a man knows that it has started; a fighter can dodge a fist without any trouble, if he knows it is coming, but if he has to wait until the fist is on the way, he'll be certain to get hit.

The intercepting aim or the delayed snap is the common style of upland shooting. It has been described pretty often and everybody knows it. It differs from the pure snap in that time is taken to realize what the bird has done while the gun was coming to shoulder. Though to the mind of the shooter the raising of the gun and the final aiming movement may appear continuous, yet, for the sake of making the subject clear, we will divide the movement into two parts, that of raising the gun, as in the snap, and the culminating aim.

When the bird breaks, the gun comes up pointed close to the mark, but under it. In this first movement the gun is simply raised. Now, unless the bird is a straight-away, it will be found that he has moved off to one side or the other of the line of sight. It is now to be seen where the bird is and where he will be when the gun, with its known space to move over, can cover him. This final aim is then generally at an angle to the line of flight, upward and at whatever angle is needed to cover the mark. Whatever the angle may be this final movement is straight and fast.

Much of shooting skill is dependent on throwing the gun up true. It is, of course, to be seen that the gun might be raised very wide of the mark. This would entail a prolonged aim, with a

D. W. Conway, for years one of our leading skeet marksmen. Note the ejected empty and the cheek kicked free of the comb of the gun.

chance for the bird to dodge. Therefore if the bird were flying across the gun, or at a wide angle from a straight-away, the gun would be raised, not at him but on his course, with the full knowledge that the mark would pass a given point before the gun reached it. A skilled shot may require no more than two inches of gun muzzle travel in order to cover the point of aim, after the gun is up. Meantime the bird may fly no more than two feet from the time the gun comes up until the shot catch him. The final shift of the gun will be so quick that to all appearances the entire aim has been a simple snap.

Again, in the nature of things, this intercepting snap may become a true swing, directly after the bird, overtaking the mark and passing to the lead. It always has happened and always will happen that the bird which has started in a certain direction alters his course while the piece is coming up. This leaves the gun back of him, and sometimes well to the rear. Nothing remains then but to swing the gun directly after the mark, and that is a swinging shot. Nevertheless, it is not the intention of the intercepting shot to allow the bird to pass far in front of his gun, maybe at a 45-degree angle, maybe less or more.

I'd define simple snapping, angle snapping or intercepting, and swinging aim like this: In the snap the aim is taken as the gun comes up and is not altered; in the intercepting snap the aim is not taken until after the gun is up; in the swing the final aim is not taken until the bird is covered. The swing is the most accurate, entails the least lead but is slow, the intercepting aim is about as accurate, is faster, but greater lead has to be taken; the snap is the fastest, the least accurate, and the greatest lead must be taken.

The snap is to be taken in the brush, when it can be seen that the bird will be in sight for but the briefest space. The intercepting snap may be used for all game, in the uplands generally, on ducks that have decoyed and are climbing out, on ducks that are jumped, on woodcock, snipe, quail, grouse, chickens, pheasants, and all game except passing birds that travel at high speed. Passing ducks can be shot with this style of aim very well, but not much can be gained in lead from the gun movement, and the trigger must be perfectly timed.

The swinging shot doesn't throw his piece beneath the mark but behind it. If he gets too far behind it, however, that is due to a lack of skill and judgment. The swing, then, is directly on the path which the bird has traveled. Since the gun is back of the mark in order to overtake it the piece must travel faster than the bird, perhaps three times as fast, and once daylight shows between the fowl and the gun ahead of it, the trigger is timed and pulled. During the interval between the initial trigger pressure, and the fall of the hammer, sufficient space is gained to afford the correct lead. Accuracy and lead are then dependent on the speed of the swing, and the aim is really based on this speed of swing; when the swing slows up, as in shooting at long range, the lead must be proportionately greater. This is why many will tell you that they kill ducks by simply swinging in ahead of them at thirty or forty yards, but nobody has ever claimed to be able to hit fowl at sixty to eighty yards simple by swinging in front. The reason is that unconsciously, with distance the swing slows up.

There is another style of swinging called the deliberate swing, but I think it is used very little. In the deliberate swing the gun is thrown up, not behind, but in front of the bird or right at him.

Gun now travels to the required lead and then evenly along in front, until the trigger is pulled. Nothing is gained in lead by this swing, but it would be accurate if slow, provided the bird moved with the utmost regularity, which very few birds do. No man can afford to potter along dwelling on an aim after it has been secured, not in wing-shooting. With the gun moving along the proper distance in front of an even flying mark, trigger time would make no difference, but trigger time makes a vital difference in any other style of aiming.

We get the idea of swinging from duck shooting or from shooting passing birds of some kind. Swinging on a straight-away couldn't well be done, and with a quartering bird the swing merely entails a loss of time. The English write often of swinging with the bird, but a great deal of their work is on driven game, which is much like passing fowl, except it is difficult to get the birds to fly high, and the gunner only takes such birds as come within a given radius, say 35 yards. There is this to be said in favor of swinging; that style develops a more even elevation than any form of interception. Elevation causes more grief to the experienced shot than lead. He knows, can remember, and can detect faulty lead, but if his elevation is off, he will miss without knowing why. This is largely due to trigger time. Trigger time changes with the marksman's condition, state of mind, nerves, and physical shape generally. If cool and indifferent, trigger time becomes slow, if over-anxious, too fast, and the shooter will not know precisely what has happened to him except he is missing birds that ought to be killed. It is easy to see what a delayed or accelerated trigger does to elevation, where the gun is moving up at an angle to the path of flight. On the other hand, with the gun and the mark traveling along together, trigger time will not alter the elevation, and will probably not alter the lead enough to cause a miss.

The snap shot is rarely a highly accurate marksman, and he takes his birds close to the gun, so requires a cylinder bore. His style is effective on tricky, dodging birds, and those that take to the brush. Every field shot should be able to snap on occasion, though if this is the only style he knows, he will acquire a reputation for being erratic.

The delayed snap can be used on all kinds of birds, and the man who knows or practices no other style will get along nicely, even on ducks. The delayed snap is practiced by the trap shooter, except there is no pause in his gun movements, no double movement, because his piece is already up. In the later days of live pigeon shooting the marksman was in the same nice position for a snap shot, but the man who tries to place his gun to shoulder, even though the bird has been pointed and he knows where it is, or even if he has some one to walk the game up, merely looks ridiculous. Therefore our field shot must get his gun up first, pointed somewhere close to the mark, after which he can snap as fast as he likes.

In duck shooting it is frequently impossible to shoot in any style except swinging with the bird, as in those passing overhead. The gun must be pointed beneath the fowl and then swung up on him, and in front. This is necessary with any incomer, and I have known gunners who couldn't take such birds well, but advocated waiting until the fowl had passed and then snapping them from the rear. The completely equipped marksman can either snap, intercept, or swing as the occasion demands. He simply knows how to take the shot no matter the kind of chance that may be afforded.

A great deal has been written concerning the necessity for following through, that is, keeping up the movement of the gun after the shot is gone. I have tried following through and conclude that it is pretty much a humbug. The gun will do its own following through, so long as no effort is made to stop it while the trigger is being pulled. If the shooter tries to stop his gun before pulling trigger or if he automatically checks it while pulling, that is bad. It is for this reason that the advice is always given to shoot with a moving gun. The real foundation for this advice is that a movement once started can be carried on easily and accurately, but the instant that movement is stopped another and different movement takes its place. Accordingly, if the gun is rising to cover a mark, and we stop it, or quite stop it, the gun will either begin to drop at once, or it will move to one side or the other—it will never stay where it is stopped.

That kind of thing is different from keeping the gun consciously moving after the shot is fired, and even after the recoil has driven the piece quite off the mark. That kind of thing accomplishes nothing, and is merely a revised form of pottering. Double-barrel shooting, shooting doubles, and the second barrel on a missed bird requires a form of carry through, which will be treated in due time.

Chapter 36

AIMING

NEARLY EVERY NOVICE today is being advised to shoot with both eyes open. It is good advice in a way, yet certain facts are to be considered. I have never seen a beginner who didn't instinctively or logically close or partly close one eye when he attempted to aim a gun. There is plenty of reason for that. He wants to see and needs to see where his gun is pointed. He can see the gun better, more easily, with less strain on his eyes, when one of them is partly closed. He can learn this in a minute's time, knows that it is so, and it is no use for anybody to tell him that it is not so. By and by a time will come when he will not need to see where his piece is pointed; he knows that perfectly without looking or the use of sights. That time for him is not in the beginning.

Binocular aiming is a graduate exercise. Just as well put a youngster who cannot add up one column of figures without making a mistake to adding up two columns of figures at a time as to tell him to aim with both eyes open when he cannot aim with one. Two eye aiming is the result of habits, trained movements that ultimately become subconscious or as we put it, instinctive. There is no royal road to wing-shooting skill; a child has to toddle before he can run, and it wouldn't be any use to try to teach him to run before he could walk. Habits have to form and to grow and are not born in us. Very few of us do any miraculous things. I have heard of a Scotch shepherd who could look at a flock of sheep, when asked to count them, and then he would say 33 or whatever it was. The sheep might then be carefully separated and counted one at a time invariably proving the shepherd right. Maybe our novice is another Scotch shepherd, and maybe he can slam away at a bird as the experts do and invariably hit it—but I doubt it.

At the risk of repetition, we will say again that in one-eye aiming the gun is directly governed by the eye. In two-eye aiming the gun is governed by trained movements. The two systems are essentially different though one may merge into the·other. One-eye aiming is used in rifle shooting and for all extremely close shooting. It is slow and a strain on the eye but is accurate. I

Doves incoming to the waterhole are some of the most difficult targets that fly.

know all about the master eye, and pointing the finger to see which eye takes the line; and I know all about training one eye to take up the mastery when both eyes are normal, and the trouble one has when the left eye is the stronger. I know that a man can so train himself as to make a mental note of what one eye sees and not of what the other sees, so that he can keep both eyes open and aim a rifle or other gun with but the one master eye. But between you and me and the devil with a forked tail, that is one-eye aiming just the same, and besides it puts a strain on the eye that remains open and sees nothing or maybe it puts a strain on both eyes. Therefore I am saying to you that if aim is to be taken with one eye, blink or slightly shadow the other one, unless it is a defective eye. Riflemen do this though they may swear that they do not.

The advantage of one-eye aiming is that the gun is seen definitely or the sights on the gun are seen definitely. Look fixedly at some object and point the finger at it, leaving both eyes wide open. The mark will be very distinct, but the finger will be shadowy. Now close the left eye and at once the finger jumps into prominence. You can see the nail and every wrinkle on it; you can also see if the alignment of that finger with the mark is precise and even the quivering of the finger will be noticed. Now if that finger were a gun with sights on it, you could see just how many inches or fractions of an inch you were off of dead center. If the mark were a bird it could be seen definitely exactly what the gun lacked of covering it, and the bird could now be covered or led an inch or a foot or a yard. If the movements of the piece are sufficiently deliberate the path of that movement can be seen all the way. After the gun was up it might start to cover, from say a distance of five feet, and we could see that it was now in two feet, now in one, now full on, and now it has passed to the point where the trigger was to be pulled. The eye governed the movement of that gun all the way, and it might be moved faster or slower or moved up or moved down; and if a rifle, a second aim might be taken where the first proved faulty.

If a man is really a novice, none of his movements will be trained. His legs may be a little out of position in the hurry of covering a fast bird; body balance or some muscle not in customary use may betray him; his swing on the mark may not be true; and the only way he can learn all this and correct it is to see precisely what is being done every step of the way. If he knows that the lead ought to be a foot on a horizontal line and he sees that inadvertently he had held precisely on the mark, he will at once perceive why he missed. But if he intends to lead a foot, and he

Scale quail and a fine old Ithaca 16 double gun.

Mexican wildfowl waters—the author.

slams the gun on like a binocular expert, he will be ready to swear he held exactly that one foot ahead, and the Lord knows why he missed because he doesn't know and can't tell. Even the skilled shot doesn't know so well why he missed, though he can usually tell an instant after it is too late. Instinct is a fine thing to follow, so long as it is correct, but we all know of the man who felt that camp was in a certain direction, just knew it, and it wasn't any use to tell him anything else, so he kept right on going in the wrong direction. I shoot with a so-called instinctive aim, as do most men who have shot a great deal, yet every now and then I get hold of a gun and miss about everything I shoot at. Then I have to close one eye and take the sight and see where the devil that gun is shooting anyhow.

The way to learn lead exactly, to learn gun faults definitely, to detect the reason for hitting and the reason for missing, the way to learn to shoot, is to not close but shadow one eye and concentrate the vision on the other one—to see the gun definitely by way of remembering precisely what has occurred after it is all over. No man can recall much about what happened when his piece was not seen and he merely waked up to find that he had missed. A thousand misses, the causes of which are unknown and cannot be known, are not much help in correcting faults, but one miss the cause of which is fully known and graphically registered on the mind may help us a lot. Every movement of the gun after it is up ought to be governed by the eye, and a mental picture retained of just what occurred. In this way the novice can lay a foundation for future skill, and he had better lay that foundation.

The method of aiming a shotgun with one eye closed and of

aiming a rifle is not essentially different. The gun comes to the shoulder and pauses for an instant, during which the rib of the piece or the sight or sights will be seen distinctly. Then the sight is carried to the mark or to the calculated lead. The piece may or may not cover the mark and be carried along with the flight, though that is the accepted style of duck shooting. The movement may be slow enough with a rifle so that it can be checked and amended, but rarely is with a shotgun. The aim may not be more accurate when the eye sees the gun every step of the way, but a faulty aim and the reason for it should be detected.

The weakness of one eye aiming is in the focus of the eyes so that while the gun is seen more distinctly the mark is seen less distinctly. Gun movements are slower, and more time is required to deliver a shot, which is a handicap except in duck shooting where approaching birds give due warning. In one-eye aiming the line of sight is closer to the rib, is taken more uniformly above the rib, and elevations should be more even. Numbers of expert shots close or partly close one eye in aiming, and their work is no less effective than is that of the binocular lads. Half the people who shoot with both eyes open really aim with one eye, the gun being seen as distinctly as though one eye had been closed. Only a few men really do binocular aiming, as we shall describe it.

Much of an individual's training throughout his life is such as to permit him to execute movements with the legs, feet, hands, arms and body that are mechanical, automatic, not directly governed by the eye. Tell a man to put his finger on his nose, his ears or any other part of the body and he can do it with the greatest exactness; he cannot see his nose or his ear, but he knows where they are and his finger goes to the spot without his eyes directing the movement. An expert typist doesn't see the keys of the machine, but simply knows where they are and has executed the movement of placing the finger on the proper key so many times, that the movement becomes automatic and is accomplished without even remembering consciously where that key is. A finer than normal sense takes possession of the mind and governs the movements of the fingers. Movements governed subconsciously are sometimes termed instinctive; but it is no true instinct, which would be born with us, while the subconscious movements are trained into us. Many persons through lack of time, through lack of training, through lack of natural aptitude, never acquire subconsciously governed gun movements, or typewriter movements, or any other subconscious movements except the simplest acquired throughout life by necessity. Accurate, definite, automatic, subconscious gun movements are the acme of shotgun training and shotgun aiming, true binocular shooting; and no man is a finished shot without being able to shoot in this way, though he may be a good shot for all that.

In true binocular shooting the gun is never seen until after it is discharged. The marksman doesn't need to see it; he knows where it is pointed every instant of the time. That gun is a part of him; he puts the sight where he wants it precisely in the way he puts his finger on his nose—never by any chance missing doing that very thing. However, give the man a stick of unknown length

The so-called 2¾-inch shell has this overall length only after firing.

and tell him to place the end of it on an exact spot on his nose, and the chances are he will miss the spot more or less. That means, in shooting, that he has changed guns, and the new gun didn't fit him like the old one. A few trials would enable the man to put the point of a stick on a pimple on his nose, and enough trials would enable him to point the new gun as well as the old one; but it would take time, and many birds would be missed while he was doing it.

In practical effect many do binocular shooting or binocular style of aiming, though closing one eye. I think that many trap shooters do this, and such a style is furthered by the manner of placing gun to cheek before calling "pull." The gun is placed to cheek and accurately aligned, maybe by the use of two sights, one eye making the alignment. Then the bird is sprung, and that is the last time the gun is seen until it is discharged. That is in effect binocular aiming, for if the final gun movement were governed by the eye, the piece would be seen closing in on the bird. I think the expert trap shot moves his piece too fast for it to be governed except automatically.

This semi-binocular aiming is frequently done with a rifle. A marksman can do good rifle shooting at a stationary mark by watching his sights. He knows where the bull is, and can watch his sights and see when they are coming on. Again he may align his sights and hold them in alignment by his cheek, and thereafter he will divert his focus to the bull, knowing where his sights were coming on, the rate at which they were coming on, and he could thus better time his trigger than he could where the eye was governing the gun movements and the bull might be covered unexpectedly. In the old days when I used to shoot a good deal with a heavy rifle weighing 17 pounds, which swung slowly and uniformly, I used to declare that I could shut my eyes, let the gun swing a time or two, and pull off, yet calling the shot within a few inches at two hundred yards, because I could feel where the gun had swung to. In the same way, I have no sort of doubt but what a man could put up his gun, see where the bird was and where it would be when the shot got there, close both eyes and kill it. I'll admit that this has been tried many times, inadvertently, without success, but plenty of us cannot walk straight in pitch dark either, though we might be trained into it. Anyway, I am not advocating shooting with both eyes shut, but merely shooting without seeing the gun.

The amount of training that a man can devote to the gun or the opportunities he has to shoot keeps him from attaining perfection in binocular aiming, that is, aiming without seeing his gun. If a man had natural ability, fine muscular coordination, and he began his training in his youth, I believe he could take a rifle without sights, never look at the barrel, and could compete on an equal footing with the best off-hand rifle shots having any kind of sight and using them. Moreover, he would get off his shot in half a second instead of ten seconds. Neither would he throw any wild shots. That the thing has never been done is no indication that it could not be done. Such a shot, given knowledge of lead, would not miss any birds, unless the bird did some unexpected thing, that is, in common parlance, the mark swerved or dodged. Dodging birds and intercepting tree trunks and limbs will always account for plenty of missing, and gun patterns for another percentage. Binocular shooting is a gun movement, and from the time the piece starts to cover the mark, little is seen in front of the gun except the mark. That gun movement once started, is going to be finished, and if a tree gets in the way the load will be slammed right into it—which is done plenty often enough in brush shooting.

The reason our marksman cannot change from one-eye aiming to two-eye aiming lies partly in the gun. Leave both eyes wide open again. Point the finger at some object, directly at it apparently. Close the left eye now, hold the finger rigid, and see if the finger is not pointing well under the object. The reason for this is ocular. When the two eyes are focused on an object it produces an eye strain to have something come between and

Stiff, awkward, and strained, a poor shooting stance.

interfere with the vision of one eye. Therefore, instinctively, without thinking, the object being aimed is kept low enough not to interfere with the vision of either eye. This means that if it is a gun, the barrels will be kept low enough not to interfere with the vision of the aiming eye, which must be kept just as clear and free of interference as the other eye. This keeps the gun down and it is going to shoot under, though apparently aimed exactly at the mark. For this reason I have found it necessary to so stock my guns that all of them will shoot high, about 15 inches high at forty yards. On the other hand the shooter who aims with one eye closed doesn't need a high shooting gun. The need for a high shooting gun, where a man aims with both eyes open, without seeing the gun, applies to both duck shooting and such birds as snipe and quail.

My own style of shooting on birds flying close to the ground, is not to put my cheek against the stock until about the time the gun is discharged. I have found that with the cheek pressed tightly against the comb, all of the gun movements are rendered slower and stiffer. The muscles of the neck are not accustomed to being swung and twisted violently, and the vision is disturbed by keeping the head in motion. For some such reason, when the bird springs, I drop my head just enough so that when the gun comes up and rises high enough to cover the mark the stock will barely touch cheek. Long practice will bring this about readily enough. If the comb never does touch cheek, that wouldn't make much difference, for the hands are guiding that gun and not the cheek pressed to comb. Matter of fact, since the aim is the culmination of a movement, and that culmination will not be altered in any event whether the cheek is against the stock or not.

Regarding the tightly pressed cheek and the firm grip on the gun, Fred Kimble says: "Most men, in the due course of a long, clean run, get more and more in earnest about it, and as they do, begin tightening up on the gun and cheek. Finally they are holding the piece like grim death, so much so that the gun movements become jerky—then they miss." This refers to trap shooting.

Chapter 37
LEAD

WING-SHOOTING DIFFERS from rifle shooting in at least two essentials. Primarily, the rifle is shot at a stationary target, the shotgun at a moving target; the rifle bullet is shot from a motionless gun, if that is possible, the shotgun missiles from a moving gun.

The rifle ball is directed by sights, and the marksman endeavors to hold those sights in exact alignment with the center of the target while the trigger is being pressed. The shotgun practically has no sight, and alignment is secured by the fit of cheek to stock. The rifle aim may be corrected again and again before the trigger is pulled; the shotgun is invariably let off to the first aim. The man who fails to fire with a shotgun, as his gun comes to the level, is a pottering shot, while the man who snaps off his rifle on big game is a reckless shot. Rifles may be fired like a shotgun, as in running shooting, and shotguns may be fired like a rifle as in pot-shooting. Running shooting is sometimes necessary with a rifle, but pot-shooting is rarely necessary with a shotgun. The gun movements and the systems of aiming a rifle at a still target and a shotgun at a moving target are entirely different. The man who tried to shoot a shotgun as he would a rifle can't do wing-shooting, and the man who tries to shoot a rifle as he would a shotgun will do plenty of missing.

Hitting with a shotgun depends upon correct lead, and without a knowledge of lead the more accurate the hold the more certain the miss. The marksman might hold a shotgun so directly upon the mark that he would hit it with a bullet, yet a spreading pattern of shot will cleanly miss, perhaps by feet or yards. That is why the great question in shotgun shooting is, where shall I hold, for a certain bird, at a certain range, at a certain angle of flight. No man ever lived or ever will live who could say with certainty just what the hold should be on every bird that breaks cover. On any wild bird very few men can more than approximately judge the lead, otherwise he could strike the mark with a rifle bullet, which is difficult.

We have a lot of fancy rifle shooters who do what might be

Excellent before-season practice. The small, portable trap can be set up anywhere.

termed wing-shooting, using a rifle; that is they are able to hit blocks and like objects tossed into the air and coming down. By shooting thousands of shots at such objects they learn the lead or the allowance, and can strike the mark about as well as though it were still, but I have never heard of any great bags of quail or other game birds being killed by these fancy riflemen. A bird doesn't go up a little way and then come straight down, or down at any other angle. He flyeth where he listeth, and how and when. Many years ago I read, I think in Stonehenge's *British Sportsman,* of some game keeper who in a match on live pigeons killed fifty in the hundred with a muzzle-loading rifle. All that is like the marvelous things that a man used to do when he was a boy, not to be demonstrated anymore. A few years since when dove shooting with a .22 rifle I fired at one passing with a six-inch lead and killed him—then emptied the remainder of the box of shells and never killed another. About that time it occurred to me that if I did hit another bird it would be a second accident and nothing else. No other bird flew precisely like that first one, and the six-inch lead that worked on that first dove never worked on any more. I have often thought that if I had tracer bullets so as to be able to watch the misses, I could hit game birds flying with a rifle, but have never been able to get the tracer bullets.

Every man needs a pattern spread in order to make amends for faulty lead or of a lack of accuracy in holding. Some need more spread than others. I shot quail for fifteen years with a full choked gun and nothing else, but after I learned how much easier it was to hit 'em with an improved cylinder never went back to the full choke. Lately somebody wrote me wanting to know how to make a cylinder bore spread wider, and the individual who already has a gun which covers 30-inch circle at twenty yards is full of schemes to get a greater spread. I question the sportsmanship of that sort of thing, unless a man wants to gamble on a certainty or he won't play. Upland game birds are becoming so scarce and bags so limited that I'd be willing to see quail guns confined to twenty bores and smaller, all full choke. If we could have quail guns which would cover no more than a six-inch circle at twenty yards, hitting a bird would be like beating par at golf, and would tickle us about as much when it happened. In a measure I am living up to my convictions and have no quail gun larger than a sixteen bore, and none more open than a quarter choke.

Lead of course depends on the speed of the mark in proportion to the velocity of the shot. This is modified directly by the angle of flight, and indirectly by many other things. If the bird flew at the rate of a hundred feet a second, and the shot has a velocity of a thousand feet over a forty-yard range, the distance at which the bird passed, then the speed of the bird being one-tenth that of the shot he must fly ten feet while the shot were getting to him at

Good, easy stance.

that particular distance. If the speed of the bird were no more than fifty feet a second, that would cut lead in two. That kind of calculation gives us theoretical lead, and it is not to be disputed except as to the speed of the mark. I am giving below a table showing the estimated speed of different game birds, together with the theoretical and practical lead, such lead being based on the velocity of a standard load of No. 6 shot at an instrumental velocity of 977 feet.

SPEED OF GAME BIRDS AND LEAD

Bird	Speed per second	Average Speed	Theoretical Lead (40 yards)	Practical Lead (40 yards)
Quail	60 to 80	70	8.7	4 to 5 feet
Prairie Chicken	60 to 80	70	8.7	4 to 5 feet
Ruffed Grouse	65 to 80	72.5	9.	5 feet
Dove	70 to 90	80	9.8	5 feet
Jack Snipe	50 to 70	60	7.36	4 feet
Curlew	40 to 60	50	6.	3 feet
Mallard	50 to 90	70	8.7	4 to 5 feet
Black Duck	50 to 90	70	8.7	4 to 5 feet
Spoonbill	50 to 90	70	8.7	4 to 5 feet
Pintail	60 to 90	75	9.2	5 feet
Wood Duck	60 to 80	70	8.7	4 to 5 feet
Widgeon	70 to 85	77	9.5	5 feet
Gadwall	70 to 80	77	9.5	5 feet
Redhead	80 to 90	85	10.4	5 to 6 feet
Bluewing	75 to 95	85	10.4	5 to 6 feet
Greenwing	80 to 90	85	10.4	5 to 6 feet
Canvasback	90 to 100	95	11.66	6 to 7 feet
Canada Goose	80 to 90	85	10.4	5 to 6 feet
Brant	80 to 90	85	10.4	5 to 6 feet

It is to be seen that the practical lead differs from the theoretical. Very few men make as much allowance as the theoretical lead demands, and if they attempted to do this would miss. The practical lead has been averaged from statements of a great many duck shooters as to the lead they take at 40 yards. The gain of practical lead over theoretical lead is due to swing or to the rapidity of the swing.

My own lead on a mallard at forty yards would be about three feet, unless the bird was scared, when it might be four to five feet. My lead at sixty yards as well as I can judge it is about six feet, and at seventy yards around ten feet. At eighty yards I have not been able to fix any lead because the ducks are missed so often.

Fred Kimble said that his lead at 40 yards was one length of a mallard in front of the bird's bill; his lead at 60 yards was doubled, becoming two lengths, and at 80 yards was again

Shooting hard-trapped targets.

doubled, becoming four lengths. He gave the length of a big duck as two feet. When duck shooting, lead in lengths of the fowl is more definite and more easily measured than it is in feet. To the evidence of the senses fowl become steadily smaller with distance. A bird or duck 60 yards overhead will look no larger than a pigeon and no longer. A length ahead of such bird will be taken as no more than a foot, hence the discrepancy in the lead that one man or another will assume that he has taken. In long range shooting it is difficult to give the lead in feet, but it can be taken with better accuracy through the picture before the eye; there is the bird and we picture a certain space between him and where the gun is pointed; that amount of space, whatever it may appear to be, killed the last time we tried it and the time before, so we have the picture of the fowl and that appearance of space in mind and take it, again killing.

Bogardus said that while most men needed a lead of four feet on a mallard at 40 yards, yet, because he shot very quickly, his lead was simply in front of the bird's bill. I have talked to a lot of old-time market gunners, watched some of them shoot also, and they told me the same thing, "Hold just in front of the duck's head and swing." We know very well that a hold just in front of the head on a passing duck at forty yards would surely miss him hence there is a catch somewhere. The only catch that I can see is the quickness with which the gun was handled and the swing. If the marksman waited until his muzzle had daylight between it and the fowl, piece coming on from behind and traveling three times as fast as the duck, swing being carried through, no telling what the lead became before he could pull the trigger. When his mind said pull, the deed was accomplished, in his mind, but the trigger lock might have registered a little more time.

The only gain due to swing is whatever space the gun may cover from the time the pull is started mentally until the shot is out of the muzzle. This will vary with one man and another because trigger and lock time vary.

The time of a fast lock has been measured at ⅟₇₅₀ of a second. Barrel and ignition time have been given as ½₅₀ of a second. If the bird were flying at the rate of 100 feet a second it is to be seen that he would cover 1.6 inches while the lock was acting, and 4.8 inches during barrel and ignition time. Trigger-pulling time has been variously estimated at from ½₅ to ⅟₂₅₀ of a second. I have noticed that it takes three feet of a quail's flight in order to stop a trigger pull that has been started, getting those figures from bird's being killed by some one else before I would shoot, aim having been taken and trigger pull started. I therefore conclude that it would take half of this time in order to start and accomplish a trigger pull, ⅟₆₀ of a second. In this ⅟₆₀ of a second, the duck at the given rate would fly two feet. We therefore have a duck travel of two feet five and four-tenths inches while the gun was being discharged. If the aim were taken directly at the fowl the load would fall that far behind, due to lock, barrel, and ignition time, and trigger time—this entirely aside from time over the course in shot velocity. If we added four feet for shot travel over the course, as in theoretical lead, that would throw us six feet, five and four-tenths inches behind the bird. However, if the gun movement were three times as fast as that of the bird, during this interval between thought and accomplished action, the gain of gun over mark would be seven feet and three inches. This, after deducting the time of the shot over the course, which we will take as requiring a lead of four feet, would leave the load directed three feet and three inches ahead of the mark, even though aim were taken directly at the mark. Granted, now, that the trigger pull was not started until gun was in front of the duck's head, he ought to be hit. I can see no other logical means by which swing can gain on lead. As a matter of fact, though, the shooter cannot move his piece three times as fast as the bird flies, and for this reason requires some conscious lead, which will vary with the man, his trigger time, and the rapidity of the swing which he can govern. Doubtless the old-time duck shooters who were in action every day, killing perhaps one hundred ducks a day, could swing much faster and deliver the shot to that swing much more accurately than we can who will not shoot a hundred ducks in the season. For some such reason we have the market gunner of another day with his dictum that lead was to be taken at forty yards directly in front of the bird's bill, and the modern theorist who can prove that the lead must be nine feet.

All of which sums up into this: Every man will be a law unto himself about the lead he takes and the lead he requires. The best we can do for him is to give him a hint by telling him the lead we take. After that it will all be a great gamble; it is a gamble with us who have shot a great deal, and it will be still more of a gamble with him. No matter, we are all gamblers born, and this wing-shooting is the most beautiful and the most fascinating gamble that the world of sport affords.

In the nature of things, lead is directly dependent on the distance of the mark; that is so obvious that it ought not to be said. Knowing the lead at forty yards doesn't do us a particle of good if the bird is sixty yards away. That is where experience and opportunity to shoot has an inning. We all know great traps shots who make a comparatively poor showing on game. They haven't shot game enough to know the lead or to judge distance. Distance is usually judged by feather markings and the blending of colors. The height of a fowl above the ground makes a difference in his appearance, not only as to feather markings but as to size. A duck 60 yards away but close to the earth will appear large, and his markings will be distinct, but 60 yards straight up will make him appear entirely beyond reach of the gun, for he will look small, and his colors will blend into a uniform neutral tint. Therefore do not lead overhead ducks too much, and take chances on them when they appear to be out of range, but if a horizontal shot is taken at a fowl and he looks far away, be very sure that he is, even farther away than he appears to be—add to the lead.

Like the Revolutionary War hero who told his men to wait until they could see the enemies' eyes before firing, if a duck's eyes can be seen he can surely be hit. If the green of a mallard's head and the markings of his wing coverts can be seen, he isn't far away. If it is hard to tell a duck from a drake, don't shoot. If the birds are so far away that spaces can hardly be seen between them, don't shoot. Everybody has shot at flocks at one time or another, but if the fowl are so far away that singles cannot be picked, it is an outrage on the ducks to shoot at them. Veteran shots err on the side of requiring the birds to come in too close before shooting; beginners try them entirely beyond range. Expert shots sometimes acquire a knack of waiting until two birds cross and bagging both with one shot—that is different from flock shooting, and is another gamble, a gamble as to whether both birds will be killed or both missed.

Let me say in closing that we are all given to underestimating distances in the air. We have all shot at a bird and noticed that we were slightly off when the trigger was pulled, maybe three inches of light between the bird and the sight. That ought not to have made any difference, mark being at forty yards, for we very well know that at the distance we have a 30-inch pattern to play with. But the bird went on. How could that happen? Guess for yourself as to whether that three inches was really ten inches or more. Shooting at the trap or with full choked guns on game, it won't do to hold off at all—miss if you do.

The whole thing is a sort of optical illusion. I suspect that the same principle applies to taking lead. We are convinced that the lead was a foot or two feet or three feet and it may have been six to eight feet. That is one reason why we make a mess of trying to tell the other fellow where to hold in feet. His conception of what a foot looks like in the air may be different from ours.

A great many shooters have a sort of conviction that when we swing the muzzle of the gun we give the shot a lateral movement. I noticed that Colonel Cutts, when writing of the effect of vibration, stated that the vibration of the muzzle gave the shot a lateral movement that carried them to one side as much as 20 inches. Vibration might cause the gun to shoot 20 inches to one side all right, but it would be due to the muzzle turning in the new direction and not from any lateral movement imparted to the shot.

This thing was threshed out and argued pro and con long ago. The example of tossing a stone from a moving train was cited, the lateral movement due to the motion of the train causing the missile to take a curved flight. If a man shoots at a still mark, from a moving car, his shot will retain the movement of that car, and his aim will have to be sufficiently to one side to make allowance. I have tried that often. At one time I concluded that if a man could take his gun and swing it as he does a golf stick, swinging faster than a bird flies, he could pull off back of the bird and yet the shot would curve forward and get ahead of it. Then it occurred to me that all the movement imparted to the shot by this sort of swing would be centrifugal. That is if you swung the gun at the rate of two hundred feet a second at the muzzle, all that would be done would be to add two hundred feet per second to the muzzle velocity, giving the shot no lateral movement whatever. Therefore no lateral movement can be given to shot however fast the gun may be swung, neither can anything be gained on lead.

Chapter 38

CLASS, FORM, STYLE, AND TIME

CERTAIN TERMS are common to all works devoted to shotgun shooting, yet perhaps had as well be mentioned and defined, where this has not been done.

We read of class, style, form, time, gun aiming, gun pointing, swing, snap, lead, allowance, speed of flight, angle of flight, drivers, incomers, outgoing birds quartering to right and left, incomers overhead and to right and left, and towering birds. Some of these terms practically explain themselves, while others have more than one definition, and our view of the meaning will be given.

Class is used by trap shooters in the same way that it would be in the school room; that is, a man belongs to a certain class, depending upon his skill or his previous performance. Thus we have the ninety-five-percent class, ninety-percent, eighty-five, and so on—the marksman being classified in accordance with the number of birds that he is expected to break in the hundred. Of course the field or the duck shot is not classified in this way or at all except as he may classify himself or some one may do that for him, as, expert, skilled, good, fair, and poor. Most of us can 'be expected to classify ourselves as damned rotten at times, and again, as good as anybody, not caring a tinker who the other fellow may be. If we were classified trap-shooter fashion by percentage, on such birds as quail, say, the expert would bag 70%, the good shot 60%, fair shot 50%, and poor shot 35 to 40%. An expert duck shot, shooting decoyed birds only, might kill ninety percent, when conditions were just right.

Class has another and more technical meaning, however, as applied to shooting men, to race horses, bird dogs, and perhaps other things. We hear of horses that have class, of high-class bird dogs, and of high-class men. Usually the latter is a statesman rather than a politician, and at least a man who can rise above party at times. With reference to shooting, I would define the class man as a pinch hitter, a man whose best powers are brought out in an emergency, and then only. A horse, having class, may show but moderate speed in his work-outs, possibly trailing some stable mate, but in the actual race, especially a race under adverse conditions, class tells, upsets all calculations, and that horse wins. The high-class dog may simply have what we call heart, what the soldier calls "guts," what the late J. A. Graham called stomach— perhaps after all merely grim courage. The wing-shot, if a match shooter, has the same sort of heart. He may be but a moderately good shot or he may be an expert, but in any event, this he has— when the necessity arises, when other men's nerves are giving way, our class man always can be depended upon to outshoot his stand-ard performance.

We might say with truth that the man has courage, endurance, but he has all that and more—he is the sort of man who has latent powers, powers which are called upon in case of extreme emer-gency and at no other time. I have seen men who couldn't shoot well or who wouldn't unless a bet was on; then beware of them. I used to have an old shooting chum, Billy Field of St. Louis, who would plug along, missing some birds and hitting others. Now and then when I wanted a good bag I'd say to him, "Billy, you are not shooting well today; bet you a dollar I beat you out." That settled it; Billy put up his dollar and the birds went down right and left. Again some shooter may be but moderately good until he gets into a tie, whereupon he never fails to become dangerous. He is a class man, a high-class man, a man of latent powers, called upon in an emergency, a pinch hitter pure and simple.

Style, in its general sense, implies the ability to do things with ease, grace, apparently without effort, and yet efficiently, with a certain dash and brilliance that forces admiration. Style is more or less born in us, a part of our constitutional make-up, and may or may not be acquired. The man who is obviously putting undue effort into what he accomplishes may be efficient but he lacks style. For example, the men I have mentioned who were exceptional shots, yet used up a tremendous amount of energy in accomplish-ing what should have been an easy and smooth performance. We may admire the misses of a man who has a brilliant style more than we do the hits of one who shoots with a labored effort. Chauncey Powers was an example of a trap shot, both at clays and live birds, no less in the field, who had brilliant style. Spectators liked to see Chauncey Powers shoot because he had the make-up of an engine that never had a knock in it, noiseless, no waste motion and no useless expenditure of energy. Style or the lack of it applies to every phase of life.

The term has a more technical meaning, as applied to shooting. It may merely refer to the method of aiming or the time. We some-times say that a man has a quick style, or a deliberate style, or a pottering style. His style of shooting may be snap work or a swing-ing style. This sort of style means method more than anything else.

Duck guns.

However, in the best meaning of the word style, it means brilliancy in action.

Every sport or game develops certain fixed principle which should not be violated. The sprinter has a certain method of taking position, a certain manner of getting into stride, a way of holding that stride, a correct carriage of the body, steps that are high enough and not too high, long enough and not too long. When every movement he makes is studied perfection, we say that he has form. In the same way a man may develop form in any variety of athletics, and in shooting. The man who has perfect form is making the very best use of the powers that nature has given him; he may not be an expert shot but usually is.

When speaking of shooting, the term form sometimes has a more restricted meaning. We speak of this or that man being in good form, meaning in good form for him. Ordinarily his form may be poor, but today he is doing better and we say that he is in fine form. Very few men, however expert, have perfect form, or they are in perfect form only occasionally. Form is not quite equivalent to style, for a man may have excellent form and yet lack brilliance.

Every act or action or feat accomplished has its own form which must be followed and sustained. For instance, the perfect form for a trotter, high and easy knee action, would be very poor form for a running horse. In the same way, good form for the modern trap shot, standing with butt to shoulder and catching his bird invariably at 32 yards, would be very poor form for the quail shot. Perfect form implies that no movement or action is overemphasized, and none is slighted. If any movement can be improved, then the form is not perfect.

Watching a known good performer at the traps, we may decide that he is a little out of form. Perhaps he is breaking his birds, but

The 10-gauge Fox Magnum.

is slobbering some of them, or possibly he is not catching them at his regular distance, too quick or too late or irregular. We know that he is a trifle out of form, and that sooner or later, probably sooner, he is to miss. Perhaps such a man may shoot himself into form after a bit or he may shoot himself farther out. The same principle applies to the field shot. The things that he can do today, he may not be able to accomplish at all next week. He knows that he is out of form but cannot tell why, perhaps, and the greater his efforts to get back into form the worse he shoots. When the writer finds himself getting out of form, he usually changes guns, and he and his dog form all the crowd that is needed until he gets back into form. Usually changes in form come suddenly, though not always. A man is shooting finely today and is off tomorrow, maybe to shoot poorly for a week, then, of a sudden he is shooting again like a house afire. All the time he is off he keeps thinking about it and trying to dope out the reason, which as a rule he cannot. The best thing he can do is to take the advice that Emerson Hough gave George Kleinman when he appeared to be losing a match, "George, why don't you quit thinking and just shoot?"

One of the great differences between the expert and the novice lies in the ability to maintain time. Miss or hit, the crack shot doesn't change his time or he never would have acquired a reputation for such skill. The novice fires at a bird quickly and misses. "Shot too quickly," he says to himself, and the next shot is taken very deliberately—also a miss. From then on he keeps changing from fast to slow to anything else he can think of. After while, and it may be quite a "spell" after, he learns to maintain time, the time that is doing the best work for him.

Time can be separated into gun time and trigger time. Half of off-hand rifle shooting consists in developing perfect trigger time. The marksman who is perfect on the trigger, who can let off precisely when he desires, invariably when he desires, can shoot a rifle well, not only in the off-hand but in any other position. His holding may not be very steady, but he can hit anyhow. Let me add, however, that no rifleman ever has been perfect on his trigger or probably ever will be. His trigger finger betrays him, and the trigger finger betrays the shotgun man too, right along down the line. He is covering a bird, knows precisely where he ought to hold, has the fixed intention of holding there, when bang goes his gun just before he gets on. Gun time and trigger time didn't coordinate, and there you are.

Trigger time is complicated with lock time, and time up the barrel, all of which alter lead, but which should be uniform and not affect lead, so long as one gun and one load are used. Trigger time is a prime cause, however, of erratic shooting. Most of us can become accustomed to almost any kind of a trigger pull, so long as we use that trigger and no other. There is no such thing, though, as pulling a three-pound trigger with one shot and an eight-pound trigger with the next, and still maintaining uniformity in time or uniformity in results, unless all shots are misses.

I once had a friend, an electrical engineer, to whom I stated the difficulties of shooting due to pulling the trigger. He thought that some device might be possible by which the trigger might be started electrically but at last accounts he hadn't any patent on the idea. The only way it could be done would be to pull trigger by thought, to wish it off. Pulling trigger takes time; as measured along the line of the flight it may take from one to three feet of

Duck shooting along White River in Arkansas.

space. In due course the knowledge comes to the shooter that if his lock is to yield, precisely as the sights cover the mark, the pull must be started just before the sights are on; otherwise the gun will pass the mark before the trigger yields. From this conclusion, trigger time develops, most likely unconsciously. The marksman presses the trigger just before covering the bird or other object, with the feeling that now is the time, and when the gun is discharged he also knows without analyzing the reason, whether or not he was on.

If the gun is moving and the trigger is pulled to that movement, it follows that the trigger time must be based on the speed of the gun movement. Whip up the gun and delay the trigger and there you are; whip up the trigger and delay the gun, and there you are—in either event the bird goes elsewhere. By which it can be seen that our shooting judgment might be betrayed either by trigger or gun action, which must be coordinated. We have all heard of a coordination of eye and finger, but it should be a coordination of eye, gun movement, and trigger time.

Gun time, I think, is the cause of the most trouble. Gun time is the space from the instant the shooter makes up his mind to take the shot up to the discharge of the gun. It is the culmination of several movements which merge into one another, and all of which may be performed unconsciously. Gun and trigger time are rather easily kept in adjustment, provided the target did what was expected, as in clay bird shooting. A live bird may behave according to no rule of his tribe; the shot may be delayed by his erratic action, and the usual systematic time will be destroyed. This is what causes misses. We get impatient because the bird is getting away, and finally the trigger lets go anyhow, off or on. No man exists whose trigger finger does not betray him sometimes, but the man with the iron control will not be very far off; and if he·has an open-bored gun, its pattern spread may still enable him to hit. I have always been of two minds about the open-bored gun. One is that I can hit when the aim is not precise and the other is that knowing the limited range of my piece I handle it faster than my time will permit.

Getting out of time is the great source of poor shooting on the part of all widely experienced shots. If the expert trap shot drops from his accustomed 98% to under 95%, he is a bit out of time. He may or may not know it, but the cause is there. Just why he should get out of time is another question that will be taken up in another chapter. It may be from lack of steady practice, may be from too much practice, causing him to become stale, may be from over-anxiety, may be from nervousness, may be from jealousy, may be from irritation, and from other causes, as too much money at stake or too little.

Shooting with a companion who may be a bit jealous or a bit overanxious to make a good showing is a prime cause of the field

Studying the pattern. The late Major Charles Askins, right.

shot getting out of time. If we know the other fellow is liable to whip in and take a shot which rightly belongs to us, we are nearly certain to speed up and lose correct time in doing it. I have a way of avoiding this which I find works very well. All birds killed go to my companion. He has to carry them, and he presently loses track of what I killed and what he killed, so that doesn't worry him and it doesn't worry me. At the end of the day I take a half dozen birds, if I need them, otherwise the bag is his. If I really need a bag rather than cheerful company for the day, I play a lone hand. This thing of two men "doubling" on birds steadily all day shows that something is wrong with one man or the other or both.

This thing of trying to "wipe the other fellow's eye," deliberately waiting to do it, is inexcusable. I remember doing it once by way of curing a man of a bad habit, but even so it was not justified. He was a good shot and a good fellow aside from his shooting, but keen and perhaps a bit selfish. After killing a half dozen quail, all of which should have been mine from where they broke cover and upon all of which we had doubled, with "Elmer" sure that he had killed the birds, I hit upon the scheme. I told him to take all the shots, and that I would wait until he had fired one shot, but to be quick about it so that the bird didn't get beyond my reach. When the next bird got up I repeated hurriedly and loudly, "quick quick, QUICK!" He shot quickly sure enough and missed, not even firing his second barrel, for he was certain my gun would whip in immediately, which it did not. This was kept up until he had missed several shots and become exasperated.

"Why don't you say slow once," he said. So I called as the bird broke, "slow, slow, SLOW!" And he missed just the same. His time was gone, but his temper remained, and finally he got around the end of a hedge where I couldn't see him and ducked me.

Time changes with the bird, and usually the change is made automatically. The time that is effective on ducks will not be right on ruffed grouse, or even snipe. I believe some of the clay-bird shots have faster time than anybody else—I have seen some of these lads catch a bird within 40 feet of the trap, and that is lightning speed. Some of the trap shots acquire a time so fast that they cannot use it afield, which leaves us wondering how such a fine trap shot can fall off so badly on quail.

Chapter 39

MECHANICAL EXECUTION

MECHANICAL EXECUTION is not all of wing-shooting, but there is no such thing as reaching expert form without the ability to repeat an act over and over again without variation. Once, twice, five times the shooter may do the trick perfectly, but the sixth time he may notice that he was a bit off, and he was farther off when the shot reached the mark.

Mechanically, men differ and one man may be what we call a natural mechanic, while the next man, though he may be an intellectual giant, is mechanically a weakling. Mechanics can be acquired; it is merely a matter of training, and the less our natural ability the more rigid the course of training. In any event the gun is a mechanical weapon which rarely makes amends for poor holding, though a lot of us keep on searching for just that kind of a gun.

Mechanically, within limitations, we have just one splendid class of wing-shots. Our best trap shooters have very nearly reached human perfection in handling a gun at the traps. The man who breaks one hundred little flying saucers straight, or two hundred or three hundred is so schooled and trained in repeating a performance that we must give him high credit. I have said above "within limitations," and of course the trap performer goes through simple maneuvers. He takes his position with his feet just so, and if he is a careful man and found a pebble under one foot he would kick it out of the way before calling "pull." If he had any coat on other than his old accustomed shooting jacket he'd be lost. Now he puts his gun to his cheek, and Jim Elliott used to take his finger and thumb and measure just the distance from point of comb to his nose. Cheek is held rigidly in position while the body is flexed and bent, dropping and raising the gun as when the bird is being covered. Then he calls "pull," and with one swift, accurate, perfectly timed movement covers the bird, after it is sprung and its course marked. He breaks the bird invariably, unless conditions, such as a high wind, interfere with his mechanical execution.

These men become so mechanically perfect that watching them is tedious and trying, to every one who is not shooting. The man

311

who is one of them, who has gone through the entire course of rigid training, will be interested, because he knows just the strain the shooter is under, but the spectator doesn't know and he soon gets so he doesn't care. He feels as he would feel if observing the work of a machine which could be guaranteed to run all day and never miss a cog. Every movement of the trap shot is simplified, so far as that is possible. He does nothing that is not absolutely essential, and he does that after a fixed form. His training embraces other things, as tremendous concentration, but concentration is outside of this chapter. He knows where to hold also; but that is not very hard to learn for the simple flights taken by a clay bird, and the bulk of his training lies in mechanics.

The simplest form of mechanical execution, as applied to the gun, is off-hand shooting at a stationary target with a rifle. The whole thing is as plain and simple as a nose with a bump on it. The bull is there, clearly outlined in black and white; the rifle is sighted in and is accurate enough to hold the inner ring; the sights are fine enough, taken in connection with the man's vision, so that he could pull a ten for every shot, where nothing else interfered. Our marksman has just two things to accomplish, hold for the center and pull the trigger—both performances purely mechanical. Can he do it? Nobody ever has, though Dr. Hudson came pretty close to doing that very thing. Can you take a pin and holding it half inch from a piece of paper jab a hole in the paper and then repeat ten times without enlarging the hole? Try it. If you cannot that is a lack of mechanical training for the movements are simple. It is the same thing with rifle shooting at a target, the movements are so simple that if a man were perfectly trained in his holding there would be no movement of the gun after it covered the target, leaving only trigger pressure, which is simple also when the piece cannot move. Yet the training demanded by off-hand rifle shooting is immensely exacting. It seems that in the human make-up, movements are more readily accomplished with accuracy, than an absence of movement can be sustained. Therein the shotgun man has an advantage of the rifleman, for all his acts consist of trained movements. Then, too, the shotgun shooter is permitted some tolerance, while the rifle marksman has none.

Emerson Hough, in the day when he was a sporting writer, taking in the live-bird matches in Chicago and vicinity, which he described for *Forest and Stream,* used to tell of a friend of his who shot matches for money, as most of the oldtimers did. This man used to put in his evenings before a match just putting up his gun, aiming and pulling trigger, thousands of times. He had a mark up in his room, and was training himself to hold his piece, gun butt beneath the elbow, then a smooth shift of butt to shoulder, cheek

Loading in weather 30 degrees below zero can be difficult.

going to comb, and the piece moved from this direction and that to cover the mark, trigger pulled as the sight came on. Shifting to the second barrel another bull would be covered, as in the use of two barrels on game.

There is a balance wheel in the back of a man's head or in some other part of his head that enables him to stand on his pegs without wavering, and to look you in the eye steadily without batting a lash. Nature made that man a good shot and a good shot he will be if he has a chance to practice. A second man, as all drill masters know, cannot stand still, and can't be taught to stand still. Put him to walking down a straight line and he will wobble off of it. This second man will have difficulty in training himself into becoming a clever shot; but he is not hopeless, and much can be done by systematic practice.

I remember the time when I trained myself in shotgun shooting with a .22 rifle, doing this in order to save ammunition. I'd put up a mark and shoot at it, swinging on from right, left, straight up, and quartering from either side. The gun was not checked as it passed the mark and the trigger had to be timed to the gun movement. By and by I could hit very close to the mark, however I came on.

Of course much of this work was trigger timing. If the gun moved fast the trigger pull had to be more prompt, and again the trigger had to be timed to a more deliberate movement. However, the greatest endeavor was to move the piece very fast and yet so time the trigger that the bull would be hit. No effort was made to stop the gun on the mark, which would have negatived the whole system of training. This kind of work could be done with an empty gun, but it required a bullet to prove the pudding. The man who can swing by from all directions and yet stay in a four-inch bull at 20 yards is a good one.

In the nature of things the field shot or the duck shot requires more training in mechanics than any modern trap shot with gun to cheek. The field shot may be walking along when a bird breaks cover; he may be carrying his gun in any manner to make it feel least burdensome. In any event, he won't have the butt to his shoulder or his cheek to comb. His first effort is to get his feet under him in position to shoot and to balance himself. Along with the movement of his feet, his gun butt is coming to shoulder, and must come up just so, neither too high nor too low, too far in nor too far out and it should not be jammed to the shoulder, which would give him a momentary shock. Meantime he has not been thinking of any of these things, which are to be accomplished automatically, for his mind is on the bird and he is trying to guess what it will do next. Gun up, properly at shoulder, the next thing is to cover the bird, and this must be done without disturbing the balance. No matter how much the mark twists about, the balance should be maintained. If the gun butt has come up true, if the legs are in position, if the body balance is maintained, if the cover-

Major Charles Askins and one of his favorite targets, old John Crow.

ing movement is accurate, if the trigger is correctly timed, and if the lead is right, there is a dead bird. This doesn't happen all the time, for we would be bagging 98 in the hundred all the same as the trap shot. That we have to be content with 60 to 75 birds in the hundred is much the fault of our gun mechanics.

One thing trap shooting can teach us. Whatever is to be done in the way of mechanical movements, do it in precisely the same way every time. Do not vary the position of the feet, the manner of holding the gun while waiting the shot, the position of butt to shoulder, place where the cheek strikes the comb, the rapidity of the gun movements, or the style of swing and aim, if mechanical excellence is ever to be obtained. A quail or a grouse is supposed to fly and no doubt does fly fifty feet the first second. With the shooter perhaps walking the bird up and not knowing precisely where it will break cover, even if he knows a bird is to appear, his legs must be brought under him, gun to shoulder, aim taken and the shot pulled, all in perhaps three-fourths of or even a half second. This meant that every action takes place far too quickly for conscious thought, and reliance must be placed on automatic action. The basis for this automatic perfection must be trained into us by conscious effort, however.

The minute a man consciously interferes with the subconscious or automatic, his system is gone and he will have to consciously make all gun movements, becoming slow and inaccurate. I have always found myself a poor hand to wait out a shot and allow the other fellow to shoot first. Generally this results in both of us missing. Standing with gun up, waiting for the other fellow to shoot, waiting to see whether he has missed, waiting to see if he is to use the second barrel, and finally slashing in a shot hurriedly, out of time, commonly results in a sure miss. Presently the novice may say, "Why you are missing just as many birds as I am, and I have always been told you were a crack shot." Then your wounded vanity may tempt you to slap in a few shots, just by way of showing him you can do it if you try. I have been accused of willfully missing birds, because of trying to stop them after some beginner had quit shooting. Of course this is much a matter of time and interrupted time, but if there is anything that needs to be trained into a marksman until it becomes mechanical, that thing is time.

The shooter with perfect mechanical execution is not supposed to miss anything where he knows the lead. Where he means his shot to go, the pattern goes, this time and the next time and every time. If the bird is not there, that is the fault of the bird or of the man's knowledge of the bird. Nevertheless, this implies that the mechanical adjuncts be in tune, that is, the gun. It is by no means certain that because the shooter has acquired time and mechanical execution with a certain gun, with a certain weight of gun, he is to sustain time and movements with a heavier piece or a lighter piece, or with a different stock or a changed balance. If our shooter is mechanically high, consistent, and, unknown to him, his gun has changed his time or his movements, misses will occur with the greatest regularity. If he misses a bird by overshooting or under-shooting, he will miss the next similar bird in precisely the same way, and he is not going to hit that bird by accident, because he has gone past the accidental stage.

During the past quail season on the opening day, I loaned my gun to a friend and picked up a little Winchester cylinder bore pump gun, 20 gauge. I fired fifteen shots that morning and killed three quail—the worst quail shooting that I can remember doing in thirty years. I didn't know the gun and never had shot it on quail or anything else. The first two shots were misses in the open, the third winged a bird, which escaped, the fourth killed one on a high hold. That settled it; the gun must be shooting low. I held

Major Charles Askins, his favorite dog, Poopdyke, and his favorite smooth-bore, the Browning over-under.

high, held farther ahead, held closer in, but it didn't do any good. At noon I changed to my own gun and easily finished out a bag limit for the day. I never did shoot that twenty bore again, but the next man who tried it swears that it is the best quail gun ever turned out by the Winchester factory. Probably the whole trouble was due to lost time, since I was just off a long season on doves, where I had been shooting a gun weighing 8¾ pounds. However, my own quail time, after I get broken in on the birds, is best sustained by a gun weighing about seven pounds, not much lighter and not much heavier. I change to a lighter gun only when I find myself slowing up.

On the same principle, the marksman who can maintain his mechanics and his mechanical time though changing guns which might weigh now six pounds and now ten, is a freak, if he ever existed. He is a Bob Fitzsimmons among shooting men and can do any sort of unreasonable thing that he takes a notion to. At that, he had better not become too notional.

Perfect mechanics implies no change in gun, in its weight, stock measurements, balance, and those parts gripped by the hands. For the latter reason very few men will shoot equally well with a pump gun and with a double. He will be trained to one gun or the other and the change will break him up more or less. The only change that may be demanded is that which may be further sustaining his time and mechanics. Should his muscles begin to weaken, for age or other cause, or should he become stale from too much shooting, slowing him up, changing his time inadvertently, he may regain it by lightening his gun or straightening his stock. Hence the only change that should be made is one that takes place after careful thought and a deliberate analysis of faults that may have developed.

It is true that our gun performer may adopt two different styles of shooting, say one on birds that wing close to the ground and the other for game that is generally taken overhead. On snipe and quail he might intercept his birds with a quick snap, while on waterfowl he would come on from behind and carry past. The mechanical training for the two styles would be different, and the guns used might differ widely. Both methods of aiming could be brought to comparative perfection, the one without interfering with the other, and he would feel no less at home with the nine-pound duck gun than with the seven-pound quail gun. However, if he tries to snap with a ten-pound gun his time will be off; and if he tries to swing with a six-pound gun, he will miss without knowing why.

Chapter 40

HITTING vs. MISSING

IT IS JUST AS EASY to hit as it is to miss, and a good deal easier on one's vanity. Hitting and missing are only a few inches apart, and the process is precisely the same. Any man who can miss can also hit, and any man who can hit can also miss, the difference being only in ratio. Missing is accomplished the more often because the outdoors is bigger than the target. The way to hit is to build up a repertoire of shots than can be accomplished, just as success in singing depends on the number of songs that you can sing.

We have quail shooters, duck shooters, grouse shooters, snipe shooters, dove shooters, and every one of us is better at one of these birds than at any of the others, and no man is more than fairly good on all of them. The difference, of course, is that he has learned the speed and flight characteristics of one bird better than the others. In the nature of things this will always be so. We learn to shoot one bird or another according to opportunity, to predilection, and to make-up, physical and mental. I'd expect a light, quick man, nervously alive, to do better on grouse than he would on Canada geese. A big man, difficult to disturb or throw off balance, will kill the geese, and he will like goose shooting.

I have known just one profoundly good snipe shot in my time. He was moderately tall, lanky and strong, with deep-set eyes which now danced and now glared. When hunting snipe in the big, submerged meadows, he walked fast and quartered the ground like a trained dog. He either couldn't or wouldn't walk a moderate gait. He preferred to walk a few miles, say five or six, at a startling clip before beginning to shoot. Give him two drinks of whiskey, neither more nor less, and he didn't miss any snipe at all—neither did he lose any dead ones. He wouldn't have a dog, except the beast kept to heel. Neither could anybody else get any fun out of shooting snipe with Jim. He was immensely quick, and every bird was Jim's bird. Now and then he would agree not to shoot, but he was a critical audience, badly concealing his impatience with all misses. I tried to learn snipe shooting from him, but he had no ability to impart instruction. According to Jim, he just duly noted that the bird would get away unless he shot at it, so he shot it. What could

318

be more simple than that? He had a withering contempt, however, for a man who would let a snipe fly afoot farther than he had to. This was in a day when a lot was being said about allowing a snipe to fly a certain distance whereupon he would settle down to wing as steadily as a rail. Jim could hit 'em on the jump, so can any snipe shot.

The best duck shot with whom I have come into personal contact was a man something like Jim, more rugged, but as keen as a fighting bull-terrier. He had come from England for the sake of the shooting in this country. He could shoot anything, but was deadly on ducks. In him, I saw an abnormally fast man with a pump gun, for it was nothing unusual for him to empty his Winchester on a passing flock of teal, killing with the last shot. He worried a bit because he couldn't have ten shots in his gun in place of six. Unlike Jim, he was a student and could tell you precisely where to hold for every shot that might appear. Having killed thousands and thousands of ducks in his day, he ought to have known and did know how to take them. I could hit passing birds about as well as he could, but not after they had decoyed and come well within reach of his "corn-sheller."

Both Jim and George seemed to put tremendous energy into their shooting. Every shot was started and finished like a knockout swing. I didn't like that; thought a sportsman ought to do his work easily, gracefully, like a gentleman. Nevertheless in other respects they were governed by the rules of sport. Jim wouldn't shoot a rabbit or a quail until it had flown just so far, and if it got away unshot, that was a part of the game. George wouldn't kill an unwounded duck on the water. He declared that if he couldn't get his fun out of duck shooting he'd work at something else, and pot-shooting ducks was no different than chopping cotton and plowing corn.

A big German market shooter was the best quail shot that I have seen. He used a ten-bore lever-action Winchester, cylinder bored. He was absolutely systematic about everything he did, shooting over a slow-going dog that had been taught to flush to order. When the dog got birds, Dutch Frank went up and selected his position, then ordered the dog to jump in. He never followed quail into the brush, but murdered them in the open, deliberately, phlegmatically murdered them. Of a scattered flock few birds would get away from that man and that dog. Each of these men shot too well to really enjoy the sport. They were professionals, and I doubt if professionals ever do get as much kick out of the game as amateurs. Our marksman, professional or amateur, can become so good that a hit gives him little pleasure and a miss is a source of worry. The point I am trying to make is that we do

Bill Weaver, who developed a IX scope for the shotgun, tries the device.

not have to be so skilled as all that in order to secure the full measure of enjoyment from wing-shooting.

DUCKS

Now, getting along down to hitting or missing. Can you hit a duck passing at thirty yards, hit him every time? Yes. All well and good. You know just how a passing mallard looks over the barrels, how to swing or otherwise take him, how much to lead, and you know the results before pulling trigger. Very well; in the course of a day, maybe one duck in ten will fly by just like that, and you are safe about making a bag of one bird to ten shots. Now can you hit a bird coming straight over-head, not over 30 yards high? Sometimes! Well, that sometimes needs to be amended until it is every time. I believe the overhead incomer is the easiest bird to hit of them all. Don't let the old drake see you, place the gun under him, come up with him, cover him up and pull the trigger. Time the place of hitting him so that he will drop into the boat or blind. Once being able to hit the low flying incomer, you have two birds out of ten shots.

Now what is done by the birds, the remaining birds, when that low-flying incomer is killed? If mallards, what do they do, if bluewings, how do they act, if greenwings, if canvasbacks? You need to learn this. Mallards, low down, not yet over the gun, will flare and tower; pintails will do the same even when high. Can you catch one of those towering birds? No. Well it takes a bit of practice to learn that. Those ducks will climb, but only for a certain distance, when they apparently pause for an instant before resuming their course. Climb right with the selected fowl until he gets to the top of his bound, and then fire right between where he is and the direction he means to go. It is an easy shot provided the duck is waited out, and not taken on the bound. Of course that can be done also, but will come in later. At present we want to get the duck that has towered with the shot, starting at maybe 75 feet high and jumping to a hundred feet. He can be caught just at the top of his bound, or just after he has reached the apex of that bound. At the top of his bound, shoot right at him, with a gun that throws the charge a foot high, but it is safer to wait and lead just in front of his head. This shot ought, by and by, to become a fixed certainty, with big ducks not over a hundred feet away.

Bluewing teal, canvasbacks and redheads won't flare, or they won't flare much. These are fast birds, and they may get by the gun and have to be taken going away, or the second barrel will have to be taken going away.

A fowl from overhead travels off toward the horizon, which is always down. The tendency is to swing over him. Hence on overhead birds going away or passing birds going away, hold in front and low. The lead is not so great because part of that lead is due to holding low, which throws the charge in front. No man ever shoots ducks at all without getting this shot on birds that have passed the gun. Get the knack of taking these birds, and keep on studying the flight until it can be done. Now you have four flights that you can measure and master, which means four birds in ten shots. Plenty of us never learn to do any better.

The remaining six shots of the ten would be classed as misses. Some of these are due to a change in the bird, the shot which would kill a mallard might miss a teal or a canvasback, and the difference in lead must be learned. Mostly those other six misses though are due to distance. If the bird can be shot regularly at forty yards, can he be taken at fifty yards? Maybe. Can he be hit at sixty yards? No. Well, the difference is a difference in lead and this will have to be learned. It never is learned well enough except by a few men who have many opportunities.

Outside of handling the gun accurately, which we are assuming can be done, wing-shooting depends on knowing the bird, his characteristic flight and characteristic behavior. Knowing one bird doesn't tell us much about the next one, except all game birds fly fairly evenly and upon the whole without great variation in speed. It might appear that in making a selection of game birds we had chosen those difficult to hit, but on the contrary nearly all game birds are those that are easiest to hit of the winged creation. That is one reason why they were selected and the other reason is because they are good to eat. If we wanted difficult marks we might try the woodpeckers, the swallows and the sparrows. Most game birds keep a very straight course, but they have a certain method of swerving, jumping and ducking that needs to be learned. The snipe is one bird that doesn't keep a straight course, but it is just as easy to catch a curved ball as it is a straight ball, once you know it is going to curve, in what direction and how much. Every game bird has his little book of tricks, and he never forgets anything and he never learns anything further. Once we have learned his tricks we have mastered that bird.

SNIPE

The snipe is one of the easiest birds to hit, under good snipe conditions, that we have. He has but few tricks, and what he does today he does tomorrow, after the same set fashion. The wind and the weather are all that makes a difference to the snipe. Generally he is in the open, and he doesn't have to dodge trees or anything else. His zig-zag bounds are no more difficult than though he were flying straight, once they are mastered. He will

The author's favorite "secretario"—gun bearer—during four years he shot and hunted in Spain.

make one good long jump before the gun can come up, after which he will tack on another bound. We know he will do this because he always has done it and always will. Depending on the wind and his fright or state of nerves, the bounds or whips of a snipe will extend from fifteen to twenty feet. The problem of the shooter is to gauge these "air-jumps." Usually each successive tack is a little shorter than the last, but when a tack is started the bird can be caught before he reaches the end of it, a snipe that gets up within twenty yards can usually be killed within thirty yards, at the end of his second bound. The results are about as certain as wing-shooting can become. Occasionally, on cold days, when the birds rise wild, they can't be hit, taking a sort of corkscrew flight that nobody can gauge. This is to be expected on some days, and merely adds to the fascination of snipe-shooting. However, what the shooter has to learn about snipe-shooting is not what he can't do but what he can do and that is a plenty.

QUAIL

The quail is such a straight flying little chap that it looks like anybody ought to be able to hit him. Very often he flies as straight as a bullet, level with the gun, not to be missed any more than a stationary mark should be missed. Again, with regard to the position of the gun, Bob-White may go off quartering. A hold just in front will get the quartering bird with great certainty, for he is not any harder than the straight-away. I am going to take it for granted that everybody can get the straight-away and easy quartering birds, going off from four to six feet high, from twenty to thirty yards distant. At least three shots in ten will be of this nature, maybe five, maybe more. That is a pretty good percentage when we remember that it is said five birds in ten shots is good quail shooting. I do not consider five birds in ten good shooting myself, when one hunts alone and is not bothered by a second gun.

Supposing these three shots are easy enough, what is wrong with the other seven? The nature of the ground, the cover, and the position taken by the gun, either from necessity or choice. The nature of the ground! Know what that means. Have the dog make his find at the foot of a hill, and do you know what birds will do when they break cover? Nine times in ten they will dash right up and over that hill. A hold right at the bird is not going to kill him then, but it will have to be high, if taken as he climbs, and low after he reaches the top. There is your problem, then, a high shot as the bird climbs the hill, and then under him for the second barrel, for as sure as fate he will drop away as soon as he reaches the top of the hill. If it is a very high hill he may not go over, but still he will climb. The uphill first barrel and descending second barrel should be learned and added to the repertoire. Again there is the bird or the bevy that starts toward a hedge, or like cover. If the hedge is distant more than fifty yards, the flight may be level, if near, our quail is going to line for the top of it, and a low hold will miss him. It appears strange, sometimes, that we can be right on a bird and miss him, but he can top a pattern without any trouble, even when his rise is not perceptible. Look about at the cover and know what the bird is to do before he starts, because there is not much time for thinking afterwards. A second problem is the bevy that fairly explodes as it rises, goes right up into the air and then separates. Any time a bevy goes up forty feet high on the rise it is going to come down again, probably to begin descending immediately. Carry the gun up with these rising birds and they will, twice in three times, duck under the charge that is driven straight at them.

The other conundrum is to get into the proper position. Take it as fixed fact that no man can hit a quail flying within twenty feet of the shooter's head, and curving in flight. Get between birds and cover, possibly with the idea of driving them into the open, and the birds will fly all over you, all sides and above, and not one of them can be hit except by being very cool about it and turning on them. That means a difficult shot. Don't ignorantly or wilfully make a shot difficult; therefore let the little birds fly naturally and don't head them off from where they are bound to go anyhow. In the timber, particularly timber with underbrush, snap high and a foot too far ahead. Most misses in the brush come, not from striking the limbs, but from shooting behind and under; the shot appears "urgent" and not enough time is taken to get ahead.

In quail shooting the driving and quartering birds ought to be killed; the rising birds by covering them up, and those topping a hill or topping brush by holding a foot under and a foot ahead. The birds that tower and then wing straight off on a level demand low holding—keep that in mind and the shot is safe.

The low-flying shot is not afforded very often, except when two guns are working together, with one man on the hill, flushing the birds and another under it. When Bob is coming down the hill on you, hold low and well ahead. This leaves us the dodging and swerving birds for misses. Quail may dodge to avoid a limb, either up or down or to either side. They may in a burst of fright start out in the open, and then turn abruptly to make cover. They may get behind a tree after the allowance for lead is made, and if so the shot will plump into that tree, and the shooter will not be able to see that the tree is there until it is too late. Take quail quick, the farther they fly the harder they are to hit.

A good quail shot, with six in ten birds shot at in the open, should bag seven quail to ten shots. The other misses will be unavoidable, and he may miss more than three in ten. This kind of calculation applies to a double gun, if he shoots a repeater, half the birds will be missed, because he is taking more chances and shooting after the double gun is through. Don't snap a bird

Almost a limit.

that is in the open, there is plenty of time; don't swing on a bird that is in the brush, there isn't enough time.

WOODCOCK

From the wing-shot's standpoint we have two varieties of wood-cock shooting; taking them any time throughout the day, perhaps over the point of a dog; and taking the birds in flight.

Flight shooting occurs in the late afternoon, just before dusk after sunset. It is rare luck to discover a woodcock pass. The birds may have lain all day in some impenetrable marsh, but at sun-down come out, winging for some field where they intend to pass the night foraging. The woodcock is a night feeder, doing very little boring throughout the day. He is very likely to pass the day in dense cover, the night in quite open fields and it is when passing from his resting grounds to his "feed-yard" that we catch him in flight. The birds usually wing by on a clearly marked line, one bird coming after another in ghostly silence, no sound of wings; but the flight is from thirty to fifty feet above the ground and very steady, as is true of snipe under similar conditions. It is all a matter of lead and good holding, with a gun that is not much choked since it is mostly snap shooting, the bird coming and going with only one open space in which he may be taken.

Down in the Mississippi and Louisiana cane-brakes, where the stalks grow tall and dense, with water-filled openings winding about, cock dash out into the open, very much after the same fashion that quail do from a hedge. They come out with a twitter straight into the open space at the first bound, then turn, fly straight away, low to the ground, for thirty to fifty yards, and back into the same, entering the cane near the ground. These shots are very easy, but a great many birds are never seen, though heard, as when the cane is thin enough for them to climb up through it.

In ordinary woodcock shooting, to which gunners are accustomed in the East, the birds are found in cover, very often in alder slashes, sometimes in higher and more open ground. Typical woodcock shooting is among the alders and other dwarf timber. The cock comes as nearly having a set behavior then as any game bird ever does. They climb up through the short growth, top it, and then drop away. When the dog points, take a good look at the cover before flushing. If there is opening or a thiner spot among the alders, the gun should take a position to cover it, for the cock will probably go out right through that opening. The dog should be taught to flush to order. The only trick about the shooting is to catch the bird at the top of his bound, and not sooner or later, very much like hitting a tin can that somebody has tossed into the air. It is really hardly necessary to advise the hunter to shoot when the cock tops the brush because more than likely that is the only place where he will be seen. The hazard comes from the bird not showing in the opening at all, not showing long enough for a shot, or from intervening limbs and brush. A 20-bore gun is powerful enough, with open barrels and No. 8 shot. The most difficult problem in cock shooting today is finding the cock.

DOVES

The dove is a Western and Southern game bird. In the West he is an off-season bird, being shot at a time of the year when it is not legal to take anything else, so he gets plenty of attention. In the South where doves winter, they are shot in the pea-fields, either by being jumped or taking stands and pass shooting as the trim little chaps wing by. At times the birds are even driven, English fashion, the guns lining up along or behind some fence while a line of beaters are sent around to drive.

In the West in the semi-arid country, most shooting is at water-holes or on a pass leading to a pond. The shooting is then not essentially different from pass-shooting ducks, except that the dove is rarely taken at such long range, doesn't fly quite as fast as speedy fowl, and the lead is not so great. Duck guns are in common use on doves, though 16 and 20 bores will do very well. Number seven and a half and eight shot are in common use.

The dove has his own scheme for escaping when he knows himself in danger. He cannot tower like a duck or drop out of a tree like a grouse, but he can swerve with the greatest abruptness. One whip of his wings and he will be three feet out of the line on which he was coming, and he may tack with the next whip of wings, or go right along in a beautiful curve. The secret of good dove shooting is to so hide that the birds can be taken unawares, without knowing that danger is near. If they see the gunner, right now the dove is going to make the shot hard. The easiest shot is the passing bird, passing at right angles, unsuspicious. It is merely necessary to lead him properly, and the lead is not very great, a foot at twenty yards, to four feet at forty. It is best to half-snap; that is, to intercept the mark, for the dove often changes his course too abruptly to make a steady swing effective. Get the first shot off quickly, then do not be too quick with the second barrel, but let him get over his flurry and bear away on a line. Now hold under and in front, the same as with ducks, and the shot is certain, provided the bird is within easy reach. Doves can rarely be killed at as long range as ducks, and fifty yards is a long shot.

The incomer is a hard shot in dove shooting particularly if he gets sight of the shooter, which he usually does. He may simply curve off at a tangent, but he may also let go all holds and drop nearly to the ground and at the same time curving out and away from the gun. Wing-shooting is a peculiar business, and if we cannot tell what the bird is to do next, we can't hit him. There is where the elusive dove has his inning, for there are times when nobody can tell what he will do next. The only advice I can give is that when he is doing things with a speed beyond calculation, wait him out—get him in close before the gun is moved and then wait him out. The hold is the same as in duck shooting, when the bird will maintain a straight course for a sufficient length of time.

Jumped doves are simple. They go off low along the ground,

sometimes climbing, but not abruptly, and the shots will be drivers, as a rule, straight away and quartering to the right and left. More jumped doves are missed through faulty elevation than from the wrong lead. Doves beneath the level of the gun, and they sometimes skim the ground, require holding a bit high, and the same with those that are climbing at an angle of twenty degrees.

GROUSE

Grouse are called the king of game birds, for the reason, maybe, that more shells are expended to the birds bagged than is true of other game. He is a hard bird to hit, but I am inclined to think this is more due to cover than anything else. Any bird would be difficult in undergrowth and heavy timber. I used to shoot ruffed grouse in Missouri, along old rail fences overgrown with grape vines and briars. When the birds took to the open they were little more difficult than prairie chickens. However, when in timber, winging among the branches, dropping out of trees, fanning the leaves, maybe, into a white flare of light behind them, the grouse hunter needs a rabbit foot, and a gun that points itself by instinct and is not abused when it misses. The only advice I can give the grouse shooter is to take more lead than the shot seems to demand. The cute scamps are seen only momentarily, perhaps, and the tendency is to shoot right where they are and not where they will be an instant later. If the opening across which the grouse dashes is no more than five or six feet wide, at a distance of thirty yards, shoot into the leaves on the side opposite from where he enters.

RABBIT

Shooting rabbits with a quail gun, with all of mine throwing the pattern high, I have to be careful not to overshoot. The eye seems to take the high line of a rabbit as his "line of flight," and with every jump he ducks under that line. It follows that the high shooting gun which works nicely on winged game is not the best for rabbits where the arm ought to shoot to its sights with the center of the pattern.

As to the lead, not many rabbits are missed by shooting ahead of them, and plenty are by dropping behind. Somebody has told me never to see anything but a rabbit's head and hold for it on all crossing and quartering shots. A rabbit, going full tilt, needs a lead of a foot at twenty yards if crossing, from that to five feet at fifty yards. I have learned the exact lead by shooting at them with a .22 rifle, noting where the dirt was cut up by the bullet. On straight-away rabbits see them over the top of the barrel, unless the mark is very close and you are shooting down on him.

Most frequently a rabbit is missed when slowly hopping about in the brush and weeds. He may show himself for but an instant, and a shot right where he apparently is won't touch him. It is necessary to get ahead, on his next bound, even should he then be out of sight. I have one shooting chum who is a phenomenal shot on rabbits that are already out of sight in the weeds and grass. By some sort of inexplicable instinct, he appears to know right where that rabbit will be on his next bound after disappearing. Shooting, he confidently goes forward and picks up his rabbit. For me, I'd feel assured that rabbit was missed, and he would be.

As to the style of shooting or aiming, I think a rabbit ought to be snapped, without the swing through of the duck shot. His bounds are too irregular to make the swing highly effective. Raise the gun and intercept him. I have seen many a rabbit killed when the time was too short for any kind of an aim—merely got the gun to the shoulder and let go at him. Of one thing be sure, if he is about to disappear and the shot is hurried, don't pull behind him, for that is the tendency on both winged and running game, where it is to be seen that the mark is about to escape. With a grouse or a quail passing behind limbs or a rabbit disappearing in the brush, double the lead that would have been taken had he remained in the open.

Rabbit guns are carried with the tubes pointing towards the ground, not up or at any angle where the load could carry to a companion. Rabbit shooting is the most successful when two or more men go in a party, tramping abreast or taking different sides of hedges and draws, but that means additional care in handling the gun and as to where shots may be directed. I believe that more shooting accidents occur in rabbit shooting than in any other form of small-game hunting. If any man ever lets his gun go off accidentally or shoots close to another, meet him at lunch and talk rabbit shooting, but go shooting one day earlier than he thinks you will.

As to the sport of rabbit hunting, it is all in the mental attitude. Commonly the quail shooter will not fire at a rabbit, but I have gone out especially for rabbits when quail didn't appeal to me as being much game. Go rabbit shooting when the other fellow has killed two or three rabbits, with as many misses for you, and if you don't get keen about hitting the next one that jumps, I am bad at guessing.

As to the ethics of rabbit shooting, I once knew an Irishman who wouldn't fire at one under twenty-five yards, but I think he had been trained in a more open country than we have. Usually it is wise to catch bunny near or far as the occasion demands, only don't shoot him sitting in his form. He is too fine a little beast to deliberately sacrifice him, to deliberately forego a shot that may be recalled with pleasure, simply for the meat he carries. A sitting shot is always an opportunity gone that will not come back.

I'd get a lot of kick out of the work of a good rabbit dog myself. The musical cry of a beagle, driving fast and true is of itself plenty of excuse for a day spent in pursuit of cottontails. Neither need the dog be a thoroughbred beagle; any kind of a hound will do or any other kind of a dog which will follow a trail and not lose it. Of course everybody knows that a rabbit with a dog after him will make some sort of a circle and come back to about where he started. There is both fun and good honest sport in taking a stand and waiting for the dogs to bring the rabbit around. The man who cannot enjoy the running of a pair of beagles or a pack, is a stranger to me. I have hunted the rabbit in Mississippi with a pack of two dozen beagles, no guns carried, but I always feel more at home with a gun in my hands, and it is better sport to shoot a rabbit than to run him to death.

Chapter 41

USING THE SECOND BARREL

OF FIFTY FAIRLY GOOD SHOTS perhaps not more than one is a first-rate second-barrel shot. It requires more than double the nervous energy to place two barrels well than it does one barrel. Just so much nervous energy or concentration being stored up in the shooter, he will expend the most of it in the first shot; or he will save it on the first shot and expend it on the second. Neither plan leads to perfect two-barrel work. There is no royal road to any kind of skill, and the only way to learn to shoot that second barrel is to shoot it. Taking such birds as quail or snipe, the only bird that ever ought to be allowed to get away unshot with the second barrel is the one that is absolutely hidden by brush or some other cover.

Did you ever fire at a bird, miss him, and fail to fire the second barrel because you thought the mark too far off? Well, that was wrong. When a bird is missed it is no time for thinking, but for shooting. Any bird that was close enough for the first barrel is close enough for the second barrel, provided it is driven in promptly. Any time a quail or like game gets away with only one shot, the shooter lacks training. Any time the gunner misses a bird and picks another one that is closer for his second barrel, that is wrong. No skill is to be developed that way, only bad habits.

The best second-barrel shots that I have ever seen were the old live-pigeon shots. They did what was called using the second barrel for "safety," shooting it whether or not the pigeon appeared to be killed outright. Some of these men could kill a bird no more than four feet from the ground and strike him again before he hit the earth. Some of them missed him too, with that snapped second shot, and the really safe man was the one who allowed the bird to fall and then plastered him with that second barrel. These men had to play safe, for there might be a thousand dollars a side on a hundred-bird match and a good many other thousands on the outside where such men as Elliott and Brewer were shooting.

The point is that these men acquired the habit of using the second barrel. What is a habit anyhow? It is the ability to do a thing automatically, without conscious thought, the subconscious

331

Spanish sporting-arms and munitions manufacturers. Center is Esteben Orbea, whose family has made arms in Eibar for five hundred years.

mind governing. The man who has a habit of doing a thing doesn't have to think the matter over and conclude to do it, but does it with the same certainty that his teeth clamp down on a bite of steak when he gets it in his mouth. An automatic performance is far faster than a conscious performance in which every movement is reasoned out. No marksman ever acquires a high degree of skill who cannot shoot, and shoot exactly right, without thinking. The subconscious mind takes control, alike in shooting and fine mechanical work. The mechanic who had to see, stroke after stroke, just how deep his file had cut, never could use a file. The finished marksman who had to go over this process mentally, as, "Here comes a duck forty yards off, I'll bring up my gun from behind, swing past and lead him four feet and kill him," probably never would hit that duck. Seeing that duck passing, all conscious efforts cease; and he merely shoots, whereupon the duck falls. He doesn't remember his lead or any of the thought processes back of that lead, because he shot from habit, which is far faster and more accurate than taking every step through the dictates of conscious reason.

Habit comes from doing a thing so often that eyes, muscles and nerves are educated into doing it that way and no other way. All we need to do is to quit interfering, and everything will go off according to Hoyle and in perfect time. The habit of using the second barrel will come from using the second barrel and in no other way. We will have to acquire the habit of using that second barrel, if we lack it, and that simply means using the second barrel on every possible and a good many impossible occasions. One time, finding myself weak with the second barrel, I resolved to shoot it on every bird. I shot that second barrel at every bird missed and at every bird hit, trying to catch him before he struck the ground. This was on quail and they were plentiful. In two days I so acquired the habit of driving in the left barrel that no bird missed with the right ever got away in the open without taking chances on the other barrel also, and that follow-up barrel went in fast. I have missed a quail with the first barrel and caught him with the second, within fifteen feet. The gun had something to do with that sort of speed, as we shall see presently.

The ordinary performance of the average wing-shot is to take as good an aim as he knows how with the first shot. Then, mentally, he takes it for granted that the bird is killed and relaxes. All at once he is amazed to see the bird flying on untouched, whereupon he tightens up and rushes in a second shot without much aim, half panicky, and all too late. The second barrel is to be fired from a definite preconviction that it is going to be needed and is going to be fired. The aim is maintained on a dead bird precisely as on one with his wings under him, and nothing whatever is going to stop that second barrel except a dead bird falling under the tubes. If you cannot acquire the second barrel habit any other way, don't let the fact that the bird is dead stop you from shooting at him either. The substance of all this is that the second barrel to be fired is fixed in the mind before the first is fired, kept that way while the first barrel is being fired, and is not an after-thought and doesn't require thinking to do it. If lacking in second-barrel precision and second-barrel habit, which amounts to the same thing, shoot twice at every bird that gets up throughout an entire season and you will get the habit.

Perhaps a word of warning would be in place here. There are men who snap in a first barrel very carelessly, knowing they have a second barrel in reserve which is held accurately and deliberately. This is not good wing-shooting either and leads to plenty of missing. This reminds me of what an old pigeon shooter used to tell me, Billy Field, who had a reputation for being a reliable double bird shot. He said, "Now you get that first bird first, don't miss the first bird whatever else you do." That holds equally true in the field, don't be careless with the first barrel, but get the first bird with the first shot if the thing is possible. That is the only way to make doubles, remember, and making doubles is what we are trying to teach.

I have said something about the gun being a factor in second-barrel work. In these days many appear desirous of obtaining the lightest field gun possible to procure, for a given gauge. They want full power but little weight of arm, possibly a 12 bore, shooting 2¾-inch cases and heavy loads, with the piece weighing no more than six and a half pounds. It is almost impossible to do good, accurate, prompt, second-barrel work with any such gun. On discharge it will kick high above the mark, obscuring or partly ob-

Duck silhouette used during patterning tests.

scuring it, and at the same time loosening the face from the comb. Such a gun shocks a man, and for the fraction of a second paralyzes him. The gun has to be brought back to the level of the mark, the face has to be readjusted to the stock, and meantime the bird has been getting away so rapidly that the second shot has to be snapped in, or perhaps is not fired.

Duck shooters handle flocks so often that of course the second barrel is to be used, hence the duck shooter, next to the old live-bird shot, is the best second-barrel man I know. He may shoot three or more barrels, as matter of fact, commonly using a pump or an automatic. Nevertheless, from my observation, the pump gun is not as good as the double in stopping with the second barrel a bird that has been missed with the first, this in regard to quail shooting. On passing birds, like ducks and doves, the repeating shotgun comes into its own. I have seen more than one duck killed after having been missed twice, and it is the same with doves. The quail is too fast, and in the woods we soon get out of the habit of trying to get more than one shot at him if the gun has to be pumped between shots.

The duck shot keeps up his second-barrel work pretty well, because circumstances make it necessary to use it, and it is the same way in chicken shooting, but the quail shot who does much of his work in the brush soon gets to depending on the first barrel only, since the one shot is the only opportunity he gets. However, the second barrel habit is a good one for him also. I find from personal experience that when that second barrel is to be fired I watch more closely where that first shot went. A part of our missing is due to the mind assuming the thing accomplished before it is, and we are not alert to see precisely where that first shot did go. The thing to do is to hold for the bird, then carry right through to where that bird should be if alive. That means if the first shot is fired at a given range, thirty feet beyond on the line of flight the second barrel would whip in. By the time recovery is made from recoil, when the trigger shift has been made or the gun pumped, it should then be found pointing this thirty feet in advance, and not at the spot where the first barrel sent its charge. If this cannot be done, if the arm cannot be carried through and thus be found in position for the left barrel, then not much will be accomplished by this barrel.

As to the super effort required to shoot both barrels well, I have made a test of that, finding that if the first barrel were snapped in without much effort, the second could be fired very accurately. I tried this out by not aiming the first barrel, but simply shooting, then holding well with the second and killing reliably. It might be well to try that out if the second barrel is not doing what it ought to. The main thing to be proven by this is that there is lots of time for that left barrel, provided the mind is fixed on shooting it. Everything considered, it is all a matter of the mind and of habit. A prolonged concentration of effort is not easy, but neither is good wing-shooting easy, for the matter of that.

The principle involved in second-barrel shooting is, be ready for it, be agreeably surprised if you do not have to use it, and don't be caught "off balance" if you do have to use it. I have seen more than one man put up a quail at his feet, shoot at it, miss it, and just stare after the disappearing bird without another thought of his gun. You would think that no such thing ever happened to him before, but it did and will happen again if he doesn't learn better.

I have been speaking here of second barrel, and apparently of double guns, but this doesn't mean that the arm must have two barrels. In fact I can do better work with a pump gun in placing

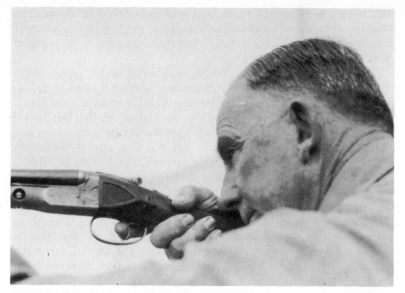

One of the finest wing shots, Bill Coleman, Seattle advertising tycoon.

the second barrel than I can with a double gun. Either the delay caused by pumping the gun or the need for concentration during this effort steadies and balances me, resulting in a more accurately placed second shot. In trying to analyze second-barrel misses, also by seeing where the charge had gone, as over water or among trees, I found that most of the misses went high. I doped it out at last as the result of recoil which raised my head, and when cheek was loose from the comb, with a sighting line well above the barrels, the bird might be seen right over the muzzle, yet the entire pattern go above him. Frequently this kind of missing is attributed to distance—bird too far away, but most likely he wasn't. The gun that disturbs me the least is a 20-bore pump, with which I am nearly certain to maintain a true elevation. With the second barrel misses are ordinarily due to shooting too high and shooting behind. Shooting too high is due to the cheek being above the comb, as said before, and shooting behind is due to nervous anxiety—the fear that the bird is escaping. This last happens also in brush shooting when it seems the bird will certainly be covered in another instant by a tree.

One reason why the pump gun is apt to improve second-barrel hitting with many is that a lot of us grip our guns too hard in aiming. The springing of game tenses nerves and muscles, we jam the piece against the shoulder until it vibrates, shooter as well, and then the gun is held with such rigid force that it cannot be directed on the mark. That is for the first barrel of course, but it makes that first barrel slow and the next one hurried. However, it is the same with the second shot, having missed with the first, only worse. The gun will not cover the mark as it should because of the stiffness with which it is held. The trigger finger gets its share of that same force, and away goes the load which, it can be seen with half an eye, was not on the mark. For this reason one thing that should be done is to have the second barrel, if a double, pull a pound heavier than the first barrel.

Talk to yourself when you find this severe gripping of the gun is handicapping you. Say, "Hold your horses, old fellow, this is not a matter of life or death and anyhow it is no use to hurt yourself worse than you do the bird." Just notice now and then, by leaving the gun empty, how darned easy it is to cover that bird with both barrels, knowing that no shells are in the gun, and then try to grip and aim the piece just the same as though it had no load in it.

In training for second-barrel shooting, fire the first barrel quickly, and have it absolutely in mind that this shot is to miss and you are going to kill him with the second barrel. You can do it then. But you can't do it if the shot comes as a surprise. Now get this, you are training to acquire the second barrel habit. In doing that kind of training I have purposely missed with the first barrel, then driven in with the second almost where the first barrel should have gone. Again I have gone out and for a half day would try to catch every bird killed with the first barrel before it could strike the ground. That is the precise training of the old live-pigeon shot, and it works. In any event, if you are to become a second-barrel shot, always be ready and always have it in mind that this second barrel is to be used.

It is very much the same way in making doubles. Have the second barrel well in mind all the time, but whatever you do, don't pick out a bird to be killed with the second charge before the first one is fired. Shoot and hold the gun to the cheek, looking for a bird over the tubes. The chances are he is seen promptly, and covered still well within range, but if the gun gets away from you and has to be readjusted for that second shot, the shooter will have just one thing left in his head: "The bird is getting away, getting too far off, TAKE HIM QUICK!" The result being that he is not taken at all.

Much good drilling is required to effectively time the second shot. I sat in a blind one day with a good duck shot. The birds were not coming in to us, but another blind a half mile off was very busy. At brief intervals would come a bang-bang, or maybe bang-bang-bang, almost too fast to count. "None of us are killing anything," Jim said laconically. "We are not getting any shooting, and they are shooting so fast that they can't be hitting anything." We can almost stand out of sight of a gunner and tell by the measure of his reports whether or not he is a good shot. There is nobody that can fire a gun, if it is a double gun or an automatic, any faster than a novice—because all he has to do is to pull the trigger. Nevertheless, the expert is very fast with his second barrel, very fast and very effective. The one does his prompt work because he has studied efficiency, no lost motion and not a movement that could be spared. The other man is obsessed with the notion that if he can pull five shots in a second, one of them will hit. In the same way half of the second-barrel shots fired, very much surprise the shooter if they hit anything.

Every shooter needs to study himself a bit, too, in deciding upon the boring of his barrels. For myself, I aim more accurately with the first barrel than with the second. For this reason I want that left barrel just as open as the right, notwithstanding it is to be used at longer range. Another marksman might reverse things, taking a very deliberate and a very careful aim with his left barrel. The gun, therefore, in the way it is bored needs to be regulated to the style of its owner: if slow, the second barrel might be full choke; if fast, more or less open bored.

In the use of the second barrel the single trigger helps a little but not a great deal. The aid comes not so much from greater quickness as from not being obliged to shift the hand or to allow the grip to change. This is accomplished just about as well by shooting the left barrel first, whereupon the piece kicks back through the hand, bringing the front trigger right under the finger. Shooting the right barrel first is only a follow-the-bell-wether business. When a shot is in the offing, when you can see it coming, place the pulling finger between the two triggers, and the gun will come to the shoulder with less effort, or a longer stock might be used, and the second trigger will fall under the finger without any conscious shifting of the hand.

Now, take it for granted that there will be no such thing as shooting well with the second barrel except it be shot from habit. Get the habit until that left barrel follows the right automatically. That means training. Snipe are a good bird to train on, if plenty of them are missed. Lacking the snipe, English sparrows will do. Never fail to try the sparrow with the second barrel if he is missed with the first, and when killed by the first barrel hit him again before he strikes the ground. Market gunners used to invariably drive a second charge into winged duck before he reached the water, knowing how much trouble that would save.

Chapter 42
FLINCHING

FLINCHING WILL PROVE of many descriptions that are too numerous to mention. I have never heard of the man who didn't flinch at some time, and if I had heard of him, I never should have placed a bet on his veracity. No two men flinch in precisely the same way, hence the difficulty of duly mentioning just what the trouble may be.

The most common manner of flinching is to first shut one eye to aim, and then shut the other eye to shoot. Results are rarely good. A flinch with both eyes shut doesn't necessarily, and invariably and *per se,* result in a miss. I have tried it, as an experiment if not in due course. Getting the gun up and starting the final aim, I have shut my eyes, finished the movement, shot and sometimes killed. I do not recommend the proceeding as a permanent practice, however. If you think the thing cannot be done, try it on a stationary mark.

One common manner of flinching is to do everything about right until just before the gun goes off, then shut the eyes and pull trigger, at the same time jerking the piece, probably down. Of course flinching is a fatal habit in the rifleman, and he has had more to say about it, how it is to be avoided and how cured, than anybody else has said. Instructions for a cure include pressing the trigger so gently that the tyro never does know when the rifle is going off until it has gone. That works out in some form of rest shooting, or firing from the prone; but it doesn't with a shotgun, or with any gun that is fired while it is moving.

The best instruction to give the rifleman, particularly the off-hand marksman, is to get him so interested in calling the shot that he forgets what happened and what is going to happen until it is too late to flinch. Tell him to see and remember and tell you precisely where the sights were when the gun went off, the direction the piece was moving, if at all, and where the front sight went to when recoil took charge. When he gets so that he can do this, and can make for his instructor a diagram of all gun movements from the time he pressed the trigger until movements ceased, the shots that go out of the black will not be due to flinching.

Repeating scatterguns are long-odds favorites in the duck blind.

The same system will work with the shotgun man. Tell him to pay no attention to killing the bird but to note carefully how many inches he was off the mark when he fired; in inches where the gun jumped to, and where it came to rest, whether above or below the mark. It is not necessary for a shooter to remember any of these things if he is hitting, but if his missing might be due to flinching, then he had better pay attention to what the gun did when fired. A flinch with a jerked gun ought to be detected pretty promptly, if not by the shooter, then by a companion. However, there are other, perhaps minor forms of flinching which may not become known.

Occasional flinches occur with everybody, but it is flinching from habit that hurts. Habits are governed by the subconscious mind, and that phase of the mind rules peremptorily. What the subconscious mind does is not done "by your leave, Mister." Hence you may say to yourself, "Now I won't flinch this time," and then go right ahead and do so, once the habit is established. The thing then is to avoid acquiring the habit.

Flinching is induced first by punishment. Only the hardy can take punishment without a tendency to flinch, and particularly punishment in the face and about the eyes. Strike a man in the body and he may not mind, but start a punch for his eye and he'll have to be a trained prize fighter if he doesn't blink. A man can become inured to most anything that doesn't kill or cripple him, and so he can become inured to recoil; but he isn't doing much else while he is about it. If he means to learn to shoot and not simply to fortify his system against small shocks, he had better start in with a gun that can't develop flinching from fear. A man who has the flinching habit may dodge when shooting a 410, but I have never seen the novice who did, after firing a few shots.

Not a single man in a hundred could begin shooting with one of the present light, heavily charged ten bores and not develop flinching, but once his shooting habits are fixed, with no flinching in evidence, then he can take up the big guns.

Flinching is not altogether and in every instance due to punishment. When a man aims at a flying mark with a shotgun or a stationary mark with a rifle, keenly anxious to pull a good shot, shooting with the utmost determination, he is putting his nervous system under a strain. If it is a new strain, one to which the nerves are not accustomed, they will rebel, and the marksman will relax his grip or tighten his grip, either of which means a flinch. Slow shooting, too, puts a lot greater strain on the nerves and even on the eyes than does prompt shooting. The clear keen vision is only temporary. Look at some object very steadily, without blinking, and it will begin to fade, then come back clearly. On a long aim the object being shot at may fade at the crucial moment. Therefore the strain on the eyes of a prolonged aim is far greater than with a quick aim. The rifleman knows this, but it takes the shotgun man a long time to learn it, if he ever does. Here we are

The time to start the young fry.

then for the man with a tendency to flinch: press the cheek lightly against the stock, never so hard as to, for that reason, put a strain on the eyes; never grip the gun too hard; never prolong the aim, and shoot with the least strain possible and yet be effective.

There is a form of flinching that is not often recognized and in fact may not apply to many, but I have noticed it in my own work. Just before the aim is concluded the mind quits the job. The gun has come up, the allowance for lead has been made, the gun has nearly reached the point of aim, and to the mind has reached it; there the mind quits, the job is finished, the bird is killed—except the shooter wakes up and finds much to his amazement that the bird is not killed. This is most likely to happen in double bird shooting. The mind jumps to the second task before the first one is concluded.

An old trap shot used to say to me, "Son, you kill that first bird first. Make sure of that first bird and never mind the second one. If you don't you will miss with the first barrel." Just that kind of a thing may happen and does happen when only one bird is a-wing and practically it is a flinch.

Misses are made in wing-shooting from all kinds of causes, from faulty lead, from poor mechanical execution, from a trigger finger that works too fast for the gun movement, from a poorly fitted gun that is shooting high or low without the marksman being aware; but the misses that are entirely inexplicable are usually due to flinching.

I was shooting with a very good quail shot, once on a time. He had just purchased a new automatic shotgun, and was using it for the first time. He missed just about every bird shot at, no matter how easy the shot might be.

"Why," he told me, "I know I was on. I could see that bird whipping along right square in front of my gun before I pulled the trigger." So he could, I have no doubt whatever; but just at the time he was pulling that trigger his mind left the bird and went to the queer way that new gun of his intended to act the instant the trigger was pulled. Another man missed more understandingly because in attempting to get speed from a repeater, he started the pumping process before the first shot was out of the barrel.

The pump gun works out the other way for me, and if I have any tendency to flinch, it will cease right now when I take up the pump; and it so happens, also, that I can do better second-barrel work with a repeater than with the double gun. Probably the brief interval necessary to function the arm enables me to regain balance, and the fast action entirely takes the mind off such an inconsequential thing as recoil. The other reason is that my cheek goes back to place more accurately with the pump than it remains in place under the jump of the double barrel.

Flinching with a rifle, and also quite possibly with a shotgun, may be caused by simply unlocking some tied-up nerves and muscles. Finding his piece swinging on, the marksman tries to pull the trigger, but instead of the trigger muscles alone obeying him, he finds that he has set a lot of other muscles to work at the same time, and away goes his gun, with the trigger yielding at the same instant. The trigger finger needs a tremendous amount of education.

Chapter 43

WHAT CONSTITUTES GOOD SHOOTING?

WE ARE REFERRING here to good performances in the field or on the duck marsh, and are not considering trap shooting. Everybody knows what a good clay-bird shot is, and nobody else classes with them in percentages of birds killed and missed. Good clay-bird shots run around 98%, and the question is how close do field and duck percentages run to anything like that.

To find really brilliant duck performances I suppose we would have to go back a generation or so. There should be some fine duck shots yet off the coast of North Carolina, and on the Gulf Coast of Texas, as well as in Louisiana Marshes. There we would find duck shots who are really professionals, in the sense that one way or another, either by guiding or by shooting, they make a living by hunting, just as the great duck shots of the latter part of the last century were professional market hunters. We are desirous of looking at the question from the standpoint of the amateur, the sportsman, the man who shoots for sport only. Very few amateurs today can become really expert because they haven't enough game to shoot at. Killing a few dozen ducks in a year is not going to make us deadly shots, any more than shooting two hundred clay birds in a year would make us 98% men.

Men change but little and guns have not changed much, but shooting conditions have changed a great deal. I can recall the time when as a boy I went out with a market shooter and he wouldn't let me fire at a duck more than forty yards away. All day he kept saying, "Wait, wait, too far!" That tells the story of conditions; the gunner merely had to wait in those days and the ducks would come in close enough so that shots were never missed through fault of pattern or for any reason except poor holding. Today we might have to take a half a chance or any chance at all in order to make a bag, the bag alone counting and not the shells we might have to expend in getting it. The old-time market gunner had one problem before him—counting the cost of shells against the number of birds bagged so that his balance would come out on the right side and he could continue shooting. I have listened to those lads of the duck boat and decoys tell of

344

their troubles, when the duck market dropped on them, and they might pick out ten dozen mallards and a dozen mixed ducks, sending them in to the commission houses, and getting back a report and pay for eleven dozen mixed ducks, where the mixed ducks sold for a dollar and a quarter a dozen and the mallards for three dollars a dozen. For some such reason it was the habit of these professional duck shots, when fowl were in numbers, to pick out nothing but mallards, canvasbacks and redheads for the day's bag, all of which were quoted at mallard prices.

I have read in Long's *Wildfowl Shooting*, that in less than three weeks, 17 days in fact, no shooting on Sundays, his party of four guns killed 2,760 ducks, mostly mallards. Of these Fred Kimble killed 1,365 in fifteen days, shooting a single-barrel muzzle-loading gun. Under these conditions, either Kimble or any of the rest of us would have learned to hit ducks, With any quantity of fowl apparently, with many good shots in existence and considerable rivalry, duck matches used to be shot, with money up, and I have not heard of any of these matches wherein Kimble killed less than one hundred ducks, whatever the day might happen to be. Twice Kimble made runs of 54 ducks, once on mallards and once on bluebills. Kimble had the reputation and I suppose was the best duck shot that America has ever developed. From what I can gather he averaged about ninety percent on ducks throughout a long season.

In the next generation, from 1880 to 1900, many good duck shots appeared in the West. Of these Charlie Grimm and Fred Gilbert of Iowa become well known. They acquired skill at a time when Iowa had numbers of water-fowl. Both of them became fine trap shots as well, at live and clay birds. Chan Powers had a great reputation as a duck shot in Illinois. He had a duck lake of his own on the Illinois River, and ample opportunities for practice. In the South, heading a notable group of Texas duck shots was Colonel Oscar Guessaz. The Texas men had such fine duck shooting that they took to smallbore guns by way of making the sport more difficult. Many of them used 24-gauge guns, and these arms might be called the forerunners of the smallbore shotgun in America. From what I have been told by Mark Dyer and others who have seen the Texas men shoot often, also Chan Powers and Dick Merrill who shot with them on the Gulf Coast, the men mentioned here averaged about 75 percent on wildfowl during a season.

Twenty years ago in Oklahoma we had one duck shot who could do as well as 75%, and watching him shoot at times one would go away with the impression that he didn't miss at all. Asked about this very thing, he said that while he hadn't kept count he believed that one duck missed to three killed would be about his gait. On occasions, he said, when ducks were plentiful and working well to decoys, he did very little missing; but if the birds were scarce, when he needed a bag and had to take chances, plenty of missing was done. Perhaps we have some 75% duck shooters yet, but they must live in a. duck country, where the

The late Major Charles Askins, father of the author.

birds winter; or some amateur with means and unlimited time might possibly develop such skill.

The novice will do well to bag 30% and when he has reached forty is beginning to learn how to shoot ducks. I have seen 25 shells expended and no ducks killed at all. This from the kind of chap who will shoot at ducks three hundred yards away on the chance that he might cripple one. This lad burns out the ducks and I once saw him burnt out himself. He located his blind within three hundred yards of two good duck shots, all rigged out with blind and decoys. Not a flock of ducks was allowed to decoy to the two hunters or even to come near them. Finally, when a fine flock of pintails had started to come in and were driven off by our novice, the hunters deliberately fired four shots well elevated into the scare-crow blind. The spent shot clipped into the sand and may have had some force when they got there. At first the "wild" wild duck shooter contented himself with loud protests, but at about the fourth volley concluded the scoundrels were actually shooting at him, shook his fist, got up, and beat it out of there.

I do not know any webfoot easier to bag than a goose if he gets on top of you, but getting him on top of you is a problem. Looking back over my goose-shooting experiences of thirty-five years I doubt if I have killed more than one bird in four shots. Even when the big fellows did come in close I have wasted plenty of shells. For example, the last flock of Canadas that came over me were massed in a flock less than twenty-five yards away when I commenced to shoot. I had an automatic shotgun, and the first two came down all right, and then I emptied the gun without getting any more. Possibly this is a common experience where a man gets a goose only now and then, and is anxious about it. Knowing only Western goose shooting, with the birds shot at if they come within 60 yards, I'd think one bird to three shells about as good as the average man could expect. The trouble is that the big fellows are so often quite out of range when they look close enough, and any time a Canada honker looks 60 yards off, figure the distance at really 80 yards and let it go at that; barring an occasional broken wing with BBs, geese are not killed at 80 yards, even though they look impossible to miss.

I have made some ridiculous misses in goose shooting. One morning I saw a goose coming in. There was no cover and I threw myself flat on the ground. Pretty soon I looked up and saw that goose, apparently very close. But I had been told, just as I have told you, that geese are always farther away than they look, so I held six feet ahead and missed, held the second barrel six feet ahead and missed, then sat up and took a good look. That goose hadn't been more than twenty-five yards away for either shot and a lead of two feet surely would have killed him.

While I may be wrong, I suspect that the average man has missed plenty of geese, and does very well to bag 30%. Half the missed fowl will be out of range, and a certain percentage will be hit and not killed. Not one duck hunter in a thousand gets much practice on geese.

Conditions make all the difference in duck shooting, in snipe shooting, on chickens and grouse. An English authority says that on driven grouse, in August, the kills to shells expended would be about 80%, falling off by the middle of September to 40%. Quail are less variable than other birds, perhaps. Bob-White is the one bird that almost always rises well within reach of the gun. Shots are rarely missed therefore through the bird being out of range. However, it is in a measure the old story, for early in the season the birds can be shot mostly in the open, while in

Bill Askins, son of the author, during Chukar partridge hunt near Villar-robledo, Spain.

winter it will be necessary to follow them into the woods or other cover. The difference between cover shooting and open shooting is fully fifty percent, in birds killed to shells expended.

It still remains true that when quail scatter and get up singly in the open, a good shot ought to bag not less than 70% of his birds. However, quail are becoming too wise to scatter in the open and are rarely found so far from cover that they cannot make it into the brush on the first flight. Thereafter it is a matter of firing through thin brush, of making a snap shot in small openings, of covering a space between trees and trying to catch Bob as he dashes across. Misses will come plenty often enough. Fifty percent in heavy cover is fine shooting and forty percent good enough. Taking the season through, with much of the work in December, the man who goes out with a box of shells, follows the birds into cover for half his shots, and bags ten quail with his shells does very well. If he gets fifteen birds to his twenty-five shots, he has exceptional skill, while above fifteen birds to twenty-five shots means that the marksman has found enough game so that he can get his bag without entering cover.

Everybody can hit some quail, for the birds rise in the open and often wing straight away or gently quartering so that with an open-bored gun not much knowledge of lead is required. But I have never seen anybody who didn't miss birds in the timber, even in thin timber. Bob may be shot at when he is in fair view, flying just right, perfectly covered, but in making the shift to get ahead of him, a tree or a limb will catch the shot. This happens to everybody, and the man who says he can kill all the birds he shoots at, or that he knows somebody who can kill all the birds he shoots at, may not be honest about what he says. I have never met such a quail shot.

Having watched men shoot quail for a great many years I'd conclude that the beginner can bag about one bird in five, the better trained wing-shot one bird in four, the fair shot brought up on quail 40%, the good shot 50% under all conditions, and the rarely seen expert quail shot sixty to sixty-five percent. Better than that is not done except by the man who picks his shot and stays out of the brush.

I read, once on a time, in looking up snipe records, of some man in Louisiana who killed 720 jack snipe in one day. He must have been some snipe shot! However, under some conditions snipe shooting is easy. Take the short-grass prairie country, as we used to find it in the Nebraska sandhill country, short grass with intervening shallow marshes, the birds getting up and just topping the grass, winging out and back into the marsh, and there isn't much excuse for missing a snipe under thirty yards. The finest snipe shooting used to be had in the spring of the year, on warm days in April and May, when the long bills got up under protest, very close to one's feet, lazily tacking as they went off, dropping

Walking 10-12 miles over rough terrain, the Spanish beater eats bread and cheese and drinks his inevitable vino at noontime.

back within forty yards; and it has sometimes appeared to me that every bird ought to be killed.

Again in the same country, on a frosty morning in the fall, snipe may be rising wild and going clean out of the country on the first flight. I have seen them when the rise and 'scape of one snipe would start twenty more into action, nearly all beyond reach of the gun, and not a bird dropping back. The flight was stronger too, much of an up-and-down whip, very often climbing, with a true corkscrew movement. Snipe are going to be missed then. I used to consider myself better and surer on snipe than any other game bird, yet the last eleven snipe that I remember shooting at, of these wild rising cantankerous little scamps, I bagged only three birds.

Today most men are not getting enough practice on snipe to do well. The fact that the shooter knows how to take quail or ducks or chickens doesn't mean that he can hit snipe unless he is trained on that bird. I have seen so many snipe missed that I know this is true. Attempting to strike an average of what the ordinary shot ought to do, considering the amount of practice on this bird that he has probably had, I'd say 40% would be a very fair performance. But the man whose hobby is snipe shooting, who has done a lot of it, can bag 50, 60, or 70%, according to the weather and other conditions. In a general way we might look at it like this; the gunner who refuses to take a snipe if it breaks cover over twenty-five yards away should bag 60% of his birds; when snipe are wild, taking everything that rises within forty yards, snapping quickly of course, the percentage will be cut badly; but that sort of a lad will get snipe.

Ruffed grouse are supposed to be the hardest of all game birds to bag, in proportion to shells expended. This is perhaps due to the partridge being a timber bird, rarely shot in the open. Years ago I used to get fair ruffed grouse shooting in the Ozark Mountains, and found that if the birds could 'be caught in the open, as sometimes happened, along old rail fences, overgrown with brush and wild grapes, they were little more difficult than prairie chickens. I remember that I made a double on ruffed grouse, the first that I ever shot. The birds came out of a fence row, dog pointing on the opposite side, and went off low and straight. I killed on one day under such conditions eight grouse, with few misses. About that time I began to have a contempt for the bird or for the men who said he was so hard. Later I followed a covey into scrub post-oak, and learned just what ruffed-grouse shooting was like. One bird was pointed right at the root of a three-foot red oak. He got up in ten feet of me, deliberately ran around the tree with his topknot up and took wing on the other side. The fastest kind of jumping didn't give me a shot before he was in the dense brush. Again the two dogs treed one, and the old pointer had a trick of barking when he treed a game bird. I walked up, saw the bird no more than eight feet above the ground, standing up on a limb, and had to raise my gun, threatening to punch him out before he would fly. When he did fly he dropped right along the ground, and all I ever did see was a fluttering and flashing of the heavy carpet of leaves behind him. Couldn't get a distinct view of the grouse at all, and I missed him.

Woodcock are rare in most sections of the country, highly appreciated, shot at when only a glimpse is obtained; and the man who bags 50% through the season does well. Cock are easily hit, were they plentiful enough so that only good shots would be taken. The best and easiest shooting that I have had was in the cane, sending in the dogs and taking the birds as they came out, twenty to thirty feet high, crossing an opening. Cock are missed through trying to take them when covered by limbs, through snapping too quick, and through shooting while the bird is still climbing.

Doves are a sort of miniature duck in their flight, not quite so fast, and having more ability to dodge. Every man will have some flights that he can hit readily and some that he misses with like certainty. For me there are two or three easy flights. The first is the driver, jumped doves getting up close to the gun, from stubble or peas. These birds are less difficult than quail. The second shot that ought to be killed is the passing bird, passing at right angles to the gun, within thirty yards. If this dove doesn't suspect danger, a lead of from one to two feet will get him with the same certainty as though he were at rest. The next bird that should be killed is the overhead incomer. A lead of just in front when under thirty yards, up to three feet in front at forty yards high will drop him. The hard birds are those that come in dropping away, swerving, now caught by the wind when they appear to let all holds go and are just carried away. Nobody can tell what such a bird will do next and plenty of them will be missed. Everything considered, taking all doves as they come, in passing or waterhole shooting, I'd think 60% about average dove shooting.

Chapter 44

FREE SHOOTING

THIS IS A RICH COUNTRY. Untold millions are spent annually for the sport of shooting. However, there is no system or method in what we are doing. We are wasting our money in traveling to this and other countries, searching for the odd corners that may remain undisturbed. Paradise lies over the hill, and we go over the hill and the next one, never finding it. No small-game paradise is left in America, and few such spots in all the world. We travel a thousand miles and spend a thousand dollars, trying to find a land of dreams, and when we get there discover, "Posted" "No Shooting," on both sides of the road. A game paradise lies right in our country, in whatever state we may live, or we could make it a game paradise if we took the land owner into partnership in the production of game.

The supply of game must be increased. There is no other way out, for shooters are steadily increasing while game is just as steadily decreasing. Free shooting is about gone—no matter how much we would wish it otherwise—we must awaken to the reality. Game cannot be produced on land without the consent of the owner, and unless the land-owner can look on game as a "crop" capable of producing financial returns, he will be inimical or at least indifferent. This is human nature. Game breeding has proven simple and practical on game farms. But what to do with such game after it is bred is a problem. Usually state-bred game is placed upon the farm of some one who is friendly—friendly but uninterested; and what subsequently becomes of it nobody knows.

In the conservation of small game we have always had two schools in this country; the one active and backed by state law, the other destined to make itself felt in the future. The active school declares that game belongs to the state, and that no individual has any property rights in wild game until after it is shot. Game is to be taken only at such seasons as the state may dictate, by the means the state may dictate, by the people the state may license to do the killing. The land upon which game may be found is not considered, under law, as having any title to it whatever.

On the other side is the farmer or other land owner. Many of our convictions are the result of heritage. Back in England or other

European countries the game belonged to the man on whose land it was found, and nine farmers in ten in this country have a firm if secret conviction that the game found upon their land belongs to them. No one will be permitted to shoot that game without permission from the man who is convinced that as a matter of right and justice he owns it. The laws uphold him in preventing the game found on his place from being shot without his permission, but the law that backs him is based on English Common Law, in contravention of the theory of the state ownership of game.

The theory of the state ownership of game, now accepted as the law of the land, carried to its limits, would license the hunter to shoot state-owned game wherever it might be found. Carried to such an extreme, the law of state ownership would not work because it conflicts with that common law, which is far older than any game law, holding that a man's home is his castle, which he has the right to defend by any means in his power, and that his farm is the outer works of his castle, to be defended as well. The common law is an English heritage, the heritage of every free man, and no law passed in contravention would stand. Hence we have and always will have trespass laws, and no man ever has had or ever will have the right to shoot upon the lands of another without permission. Some states go so far as to require written permission before a hunter can shoot upon the lands of another.

The theory of the public ownership of game has been made the law, its soundness passed upon by the highest courts, on the principle that the public interests are paramount. Otherwise laws could not be made to apply to the landowner who would take game at will during all seasons. That the public interests are paramount is recognized by all civilized countries, and land proprietors are not permitted to take game except during fixed seasons as stipulated by the state, no matter if game is recognized as an asset of the land, Here is where we differ from other countries, and here is why English farms that have been in cultivation two thousand years still produce plenty of game, and our farms that have been in cultivation perhaps no more than fifty years have little or none; the game on every English farm is an asset, the game upon every American farm is a liability, and there is the difference. We cannot produce game without land on which to raise it, and no man is going to feel very friendly towards the game on his place so long as it is a mere liability, a nuisance, a cause of trespass, a source of trouble and no income.

The American farmers have been governed heretofore by a live-and-let-live spirit, by a generosity that made it appear small to forbid hunting upon lands where no damage was done and none likely to occur. That was free shooting. That time is passing. The farmer is no different from what he always was, but shooters have so increased in numbers that tolerance ceases to be a virtue. Perhaps in the old days one or two shooting parties might appear on the place in the course of a season. They were regarded as gentlemen sportsmen and made welcome. As the old-time plantation owners used to say, "Shoot until you hear the bell and then come in to dinner." But now a dozen "gangs" might tramp over that farm in one day, and purely in self-defense the owner must forbid free shooting.

The situation as it stands is that there is very little attractive free shooting to be had anywhere in the United States. We have about fifteen million licensed hunters, the most of whom have no worth-while shooting in sight. In the last twenty years game birds have decreased to one bird in four, and hunters have increased many fold. The habit of free shooting persists, and small-game shooters invade lands without permission and are chased off, go on to the next farm and are chased off, causing grave annoyance to farmers and securing very little game. This situation must become worse because, with the best intentions in the world, the shooters do not know how to better it, and the land owners are becoming bitter with their grievances. What is the remedy?

One remedy in line with the state ownership of game would be to raise license fees to such an extent that game departments could afford to ease shooting grounds on which the licensee would have the right to shoot. If the present resident license fee would be raised to twenty-five dollars, with the same number of hunters we now have, sufficient funds would accrue to lease large bodies of land. Twenty-five dollars a year is no great sum for a small-game shooter to expend on his attempts to find something to shoot at. If he knew that he could have a week of nice shooting, welcome everywhere he went, enough game to reach a limit daily, no irritated land owner to contend with, the money would be well spent and the hunter willing to spend it.

However, I am convinced that high license fees and shooting grounds owned or leased by the state will not work. Why not? For the very simple reason that this is a democratic country; votes control it, and office holders are. elected. The first man who advocated a license fee of twenty-five dollars, no matter what good use he expected to make of the money, would find himself out of office, and all his fine plans would go with him. The shooters themselves would do the mischief, under the plea that the poor man was being shut out. The scheme of a high resident license and a place and game to use it on, never would be given a fair chance or any other kind of a chance to show its worth. It is possible that a double-base license might prove practical, as an entering wedge.

It is quite conceivable that if five dollars were charged for a free-shooting license, and twenty-five dollars for a license to shoot on well stocked state grounds, more and more gunners would come to see the advantage of plenty of game to shoot at even if it did cost a little more money.

I am not expecting anything like that to happen; politics would beat such a law or it might be declared unconstitutional on the grounds that it was class legislation. Probably the course that will ultimately be taken is the one of least resistance. In this country it is against the law to sell game, and there is a well defined public opinion against any money being made out of game birds in any way whatsoever. It is true that shooting grounds are being leased by clubs, also marshes, lakes, and streams, where these can be controlled privately; but the public is unfriendly, and there is constant friction, which went so far, I am told, as to cause the legislature of North Dakota to repeal the trespass laws. From the game-conservation point of view, club grounds are really sanctuaries, because club membership is limited, game rarely shot very hard, and the surplus game feeds surrounding areas. Nevertheless and not withstanding, game is steadily decreasing and shooters are steadily increasing, and the end of free shooting is in sight.

The course of least resistance referred to is the English plan, the plan of game protection and game propagating found all over Europe. It is true that we do not like any such plan, that it leads to shooting classes wherein the man of means can shoot quantities of game and the man with little money none. However, that is not all the story or more than one side of the story. Any man in England who owns land can shoot the game on that land if he likes. It is true that he very rarely elects to do this. The game is worth more to him alive than it is dead, even granted he has every right to sell it when dead. The English farmer and our farmers are not far from being in the same boat, and need to make every edge cut. If an English farmer which would be no less true here, has three hundred acres of land and can obtain three hundred dollars for the game dead, or six hundred dollars for that game alive for some one else to shoot, he is going to sell it to the man who is willing to pay for it alive. It is not class legislation that prevents the farmer of Europe from shooting, but money—money that he needs—crop money. Our farmers ought to make enough money from the game produced on their places to pay all taxes, and it will come to that afterwhile. Will the shooting public ever be willing to pay for the game shot? I think so.

The American farmer could be paid for the game produced on his place and still not interfere with the state ownership. The shooter would not be "buying game on the hoof," but would be paying the land owner for his trouble in helping to raise game, for the feed that such game had eaten on his land, for the damage to his crops and the inconvenience caused him by hunters going over his place. And he is entitled to that. To raise a good game crop the land owner must leave feed and cover for the game, which makes his farm just that much less productive in marketable crops. Yet, apparently, we want them to make this sacrifice without return.

Make it worth while to the land owner and he will cooperate to bring back good hunting, bring it right to your back door and not to some mythical far-away Paradise which is always at the end of the rainbow. The land owner will then get money for his game crop just as he does for his other crops, and the hunter will get game for less per piece than he now pays for it in dollars and cents.

How much is game worth to the shooter in this country? Is it worth two dollars a bird for quail? Is it worth five dollars apiece for ducks? Is a pheasant worth five dollars to the man who bags it? It seems to me that the average shooter who doesn't live in the country is paying a great deal more than two dollars a bird for quail right now. Can this be remedied? Yes. The farmers alone can remedy it and they will some day.

What does it cost us to shoot anyhow? Some man may answer, nothing, except for gun and ammunition and a license. This may be true in some instances; it doesn't cost a poacher in England anything to shoot except for his gun and ammunition, but in effect he is stealing. Game is property in England, worth at times a fourth as much as all the remaining crops raised on the place. Are we ever liable to reach such a state of affairs in this country, will wild game ever become property, a tangible asset of the place? I think so. Perhaps we shall not call game property, but it will be so in effect, adding perhaps one fourth to the actual value of a place.

It has been estimated by those running game farms, by game keepers, by those cognizant of just how much and how little trouble it is to produce game, that game birds can be increased in this country a thousand fold. This might be a prejudiced statement, an exaggerated statement, or it might not be. In any event, the question is, how much does it cost us to shoot game right now, under present conditions of so-called free shooting?

William H. Whitney went to Scotland and paid forty thousand dollars in annual rental for one grouse moor. We have a number of big-game hunters who go to British East Africa and pay an average of ten thousand dollars for two months' shooting. It costs two thousand dollars a month to shoot brown bear and similar big game in Alaska; and six weeks in British Columbia costs fifteen hundred dollars, they tell me. Such hunting trips are taken by men of means, of course; but how about the man of modest income, living in such states as New York or Ohio, where quail have been shot out and none are being produced? This gunner goes South for a shooting trip, at a cost of hundreds of dollars, for an annual bag of no more than a few birds.

Now the question is, wouldn't it be wiser to spend our money nearer home? Couldn't the farmers raise all the game we will want to shoot and far more than we get to shoot if we paid them one-fourth of the money we now spend? Take the turkeys; this was once a great turkey country where the birds ranged in hundreds, forty years ago. We still have the timbered sections in which the birds once ranged. Granted the eggs could be had, and wild turkey eggs can be had from game farms, we could hatch turkeys and turn them into that woods at a cost of no more than five dollars a bird, when the turkeys were ready to shoot. We can't do anything like that because the turkeys would all be shot illegally—nobody could protect them because it wouldn't be to the interest of the men who own that timberland to waste time in protecting turkeys. But suppose a club of us organized the farmers who own a stretch of that timber, gave them the eggs for hatching, instructing them to tag the birds and turn them loose to take care of themselves, but that we would pay them ten dollars apiece for every bird killed within club bounds when the season opened. Is it possible that those birds would not be protected against poachers or any form of illegal shooting? Wouldn't the farmer be just as angry if one of those birds were killed illegally as he would be to have a prime heifer stolen? Believe me, the poacher would have to kill a turkey on the run and then keep running. Those wild turkeys would be protected, you get me, and every farmer's boy would become an efficient game keeper.

Can the farmer produce quail? He can raise two hundred quail on every quarter section of land south of latitude 40 if he sees good reason for doing it. Tell him that he is to have two dollars for every bird shot on his place and see what happens. He knows precisely what is required or can readily learn. A little draw where the wild grass is left standing, a hedge, a grass-grown fence with a few bushes, a half acre of Kaffir corn or cane uncut, an acre of field peas, and the birds will raise themselves. Keeping vermin down would be the job of the farmer's boy.

The majority of farmers shoot very little. A farmer may protect a bevy or two of birds for sentimental reasons, because he likes to see the little brown chaps about the place, but these birds will not be shot if he can help it. He must be given a financial interest in the game. Pay him for his birds, and be they quail, prairie chickens, turkeys, pheasants or ducks, he will stock up with game precisely as he now stocks up with domestic poultry. Enough small game can be produced in America so that every one of the fifteen million shooters we now have can have ten birds to shoot at where he now has one. Everything else has been tried and nothing will work except that we pay the land owner for the game he produces. Show the farmer that a marsh he may have on his place is worth twice as much to duck hunters as it would be drained and in corn, and he will raise the ducks and not the corn. Show him that he can add one-tenth to his income, one-tenth to the value of his land, one-tenth to his tangible assets, and he will produce all the game that our shooters need, right at home.

Game shooting is a luxury and not a necessity. We would all be born, work, eat, live and die, were there no guns, no game, and no shooting whatever. But for many of us a great deal of the pleasure of living would be gone. The American people can afford luxuries, will always be able to afford luxuries and have been and always will be ready and willing to pay for what they want. Show them how the money can be well spent and it will be paid. Ducks require water and food, upland game birds require land and food; the farmers have the land and have the water, lacking nothing for the production of game except financial returns for what they may accomplish. Wild turkeys will come back along every wooded stream, prairie chickens "boom" from the broken sedge land, pheasants will grow in the alfalfa, and quail will return in old-time numbers. The farmer can bring the birds back; nobody else can or will do it; but we who dance must pay the fiddler.

This leads us to one conclusion, we must organize and work for our shooting, just as we do for any other sport. If we want golf we spend huge sums of money providing suitable grounds; then we buy our balls, clubs and other paraphernalia—after which we play golf at so much a round.

We must do this in shooting. We can provide our ground by establishing cordial relations with the land owner, convincing him that we are good sportsmen, that what we want will be of benefit to him also. We must provide game for stocking in some instances, and in all instances we must see that our ground is prepared to raise a suitable crop.

Free shooting is gone. The sooner we work for it the sooner we will have good shooting. This is now recognized by many people, but in the last analysis it is the individual sportsman, cooperating with the individual farmer who will most heavily count. Good shooting can be had, can be had at your own doorstep, can be had by the "one-gallus" man as well as by the rich sportsman, but it won't just happen—it must be worked for by all of us.

INDEX

INDEX